KNIT THE COLORS OF AUSTRALIA

SWING SWAGGER DRAPE

Jane Slicer-Smith

PUBLISHER  Alexis Yiorgos Xenakis

EDITOR Elaine Rowley

MANAGING EDITOR Karen Bright

TECHNICAL EDITOR Rick Mondragon

KNITTING INSTRUCTION Ginger Smith Mavis Smith Beth Whiteside

EDITORIAL ASSISTANT Kristi Miller

GRAPHIC DESIGNER Natalie Sorenson

PHOTOGRAPHER Alexis Yiorgos Xenakis

STYLIST Rick Mondragon

ASSISTANT TO THE PUBLISHER Lisa Mannes

CHIEF EXECUTIVE OFFICER Benjamin Levisay

DIRECTOR, PUBLISHING SERVICES David Xenakis

TECHNICAL ILLUSTRATOR Carol Skallerud

PRODUCTION DIRECTOR & COLOR SPECIALIST Dennis Pearson

BOOK PRODUCTION MANAGER Greg Hoogeveen

MARKETING MANAGER Lisa Mannes

BOOKS DISTRIBUTION Mavis Smith

MIS Jason Bittner

SECOND PRINTING, 2009
FIRST PUBLISHED IN THE USA IN 2009 BY XRX, INC.
COPYRIGHT © 2009 XRX, INC.

ISBN 13: 9781933064178

Produced in Sioux Falls,
South Dakota by XRX, Inc.
PO Box 965
Sioux Falls, SD
57101-0965
USA

605.338.2450

Visit us online — knittinguniverse.com

SWING SWAGGER DRAPE
KNIT THE COLORS OF AUSTRALIA

Photography by Alexis Xenakis

contents

Welcome

I live in Sydney, on Australia's east coast. Armed with knitting needles and yarn I cross the Pacific to the Americas and the Atlantic to Britain.
I always take a window seat.

Flying over Australia, America, or England, I am mesmerized by the topography of the landscape and man's hand upon it.

In England, the Romans built a few straight roads, draped viaducts across the English landscape, paths along rivers; ridgelines and valley floors became today's streets. It has evolved into a rich meandering patchwork of green, clustered with cities, towns, and villages, peppered with chimneys and steeples.

Australia is like a tree, with lush green shoots, exotic flowers, and unique animals. Eucalyptus bark reveals hidden colors and messages, the undersides of the leaves have prickly spines and yes, maybe spiders. Fallen leaves are crystalline and crisp. You can literally pick up Australia's history like sea shells in the Red Centre, where boat races are won in the dry river-beds of Alice Springs. The wet season brings flooding rains, flocks of birds, and sudden abundance. Soon to be scorched again, the land awaits a lightning strike and wildfire to unlock dormant seed pods.

To Australians, the US unfolds west to east, from beaches and forest to mountains, with canyons slicing through deserts, sheltering rivers deep below. Man's hand has scored mind-bendingly straight lines onto this landscape, way beyond the horizon. European-styled cities, with plazas and parks sprout streets to the north and avenues to the east and west. From the sky, nature's hand presses out valleys, rivers drain, and rich undulations define jutting mountain ranges.

These images travel into my designs. Metro could be city grids, lights, and colors or sown fields and tree lines? The dry desert rivers of the Lava Drape become reflective waters in the man's sweater, simply by color changes. Drop stitches emulate the intricate patterns of bark, Mitres are undulating mountain peaks with lush valleys. The colors create their own story in stitches.

From my window seat I look down into canyons and my heart goes out to those pioneering women, in John Wayne's wagon train. Each piece of fabric from dress to Hessian sack was a treasure or tool for the new land. They carried seed for food and craft skills essential to daily living. Today, our hands work with these same craft skills, now as hobbies and indulgences. Let's knit.

To my Grandmother Mary Lister, whose only regret was being born a woman in 1902 in a man's world. She wanted to sit astride horses, and sing on a stage—to make life an adventure, whatever the destination. She placed skills at my finger tips, whilst she told me her stories and listened to mine.

The story continues, with Brett's vision, taking needles to page.

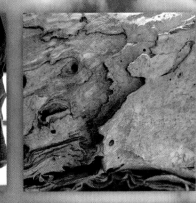

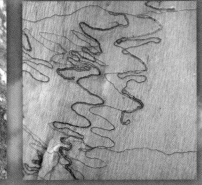

Simple Intarsia

Metro

To the East

IN AIR-CONDITIONED COMFORT

TRANS - AUSTRALIAN RAILWAY

FAST DIESEL ELECTIC TRAINS

Color blocking adds urban energy to the Metro Coat, yet the knitting pace is not too hectic. This intarsia is easy— even for a first-timer. Tapered panels and vertical play of color define this flattering coat. Choose your length—Swing and A-line lengths are shown here—then knit one of our color combos or create your own.

Use black or navy as a key to combine four colors. Trim up with collar and cuff options, or spice up with highlights of brick and fox for the bobbles and stripes.

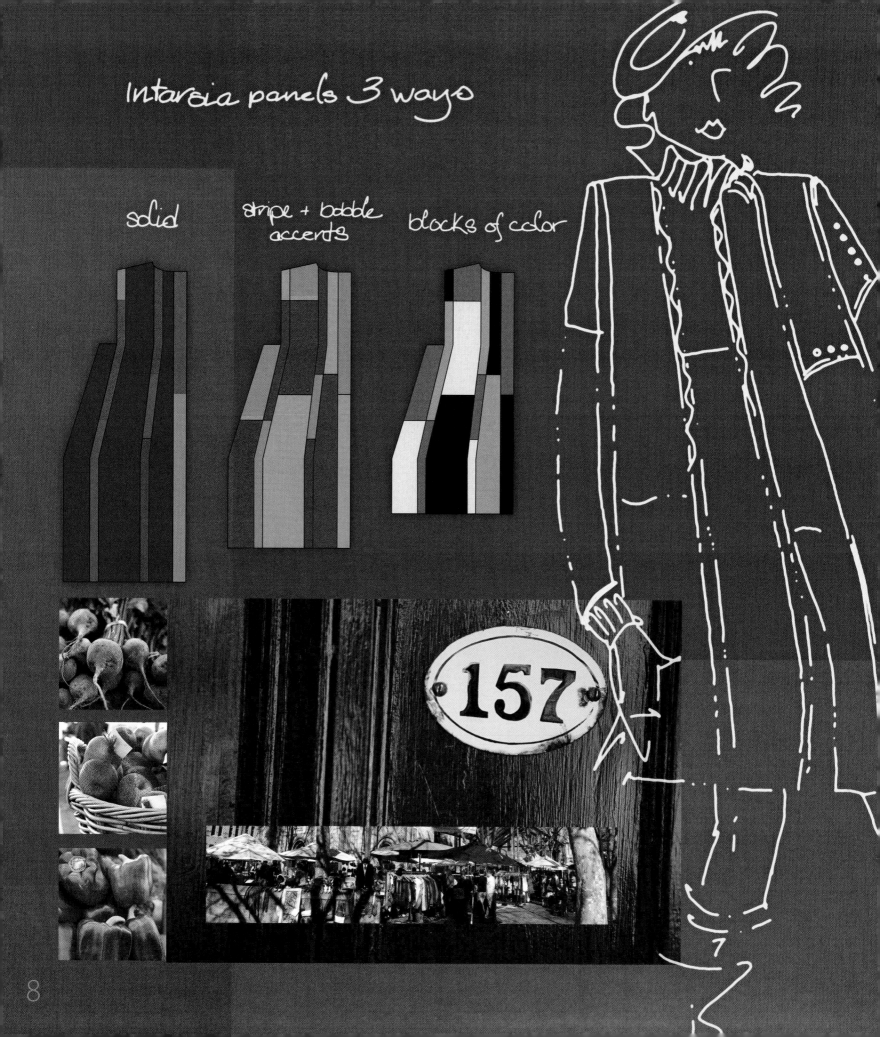

intarsia panels 3 ways

solid

stripe + bobble accents

blocks of color

157

One of my challenges is to create designs that entice you to step into my world of color. So Metro isn't only about color, it also brings the principles of Swing and Swagger onto your needles. Ease yourself into the project by starting with a sleeve: fewer stitches and fewer color changes help you master the technique. This also allows you to ensure your tension is good. And it's a time to ask yourself, 'Do my colors work?' Whether you use your favorite color as a main color or highlight, cap it off with one of our hats (locate pattern on page 156).

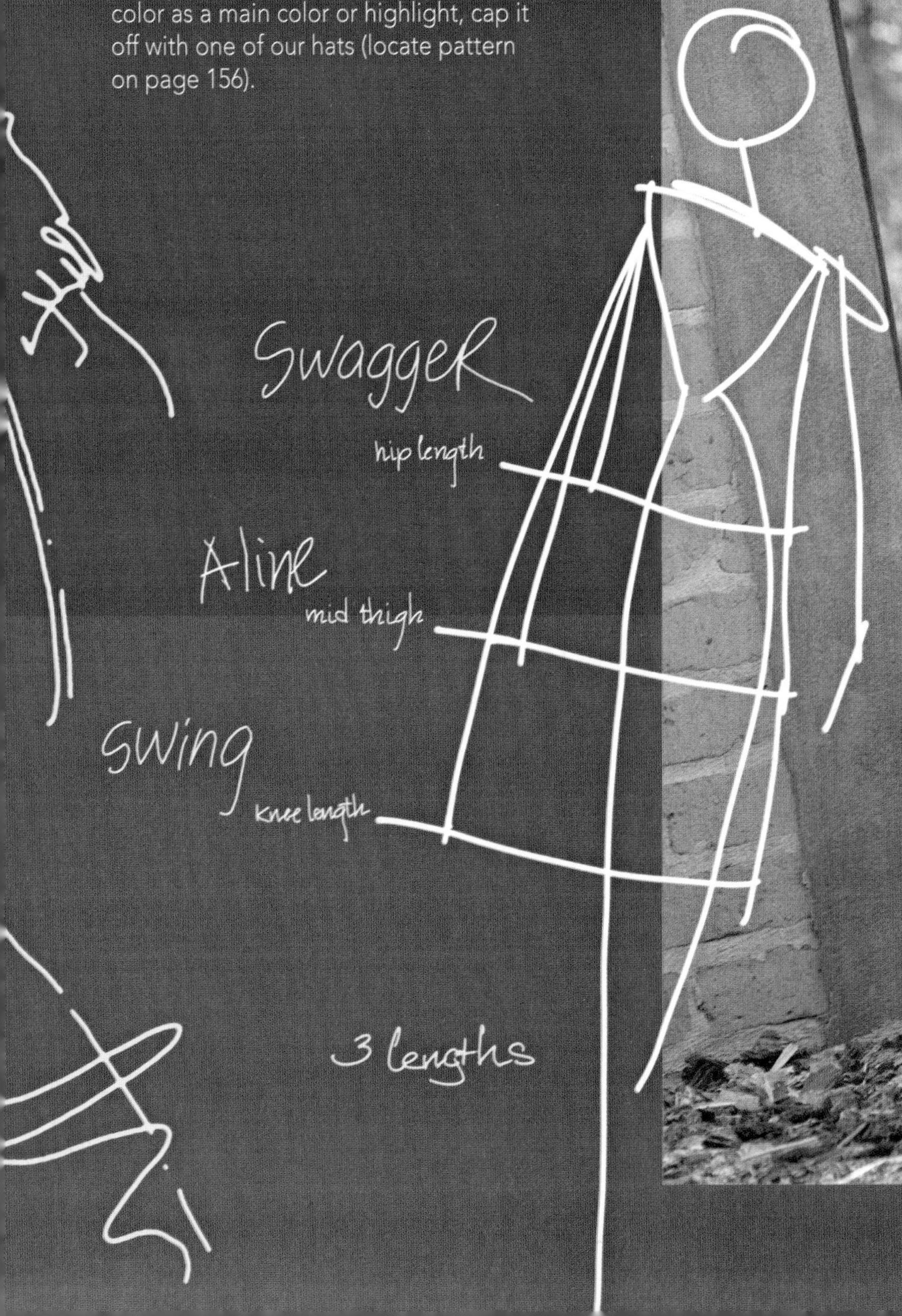

Swagger

hip length

A line

mid thigh

Swing

knee length

3 lengths

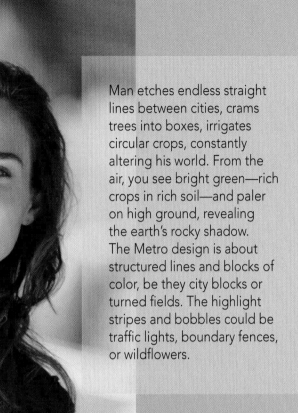

Man etches endless straight lines between cities, crams trees into boxes, irrigates circular crops, constantly altering his world. From the air, you see bright green—rich crops in rich soil—and paler on high ground, revealing the earth's rocky shadow. The Metro design is about structured lines and blocks of color, be they city blocks or turned fields. The highlight stripes and bobbles could be traffic lights, boundary fences, or wildflowers.

Choosing your own Metro colors

1 Pick 4 colors for cables and blocks: A, B, C, D.

2 Add 2 highlights for bobbles and stripes: E, F.

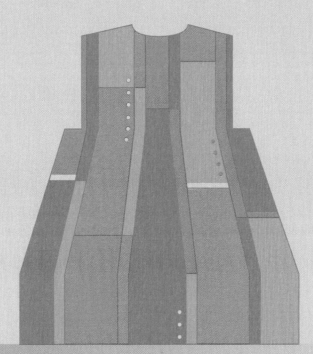

3 Proportion counts. When choosing colors, work with skeins of the block colors and strands of the highlights.

Just follow these simple steps. Choose one of the darker colors as C (collar and cuffs). The accents should be left to E and F. With a strong contrast of black to cream for cables and blocks. I'd pair a bold and a darker red for highlights. In the blue and red versions, I've used tones of one color group; if photographed (or photocopied) in black and white, they would be almost the same gray. Try this trick with any range of colors.

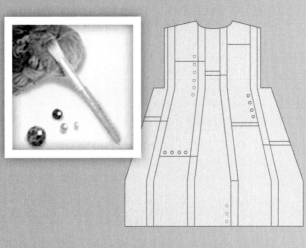

Knitter's Paintbox

When you've chosen your colors, or even before, try Knitter's Paintbox online. You'll find an outline of the Metro that's ready to color—on-screen or on paper. Use the color wheel to discover the power of opposites and create stunning colorways. KnittingUniverse.com

XS (S, M, L, 1X, 2X, 3X)
A 37 (40, 43, 46, 49, 52, 57)"
B SWAGGER 28 (28½, 29½, 30, 31, 31½, 35)"
A-LINE 31 (31½, 32½, 33, 34, 34½, 38)"
SWING 34 (34½, 35½, 36, 37, 37½, 41)"
C 27½ (28½, 29½, 30½, 31½, 32½, 34)"
D 56 (58, 60, 64, 68, 70, 70)"

10cm/4"

31
22

***over stockinette stitch
(knit on RS, purl on WS)
using 4mm/US 6 needle***

1 2 **3** 4 5 6

Light weight

Fanfare Metro
MC 1175 (1250, 1350, 1425, 1525, 1625, 1825) yds
A, C 145 (150, 160, 175, 190, 200, 230) yds each
B 85 (90, 95, 100, 110, 115, 130) yds
D 105 (110, 120, 125, 135, 140, 160) yds

Block or Stripe & Bobble Metros
A 350 (375, 400, 425, 475, 500, 550) yds
B 400 (425, 450, 475, 525, 550, 600) yds
C 575 (600, 650, 700, 750, 800, 900) yds
D 400 (450, 475, 500, 525, 550, 650) yds
E, F 30 (30, 35, 35, 40, 40, 45) yds each

For A-line length, add 7% to all colors
For Swing length, add 15% to all colors
***Add an additional 125 yds of color C for wide
collar and turn-back cuffs***

3.25mm/US 3, 3.75mm/US 5, 4mm/US 6, or
size to obtain gauge
For wide collar only: 4.5mm/US 7

SWAGGER 8 (8, 8, 8, 9, 9, 9)
A-LINE 9 (9, 9, 10, 10, 10, 10)
SWING 10 (10, 11, 11, 11, 11, 12)
19mm (¾") triangle

&

Stitch markers
Cable needle

Metros shown in Medium: SIGNATUR Pure
New Wool DK

The Metro Coat

Notes
1 See *Techniques*, page 160, for Intarsia knitting, k2tog, SSK, p2tog, SK2P, and bind off in pattern.
2 The design is given in 7 sizes and 3 lengths: Swagger (hip length), A-line (mid-thigh length), and Swing (knee length), with 2 cuff and 3 collar options. **3** Coat is worked in stockinette stitch with cable panels. Refer to diagram for color changes in cable panels and within stockinette panels for Block and Stripe & Bobble. Work color changes at specified distance from Swagger cast-on (add 3" for A-line, 6" for Swing) or from previous color change. **4** Vertically, bobbles are worked 3 stitches in from edge of panel sections and repeated every 8 rows (4, 5 or 6) times without breaking yarn. Horizontally, bobbles are centered in panel with 5 stitches between. **6** See *Intarsia Tips*, page 141, for cast on in colors.

Cable Pattern
Rows 1, 3, 7 (RS) Knit.
Rows 2, 4, 6, 8 Purl.
Row 5 Slip 3 stitches to cable needle and hold to back, k3; k3 from cable needle (3/3 RC). Repeat Rows 1–8 for pattern.

Bobble
(K1, p1, k1) into stitch, turn; p3, turn; SK2P.

Back
FANFARE METRO
With 4 mm/US 6 needle, cast on 18 (19, 20, 21, 22, 23, 23) stitches with MC, 6 with A, 31 (33, 35, 37, 39, 41, 41) with MC, 6 with D, 31 (33, 35, 37, 39, 41, 41) with MC, 6 with A, 31 (33, 35, 37, 39, 41, 41) with MC, 6 with C, 18 (19, 20, 21, 22, 23, 23) with MC — 153 (161, 169, 177, 185, 193, 193) stitches. Working in colors as established, work 4 rows of k2, p2 rib as follows:
RS rows P1, * k2, p2; repeat from *. *WS rows* * K2, p2; repeat from * to last stitch, k1.
Establish patterns: Row 1 (RS) [Knit to color change, work Row 1 of Cable Pattern over next 6 stitches] 4 times, knit to end. *Row 2* Purl. Continue in stockinette and Cable Pattern as established until piece measures 6 (6, 6, 6, 6, 6, 9)" for Swagger, 9 (9, 9, 9, 9, 9, 12)" for A-Line, 12 (12, 12, 12, 12, 12, 15)" for Swing from cast-on. Place marker.
Shape panels
Next RS row SSK *after* each cable — 4 stitches decreased. Work 5 rows. *Next row* (RS) K2tog *before* each cable — 4 stitches decreased. Work 5 rows. Repeat last 12 rows 5 (5, 5, 5, 5, 5, 3) times more — 12 (13, 14, 15, 16, 17, 19) stitches in each side-seam panel. Work 2 more sets of decrease rows EXCEPT only decrease in the 3 center panels — 15 (17, 19, 21, 23, 25, 29) stitches in center panels. Work even until piece measures 13 (13, 13½, 13½, 14, 14, 14)" from marker, end with a WS row — 93 (101, 109, 117, 125, 133, 149) stitches.
Shape armholes and panels
At beginning of the next 2 rows, bind off 10 (11, 12, 13, 14, 15, 17) stitches — 73 (79, 85, 91, 97, 103, 115) stitches. Keeping 2 stitches at each armhole edge in purl garter stitch (purl every row) and color of cable, work even until armhole measures 4 (4½, 5, 5½, 6, 6, 4)". *Next RS row* K2tog *before* the last 3 cables. Work 7 rows. *Next RS row* SSK *after* the first 3 cables — 67 (73, 79, 85, 91, 97, 109) stitches. *For size 3X only* Repeat last 9 rows once — 103 stitches. *For all sizes* Work even until armhole measures 8 (8½, 9, 9½, 10, 10½, 11)", end with a WS row. Mark center 21 (21, 23, 25, 25, 25, 25) stitches.

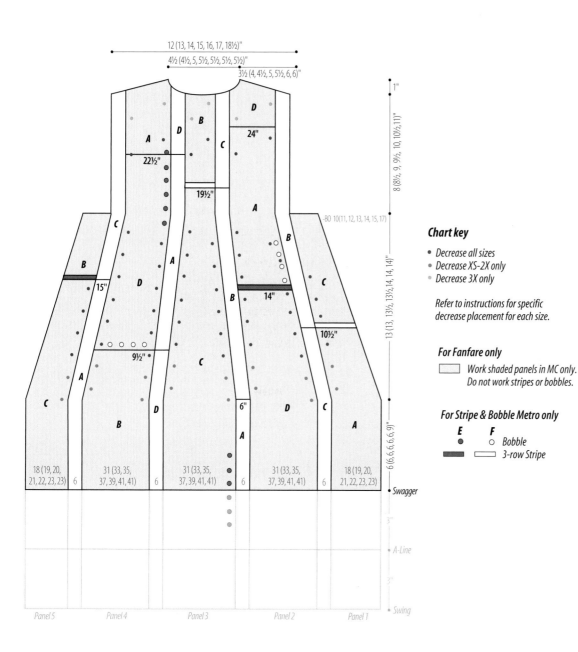

12 (13, 14, 15, 16, 17, 18½)"
4½ (4½, 5, 5½, 5½, 5½, 5½)"
3½ (4, 4½, 5, 5½, 6, 6)"

1"

8 (8½, 9, 9½, 10, 10½, 11)"

22½"

24"

19½"

-BO 10(11, 12, 13, 14, 15, 17)

13 (13, 13½, 13½, 14, 14, 14)"

15"

14"

9½"

10½"

6"

6 (6, 6, 6, 6, 6, 9)"

18 (19, 20, 21, 22, 23, 23) | 6 | 31 (33, 35, 37, 39, 41, 41) | 6 | 31 (33, 35, 37, 39, 41, 41) | 6 | 31 (33, 35, 37, 39, 41, 41) | 6 | 18 (19, 20, 21, 22, 23, 23)

• Swagger

3"

• A-Line

3"

• Swing

Panel 5   *Panel 4*   *Panel 3*   *Panel 2*   *Panel 1*

Chart key

- Decrease all sizes
- Decrease XS-2X only
- Decrease 3X only

Refer to instructions for specific decrease placement for each size.

For Fanfare only

☐ *Work shaded panels in MC only. Do not work stripes or bobbles.*

For Stripe & Bobble Metro only

E   **F**
●   ○   *Bobble*
▬   ▭   *3-row Stripe*

Fanfare Metro

Work stockinette panels in MC. No bobbles, no stripes.

Page 9

■ **MC** *Dark Navy 611*
■ **A** *Cranberry 664*
■ **B** *Brick 647*
■ **C** *Turkish 731*
■ **D** *Steel 631*

Block Metro

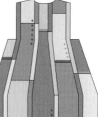

Work stockinette panels in color blocks. No bobbles, no stripes.

Page 7

☐ **A** *Raffia 603*
■ **B** *Mocca 630*
■ **C** *Mulga 690*
■ **D** *Black 613*

Stripe & Bobble Metro

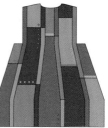

Work stockinette panels in color blocks with highlight colors in bobbles and stripes.

Pages 5

■ **A** *Brick 647*
■ **B** *Fox 673*
■ **C** *Claret 612*
■ **D** *Cranberry 664*

■ **E** *Sequoia 719*
☐ **F** *Khaki 645*

Page 5

☐ **A** *Moss 662*
☐ **B** *Khaki 645*
■ **C** *Dark Olive 697*
■ **D** *Sequoia 719*

■ **E** *Oxblood 729*
■ **F** *Fox 673*

Page 2

■ **A** *Aegean 625*
■ **B** *Peacock 663*
■ **C** *Turkish 731*
■ **D** *Purple 657*

☐ **E** *Sweet Pea 705*
■ **F** *Blueberry 704*

Page 6

☐ **A** *Pale Grey 680*
■ **B** *Black 613*
■ **C** *Charcoal 717*
■ **D** *Mid Grey 681*

■ **E** *Brick 647*
☐ **F** *Fox 673*

Shape right neck and shoulder

Next row (RS) Bind off 7 (8, 8, 10, 11, 12, 13) stitches, work to first marker, turn. Bind off 2 stitches at beginning of next WS row and 7 (8, 9, 9, 10, 11, 12) stitches at beginning of next 2 RS rows.

Shape left neck and shoulder

With RS facing, join yarn and bind off center 21 (21, 23, 25, 25, 25, 25) stitches, work to end. Bind off 7 (8, 8, 10, 11, 12, 13) stitches at beginning of next WS row, 2 stitches at beginning of next RS row, and 7 (8, 9, 9, 10, 11, 12) stitches at beginning of next 2 WS rows.

BLOCK or STRIPE & BOBBLE METRO

Work as for Fanfare Metro EXCEPT follow diagram for panel colors and bobble and stripe placement, cast on in colors as follows: 18 (19, 20, 21, 22, 23, 23) stitches with C, 6 with A, 31 (33, 35, 37, 39, 41, 41) with B, 6 with D, 31 (33, 35, 37, 39, 41, 41) with C, 6 with A, 31 (33, 35, 37, 39, 41, 41) with D, 6 with C, 18 (19, 20, 21, 22, 23, 23) with A — 153 (161, 169, 177, 185, 193, 193) stitches.

Left Front

Note Decreases begin 3" higher on fronts than on back.

FANFARE METRO

With 4 mm/US 6 needle, cast on 8 stitches with D, 18 (19, 20, 21, 22, 23, 23) with MC, 6 with A, 31 (33, 35, 37, 39, 41, 41) with MC, 6 with D, 18 (19, 20, 21, 22, 23, 23) with MC — 87 (91, 95, 99, 103, 107, 107) stitches. Working in colors as established, work 4 rows of rib as follows:

RS rows K2, * p2, k2; repeat from * to last stitch, p1. *WS rows* K1, * p2, k2; repeat from * end p2.

Establish patterns: Row 1 (RS) [Knit to color change, work Row 1 of Cable Pattern over next 6 stitches] 3 times, p2. *Row 2* Purl. Continue in stockinette, Cable Pattern, and purl garter at center edge as established until piece measures 9 (9, 9, 9, 9, 9, 12)" for Swagger; 12 (12, 12, 12, 12, 12, 15)" for A-Line; 15 (15, 15, 15, 15, 15, 18)" for Swing from cast-on. Place marker.

Shape panels

Next RS row K2tog *before* the first 2 cable panels — 2 stitches decreased. Work 5 rows. *Next RS row* SSK *after* the first 2 cable panels — 2 stitches decreased. Work 5 rows. Repeat last 12 rows 5 (5, 5, 5, 5, 5, 3) times more — 63 (67, 71, 75, 79, 83, 91) stitches. Work even until piece measures 10 (10, 10½, 10½, 11, 11, 11)" from marker, end with a WS row.

Shape armholes & panels

At the beginning of the next row, bind off 10 (11, 12, 13, 14, 15, 17) stitches — 53 (56, 59, 62, 65, 68, 74) stitches. Keeping 2 stitches at armhole edge in purl garter stitch in color of cable, work even until armhole measures 1 (1, 1½, 2, 2, 2½, 1)". *Next RS row* K2tog *before* the second cable — 1 stitch decreased. Work 7 rows. *Next RS row* SSK *after* the first 2 cables — 2 stitches decreased. Work 7 rows. Repeat last 16 rows 2 (2, 2, 2, 2, 2, 3) times more — 13 (15, 17, 19, 21, 23, 25) stitches in full panel. Work even on 44 (47, 50, 53, 56, 59, 62) stitches until armhole measures 5 (5, 5, 5, 5½, 5½, 5½)", end with a WS row.

Shape neck and shoulders

Next row (RS) Work to last 10 stitches and place them on hold (neck edge). Bind off at beginning of every WS row, 3 stitches twice, 2 stitches twice, then decrease 1 stitch 3 (3, 4, 5, 5, 5, 5) times — 21 (24, 26, 28, 31, 34, 37) stitches. Work even to same length as back at beginning of shoulder shaping. Bind off 7 (8, 8, 10, 11, 12, 13) stitches at beginning of next RS row, then 7 (8, 9, 9, 10, 11, 12) stitches at beginning of next 2 RS rows.

BLOCK or STRIPE & BOBBLE METRO

Work as for Fanfare Metro EXCEPT follow diagrams for panel colors and bobble and stripe placement, and cast on as follows: 8 stitches with D, 18 (19, 20, 21, 22, 23, 23) with C, 6 with A, 31 (33, 35, 37, 39, 41, 41) with B, 6 stitches with D, 18 (19, 20, 21, 22, 23, 23) stitches with C — 87 (91, 95, 99, 103, 107, 107) stitches.

Right Front

FANFARE METRO

Note On left front, place marker for button every 3 cable twists beginning 2 cable twists from neck edge. As you work right front, work buttonholes to match markers as follows: On RS row, work 4 stitches, bind off 2, finish row. On next row, cable cast on 2 stitches over bound-off stitches.

With 4 mm/US 6 needle, cast on 18 (19, 20, 21, 22, 23, 23) stitches with MC, 6 with C, 31 (33, 35, 37, 39, 41, 41) with MC, 6 with A, 18 (19, 20, 21, 22, 23, 23) with MC, 8 with D — 87 (91, 95, 99, 103, 107, 107) stitches. Working in colors as established, work 4 rows of rib as follows:

Row 1 (RS) P1, * k2, p2; repeat from * to end, k2. *Row 2* P2, * k2, p2; repeat from * to end, p1. *Establish patterns: Row 1* P2, [work Row 1 of Cable Pattern over next 6 stitches, knit to color change] twice, work Row 1 of Cable Pattern over next 6 stitches, knit to end. *Row 2* Purl. Continue in purl garter, Cable Pattern and stockinette as established and work as Left Front until piece measures 9 (9, 9, 9, 9, 9, 12)" for Swagger; 12 (12, 12, 12, 12, 12, 15)" for A-Line; 15 (15, 15, 15, 15, 15, 18)" for Swing from cast-on. Place marker.

Shape panels

Work as Left Front EXCEPT decrease *after* the last 2 cables on the first decrease row and *before* the last 2 cables on the second decrease row.

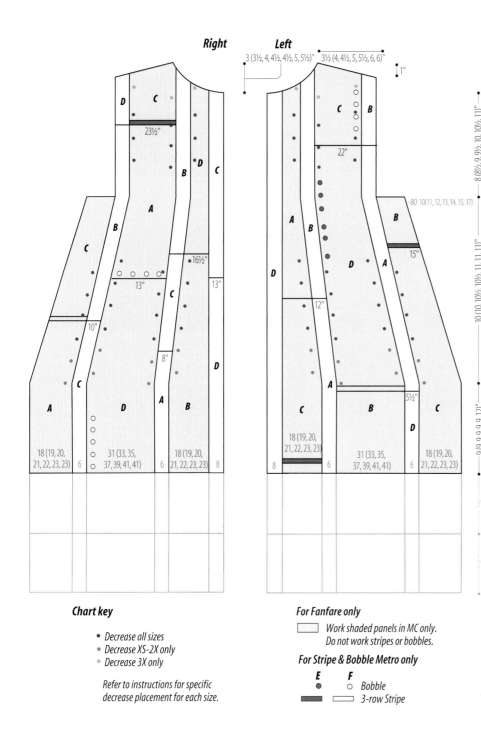

Right

Left

3 (3½, 4, 4½, 4½, 5, 5½)"   3½ (4, 4½, 5, 5½, 6, 6)"

1"

23½"

22"

8 (8½, 9, 9½, 10, 10½, 11)"

BO 10 (11, 12, 13, 14, 15, 17)

16½"

13"   13"

15"

10 (10, 10½, 10½, 11, 11, 11)"

10"

12"

8"

5½"

18 (19, 20, 21, 22, 23, 23)   31 (33, 35, 37, 39, 41, 41)   6   18 (19, 20, 21, 22, 23, 23)   8

6   18 (19, 20, 21, 22, 23, 23)   6

9 (9, 9, 9, 9, 9, 12)"

8   18 (19, 20, 21, 22, 23, 23)   6   31 (33, 35, 37, 39, 41, 41)   6   18 (19, 20, 21, 22, 23, 23)

• Swagger

3"

• A-Line

3"

• Swing

Chart key

- • Decrease all sizes
- • Decrease XS–2X only
- • Decrease 3X only

Refer to instructions for specific
decrease placement for each size.

For Fanfare only

Work shaded panels in MC only.
Do not work stripes or bobbles.

For Stripe & Bobble Metro only

E   **F**
●   ○   Bobble
▬   ▭   3-row Stripe

Fanfare Metro

Color keys

- **MC** Dark Navy 611
- **A** Cranberry 664
- **B** Brick 647
- **C** Turkish 731
- **D** Steel 631

Block Metro

- **A** Raffia 603
- **B** Mocca 630
- **C** Mulga 690
- **D** Black 613

Stripe & Bobble Metro

- **A** Brick 647
- **B** Fox 673
- **C** Claret 612
- **D** Cranberry 664

- **E** Sequoia 719
- **F** Khaki 645

- **A** Moss 662
- **B** Khaki 645
- **C** Dark Olive 697
- **D** Sequoia 719

- **E** Oxblood 729
- **F** Fox 673

- **A** Aegean 625
- **B** Peacock 663
- **C** Turkish 731
- **D** Purple 657

- **E** Sweet Pea 705
- **F** Blueberry 704

- **A** Pale Grey 680
- **B** Black 613
- **C** Charcoal 717
- **D** Mid Grey 681

- **E** Brick 647
- **F** Fox 673

Shape armholes and panels

Work as left front EXCEPT bind off at beginning of a WS row AND SSK *after* the second cable on
the first decrease row and k2tog *before* the last 2 cables on the second decrease row.

Shape neck and shoulders

Work as left front EXCEPT place 10 stitches on hold at end of a WS row AND bind off for neck at
beginning of RS rows and bind off for shoulder at beginning of WS rows.

BLOCK or STRIPE & BOBBLE METRO

Work as Fanfare Metro EXCEPT cast on as follows: 18 (19, 20, 21, 22, 23, 23) stitches with A, 6 with
C, 31 (33, 35, 37, 39, 41, 41) with D, 6 with A, 18 (19, 20, 21, 22, 23, 23) with B, 8 with D — 87 (91, 95,
99, 103, 107, 107) stitches.

Sleeves
FANFARE METRO

Note 1 When 2 colors are given, first is for left sleeve and second is for right.
2 Begin with a standard cuff or the turn-back cuff (see Options, next page).

Standard cuff

With 3.25mm/US 3 needle and C, cast on 48 (52, 52, 56, 58, 60, 60) stitches. Work 2" of k2, p2 rib, increasing 6 (6, 6, 6, 8, 6, 6) stitches evenly on last row — 54 (58, 58, 62, 66, 66, 66) stitches.

Establish patterns: Row 1 Change to 4 mm/US 6 needle and with B/C, k3; with MC, k21 (23, 23, 25, 27, 27, 27); with B/C, work Row 1 of Cable Pattern over next 6 stitches; with MC, k21 (23, 23, 25, 27, 27, 27); with C/D, knit 3. *Row 2* Purl. Continue in Cable Pattern and stockinette, increase 1 stitch at each end of third row, then every 6 rows 9 (9, 11, 11, 13, 14, 18) times — 74 (78, 82, 86, 94, 96, 104) stitches. AT SAME TIME, after 3 increase rows, establish cables with the first and last 6 stitches of the row; work additional increases in stockinette and color shown in diagram. Work even until sleeve measures 18½ (19, 19, 19½, 19½, 20, 20½)" from cast-on.

Shape cap

Bind off 5 stitches at the beginning of the next 2 rows, then 2 stitches at the beginning of every row 16 (18, 20, 22, 26, 26, 28) times, then 3 stitches 6 times. Bind off.

BLOCK or STRIPE & BOBBLE METRO

Work as Metro Fanfare except follow diagrams for panel colors and bobble and stripe placement.

Chart key
- Increase

Refer to instructions for specific increase placement for each size.

For Fanfare only

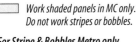 Work shaded panels in MC only. Do not work stripes or bobbles.

For Stripe & Bobbles Metro only

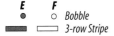
- E ● / F ○ Bobble
- ▬ / ▭ 3-row Stripe

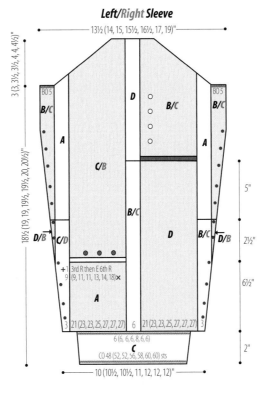

Left/Right Sleeve

13½ (14, 15, 15½, 16½, 17, 19)"

3 (3, 3½, 3½, 4, 4, 4½)"

18½ (19, 19, 19½, 19½, 20, 20½)"

BO 5 — B/C — A — C/B — B/C — D/B — C/D

D — B/C — B/C — A — D — B/C — D/B

5"

2½"

6½"

2"

3rd R then E 6th R
9 (9, 11, 11, 13, 14, 18)

A

21 (23, 23, 25, 27, 27, 27)   6 (6, 6, 6, 8, 6, 6)   21 (23, 23, 25, 27, 27, 27)   3   3

C

CO 48 (52, 52, 56, 58, 60, 60) sts

10 (10½, 10½, 11, 12, 12, 12)"

cuffs
standard rib or turn-back

Fanfare Metro

Color keys
- ■ **MC** Dark Navy 611
- ■ **A** Cranberry 664
- ■ **B** Brick 647
- ■ **C** Turkish 731
- ■ **D** Steel 631

Block Metro

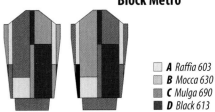

- ▢ **A** Raffia 603
- ▨ **B** Mocca 630
- ▩ **C** Mulga 690
- ■ **D** Black 613

Stripe & Bobble Metro

- ▨ **A** Brick 647
- ▨ **B** Fox 673
- ■ **C** Claret 612
- ■ **D** Cranberry 664

- ▨ **E** Sequoia 719
- ▢ **F** Khaki 645

- ▢ **A** Moss 662
- ▨ **B** Khaki 645
- ■ **C** Dark Olive 697
- ▨ **D** Sequoia 719

- ■ **E** Oxblood 729
- ▨ **F** Fox 673

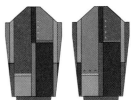

- ▨ **A** Aegean 625
- ▨ **B** Peacock 663
- ■ **C** Turkish 731
- ■ **D** Purple 657

- ▨ **E** Sweet Pea 705
- ▨ **F** Blueberry 704

- ▢ **A** Pale Grey 680
- ■ **B** Black 613
- ■ **C** Charcoal 717
- ▨ **D** Mid Grey 681

- ▨ **E** Brick 647
- ▨ **F** Fox 673

Left Sleeve   **Right Sleeve**

Finishing

Join shoulder seams.

Standard round neck

With 3.25 mm/US 3 needle, C, and RS facing, knit 10 stitches from holder, pick up and knit 25 (27, 28, 27, 29, 31, 32) to shoulder seam, 27 (27, 29, 31, 31, 31, 33) across back neck, 26 (28, 29, 28, 30, 32, 33) on left front, knit 10 from holder — 98 (102, 106, 106, 110, 114, 118) stitches. *Row 1* (WS) P4, *k2, p2; repeat from * to last 2 stitches, p2. *Row 2* P2, *k2, p2; repeat from *. Work 1½" in purl garter and rib as established, AT SAME TIME work buttonhole as for Right Front at beginning of ninth row. Bind off loosely in pattern.

Sew sleeves in, sew side seams, and sleeve seams. Sew buttons on Left Front at markers.

OPTIONS

Turn-back cuff

With 4mm/US 6 needle and C, cast on 56 (56, 60, 60, 64, 68, 68) stitches. Work 6 rows of k2, p2 rib. Decrease 1 stitch in pattern (k2tog or p2tog) at beginning and end of next RS row, then every 4 rows 3 (1, 2, 2, 2, 3, 3) times more — 48 (52, 54, 54, 58, 60, 60) stitches. Work even to 3½" from cast-on. Change to 3.25/US 3 needles and work to 5" from cast-on, increasing 6 (6, 4, 8, 8, 6, 6) stitches evenly on last row — 54 (58, 58, 62, 66, 66, 66) stitches. Continue from Row 1 of sleeve instructions.

Narrow collar

Work Standard round neck but do not bind off. Change to 3.75mm/US 5 needles and work to 2½", then change to 4mm/US 6 needle and work to 4½". Bind off loosely in pattern.

Wide button-under collar

Work Standard round neck, end with a WS row but do not bind off. Change to 3.75mm/US 5 needles and continue, increasing 1 stitch between the 2 purl stitches of each rib — 122 (127, 132, 132, 137, 142, 147) stitches. Work in purl garter and k2, p3 rib to 2½" from pick-up, change to 4mm/US 6 needles and work to 5", change to 4.5mm/US 7 needle and work to 7". *Next RS row* Work buttonhole at beginning of row as for Right Front. Work to 7½". Bind off loosely in pattern. Sew a button onto Left Front along pick-up row of neckband.

collars

Round neck

Narrow collar

wear up or down

Wide collar

Button down

or leave open

Jindabyne A-line

Basket Stitch

```
12 ████████████        11
10 ████████████         9
 8 ████████████         7
 6 ██████                5
 4 ██████                3
 2 ██████                1
```
|— 10 st repeat —|

Small Basket

```
8 ███████        7
6 ███████        5
4 ██████         3
2 ██████         1
```
|— 6 st repeat —|

Cable Chart

```
8          7
6  ╲╱      5
4          3
2          1
```

Stitch key

- ☐ Knit on RS, purl on WS
- ▨ Purl on RS, k on WS
- ╲╱ **3/3 RC** Slip 3 to cn and hold to back, k3; k3 from cn

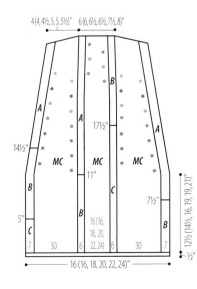

4 (4, 4½, 5, 5, 5½)" 6 (6, 6½, 6½, 7½, 8)"

17½"

14½"

11"

7½"

5" 16 (16, 18, 20, 22, 24)

12½ (14½, 16, 19, 21)"

½"

7 30 6 30 7

16 (16, 18, 20, 22, 24)"

Notes

1 See *Techniques*, page 160, for intarsia knitting, k2tog, SSK, wrap and turn for short rows, and 3-needle bind-off. **2** Each MC section is worked using a separate ball of yarn. **3** Refer to diagrams for color changes in cables. **4** Because we are working with self-striping yarn, side panels are worked with the front to avoid an underarm, mid-panel seam. **5** There are 2 cuff options: the turn-back cuff as shown and a standard cuff. **6** See *Intarsia Tips*, page 141.

JACKET

Back

With MC and 4.5mm/US 7 needles, cast on 102 (102, 104, 104, 106, 110) stitches. Work 4 rows in k1, p1 rib.

Establish colors and patterns: Row 1 (RS) With B, k7; with MC, k30; with C, k6; with MC, k16 (16, 18, 18, 20, 24); with B, k6; with MC, k30; with C, k7.
Row 2 Working in colors as established, purl. *Row 3* K1, [work Row 3 of Cable Chart over next 6 stitches, knit to color change] 3 times, work Row 3 of Cable Chart over next 6 stitches, k1. Continue in stockinette stitch and Cable Chart as established until piece measures 13 (15, 16½, 19½, 19½, 21½)" from cast-on.
Shape panels
Next Row 5 of Cable Chart SSK *after* first and third cables — 2 stitches decreased.
Next Row 5 of Cable Chart K2tog *before* second and fourth cables. Repeat last 2 decrease rows 6 (6, 5, 4, 3, 2) times more — 16 (16, 18, 20, 22, 24) stitches remain in each 30-stitch panel. AT SAME TIME when piece measures 23½ (25½, 26½, 28½, 29, 29½)", decrease for size S, M, L, 1X, 2X only as follows:
Next Row 5 of Cable Chart SSK *after* second cable. *Following Row 5 of Cable Chart* K2tog *before* third cable. Repeat 1 (1, 1, 2, 0, 0) times — 12 (12, 14, 14, 20, 24) stitches remain in center panel. Work even on 70 (70, 76, 80, 90, 98) stitches until piece measures 29½ (31, 32, 33, 34, 34½)".
Shape shoulders
Bind off 6 (6, 6, 8, 8, 8) stitches at the beginning of the next 2 rows, 7 (7, 8, 8, 9, 10) at the beginning of the next 4 rows, and bind off remaining stitches on the next row. Mark center of the back neck.

Left Front

With MC and 4.5mm/US 7 needles, cast on 85 (91, 97, 105, 118, 118) stitches. Work 4 rows in k1, p1 rib.

Establish colors and patterns: Row 1 (RS) With MC, k23 (29, 35, 43, 51, 51); with A, k6; with MC, k30; with B, k6; with MC, [p5, k5] twice; p0 (0, 0, 0, 5, 5)
Row 2 Working in color as established, k0 (0, 0, 0, 5, 5), (p5, k5) twice, purl to end. *Row 3* [Knit to color change, work Row 3 of Cable Chart over next 6 stitches] 2 times, work Row 3 of Basket Stitch to end.

Chart key

- ● Decrease all sizes
- ● Decrease S-2X only
- ● Decrease S-1X only
- ● Decrease S-L only
- ● Decrease S-M only
- ● Decrease 1X only

Refer to instructions for specific decrease placement for each size.

INTERMEDIATE +

S (M, L, 1X, 2X, 3X)

A 39 (41, 45½, 50, 54, 58)"
B 29½ (31, 32, 33, 34, 34½)"
C 30 (31, 31½, 32, 33, 33½)"
D 54 (56, 59½, 62½, 68, 69)"

10cm/4"

28 / 20

over stockinette stitch (knit on RS, purl on WS) using larger needles

1 2 3 **4** 5 6

Medium weight

MC 1475 (1575, 1700, 1875, 2100, 2200) yds
A, B, C 175 (200, 225, 250, 275, 300) yds each

4mm/US 6 & 4.5mm/US 7, or size to obtain gauge

☺

3 • 16mm (5/8") square

&

Cable needle
Stitch holder

Medium: 16 balls TRENDSETTER YARNS Tonalita in 2395 Peacock (MC), 2 ballls each Merino VIII in 334 Plum (A), 7440 Dark Teal (B), and 335 Deep Eggplant (C)

Continue in stockinette stitch, Cable Chart, and Basket Stitch as established, until piece measures 13 (15, 16½, 19½, 19½, 21½)" from cast-on.

Shape panels
Begin center panel decreases: Next Row 5 of Cable Chart SSK *after* first cable. **Next Row 5 of Cable Chart** K2tog *before* second cable. Repeat last 2 decrease rows 6 (6, 5, 4, 3, 2) times more . AT SAME TIME when piece measures 15" from cast-on **begin center panel decreases: Next Row 5 of Cable Chart** SSK at beginning of row. **Next Row 5 of Cable Chart** K2tog *before* first cable. Repeat last 2 decrease rows once. Work even until piece measures 21 (22, 22½, 23, 23½, 23½)".

Shape armholes
Next row (RS) K0 (0, 0, 0, 5, 8) stitches and place on hold, bind off 18 (24, 30, 38, 37, 31), continue across row. Decrease 1 stitch at beginning of every 4th row 0 (0, 0, 0, 4, 7) times. Continue in pattern, keeping 1 stitch at armhole in purl garter stitch in color of the cable (edge stitch) and decrease in center panel 2 times — 14 (14, 16, 18, 20, 22) stitches remain in panel. Work even on 47 (47, 49, 51, 58, 60) stitches to same length as Back.

Shape shoulders
Bind off 6 (6, 6, 8, 8, 8) stitches at the beginning of the next RS row, 7 (7, 8, 8, 9, 10) stitches at the beginning of the next 2 RS rows — 27 (32) stitches remain. **Next row** Work in pattern to last stitch, p1 in color of cable (edge stitch).

Collar extension
Work 3 (3, 3½, 3½, 3½, 4)", end with a RS row.

Shape collar
Short row 1 (WS) Work 20 (25) stitches, wrap next stitch and turn work (W&T). **All RS rows** Work to end. **Short row 2** Work 17 (22) stitches, W&T. **Short row 3** Work 14 (19) stitches, W&T. **Short row 4** Work 11 (16) stitches, W&T. **Next WS row** Bind off 8 stitches, complete row, hiding wraps; place remaining stitches on hold.

Back armhole shaping
For 2x & 3x only Place (5, 8) stitches from holder on needles. With WS facing, attach yarn, knit across. **Next RS row** Purl to last 2 stitches, p2tog. Work 3 rows reverse stockinette stitches. Repeat last 4 rows until 1 stitch remains. Fasten off.

Right Front
Cast on and rib as for Left Front.
Establish colors and patterns: Row 1 (RS) With MC, p0 (0, 0, 0, 5, 5), [k5, p5] twice; with B, k6; with MC, k30; with C, k6; with MC, k23 (29, 35, 43, 51, 51) with MC. **Row 2** Purl to last 20 (25) stitches, [k5, p5] twice, k0 (0, 0, 0, 5, 5) k5. **Row 3** Work Row 3 of Basket Stitch chart to color change, work Row 3 of Cable Chart over next 6 stitches, knit to color change, work Row 3 of Cable Chart over next 6 stitches, knit to end.
Continue in stockinette stitch, Cable Chart (changing colors as indicated on diagram), and Basket Stitch, until piece measures 11 (13, 16½, 19½, 19½, 19½)" from cast-on. AT SAME TIME, work buttonhole at 10 (11, 11½, 12, 12, 12)" from cast-on as follows: **Next RS row** Work 5 stitches in Basket Stitch, bind off 3 stitches, complete row. On next row, cable cast on 3 stitches over bind-off. Work 2 more buttonholes spaced 3½" apart.

Shape panels
Work as Left Front EXCEPT decrease for center panel *before* the second

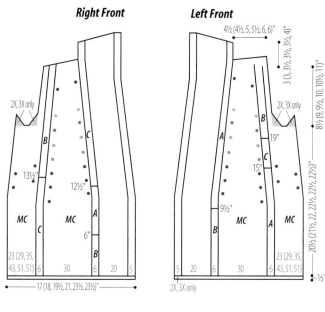

Right Front   *Left Front*

4½ (4½, 5, 5½, 6, 6)"

3 (3, 3½, 3½, 3½, 4)"

2X, 3X only

8½ (9, 9½, 10, 10½, 11)"

19"

13½"

12½"

15"

20½ (21½, 22, 22½, 22½, 22½)"

9½"

MC   MC   MC   MC

6"

23 (29, 35, 43, 51, 51) 6   30   6   20   5

5   20   6   30   6   23 (29, 35, 43, 51, 51)

½"

2X, 3X only

17 (18, 19½, 21, 23½, 23½)"

Chart key
- Decrease all sizes
- Decrease S-2X only
- Decrease S-1X only
- Decrease S-L only
- Decrease S-M only

Refer to instructions for specific decrease placement for each size.

cable on the first Row 5 and *after* the first cable on the next Row 5; for side panel, decrease at the end of the row and after the second cable.

Shape armholes
Work as Left Front EXCEPT bind off at beginning of WS rows.

Shape shoulders
Work as Left Front EXCEPT bind off at beginning of WS rows and end with a WS row.

Short-row collar shaping
Work as Left Front EXCEPT work wrap and turn for short rows and bind off on RS rows.

Back armhole shaping
For 2x & 3x only Work as for Left Front EXCEPT join yarn at side edge and knit across. **Next row** P2tog, purl across. Work 3 rows reverse stockinette. Repeat last 4 rows until 1 stitch remains. Fasten off.

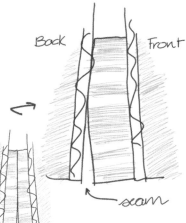

Avoid color mismatch by combining side panels into one and seaming at cable.

Sleeves

With MC and 4.5mm/US 7 needles, cast on 54 (54, 54, 60, 60, 60) stitches.

Turn-back cuff: Establish Small Basket Chart: Rows 1–4 * K3, p3; repeat from *.
Rows 5–8 * P3, k3; repeat from * AT SAME TIME decrease 1 stitch each side on Row 7. *Rows 9–20* Repeat Rows 1–8, then 1–4, decreasing every other RS row 2 (1, 0, 2, 2, 1) times — 48 (50, 52, 54, 54, 56) stitches. Place marker at end of last row. With 4mm/US 6 needles, work 8 rows of k1, p1 rib, increase 1 stitch each side on last row of rib — 50 (52, 54, 56, 56, 58) stitches.

Establish colors and patterns: Row 1 (RS) With 4.5mm/US 7 needles and MC, p4 (5, 6, 7, 7, 8); with C, k6; with MC, k30; with B, k6; with MC, p4 (5, 6, 7, 7, 8). *Row 2* Working in colors as established, k4 (5, 6, 7, 7, 8), purl to last 4 (5, 6, 7, 7, 8) stitches, knit to end. *Row 3* Purl to color change, work Row 3 of Cable Chart. Knit to color change, work Row 3 of cable chart, purl to end. Continue working reverse stockinette stitch (purl on RS, knit on WS) in outer panels, stockinette stitch in center panel, and Cable Chart as established. AT THE SAME TIME increase 1 stitch at each end of 5th row, then every 6 rows 7 (9, 10, 11, 14, 17) times. Work even on 66 (72, 76, 80, 86, 94) stitches until sleeve measures 17 (17½, 18, 18, 18½, 19)" from marker.

Shape cap
Bind off at beginning of rows: 5 stitches 4 times, 2 stitches 6 (6, 6, 6, 26, 26) times, 1 stitch 10 (8, 16, 10, 0, 0) times, 2 stitches 6 (10, 8, 12, 0, 0) times. Bind off remaining stitches.

Finishing

Block. Sew shoulder seams. With RS of fronts facing, 3-needle bind off across cable stitches of collar extension, turn so WS of fronts are facing and continue to 3-needle bind off across remaining stitches. Sew collar extension to back neck. Sew fronts to back along cables. Sew sleeve into armhole; sew sleeve seam. Sew buttons on Left Front to match buttonholes.

Optional standard cuff

With 4mm/ US 6 needles and MC, cast on 50 (54, 54, 58, 58, 62) stitches. Work 2" of k2, p2 rib. Continue from Row 1 of sleeve instructions.

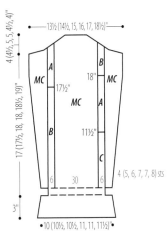

Stripe Jacket

Knit stripes into style. The
basket stitch button band
builds into a shawl collar.
Mismatched stripes join in the
back. By knitting the bands and
fronts in one piece, you'll avoid
this becoming another UFO.

Stripe Jacket

INTERMEDIATE+

S (M, L, 1X, 2X, 3X)

A 36 (39, 42, 45, 48, 51)"
B 23 (23½, 25, 25½, 25½, 26½)"
C 30½ (33, 33, 34, 35, 36½)"

10cm/4"

29

21

**over stockinette stitch
(knit on RS, purl on WS)
using smaller needles**

1 2 3 **4** 5 6

Medium weight

A 525 (550, 625, 675, 750, 775) yds
B 305 (330, 375,400, 440, 475) yds
C 350 (380, 430,460, 510, 530) yds

4mm/US 6, 4.5mm/US 7,
or size to obtain gauge

5 • 16mm (5/8")

&

Stitch markers

Medium: 6 balls TRENDSETTER YARNS Merino
VIII in 42000 Ash (A), 4 balls each in 334 Plum
(B), and 6823 Bubblegum (C); page 27

Medium: 6 balls TRENDSETTER YARNS Merino VIII
in 335 Deep Eggplant (A), 4 balls each in 8772
Burnt Rust (B), and 9779 Magenta (C); page 22

Notes
1 See *Techniques*, page 160, for intarsia knitting, wrap and turn for short rows, cable cast-on, and 3-needle bind-off. **2** When only 2 numbers are given, the first is for sizes S, M, L and the second is for sizes 1X, 2X, 3X. **3** Some stripes are worked over an odd number of rows, so you can (and may) decide to work with a circular needle to get to the end most conveniently (and with fewer cut ends). **4** See *Intarsia Tips*, page 141.

Garter Border 1 (2)
Knit 2 rows B (A) and 8 rows A (B).

Back
With B and smaller needles, cast on 94 (102, 110, 118, 126, 134) stitches, placing marker after 39 (43, 47, 51, 55, 59) stitches. Work Garter Border 1. Change to larger needles and begin working Stripe Sequence for Back in stockinette stitch, changing colors at marker as shown on chart. Continue until piece measures 15 (15, 15½, 15½, 15½, 16)" from cast-on.
Shape armholes
Bind off 15 (17, 18, 19, 20, 20) stitches at beginning of next 2 rows — 64 (68, 74, 80, 86, 94) stitches. Work even until armhole measures 8 (8½, 9½, 10, 10, 10½)".
Shape shoulders and neck
Next RS row K22 (23, 25, 27, 29, 32) stitches, bind off center 20 (22, 24, 26, 28, 30) stitches, knit to end. **Left shoulder: Next row** Bind off 10 (11, 12, 13, 14, 15) stitches, purl to neck edge. **Next row** Bind off 2 stitches, knit to end. Bind off remaining 10 (10, 11, 12, 13, 15) stitches. **Right shoulder: Next row** (WS) Join yarn at neck edge, purl to end. **Next row** Bind off 10 (11, 12, 13, 14, 15) stitches, knit to end. **Next row** Bind off 2 stitches, purl to end. **Next row** Bind off remaining 10 (10, 11, 12, 13, 15) stitches.

Left Front
With B and smaller needles, cast on 56 (60, 66, 70, 74, 78) stitches. Work Garter Border 1. Change to larger needles. **Establish patterns: Row 1** (RS) With B, k48 (52, 58, 60, 64, 68) for Left Stripe Sequence; place marker (pm); with A, k8 (10) for Button Band Chart 1. **Row 2** With A, k2, purl to marker; with B, purl to end. Work as established, following Stripe Sequences until 6 (5) repeats of Button Band Chart 1 are complete; on last WS row, move marker to 16 (20) stitches from beginning of row.
Next RS row Work Stripe Sequence to marker; then with B work Button Band Chart 2 to end. Continue until piece measures same length as Back to armhole.
Shape armhole
Bind off 15 (17, 18, 19, 20, 20) stitches at beginning of next RS row — 41 (43, 48, 51, 54, 58) stitches. Work even until armhole measures same length as Back armhole.
Shape shoulder
Bind off 10 (11, 12, 13, 14, 15) stitches at the beginning of the next RS row. Work 1 row even.
Next RS row Bind off 10 (10, 11, 12, 13, 15) stitches, work to end.
Collar extension
Continue on remaining 21 (22, 25, 26, 27, 28) stitches, working in basket stitch pattern as established. Work until collar height measures half the width of the back neck plus ½", end with a RS row.

Stripe Sequence

Button Band | Left Front & Sleeve:

	B	16R
	A	7R
	B	1R
A	C	5R
	A	12R
	C	1R
	A	3R
	B	1R
	C	6R
	A	3R
C	C	2R
	A	7R
	B	16R
	C	2R
	B	7R
	C	1R
	A	3R
	C	1R
B	A	5R
	C	14R
	A	2R
	B	1R
	A	7R
	B	2R
	C	1R
	A	5R
	C	14R
A	A	2R
	B	3R
	C	2R
	B	5R
	C	2R
	A	20R
	B	2R

Button Band | Left Front & Sleeve

Back:

B	C	16R
A		7R
B		1R
C		5R
A	B	12R
C		1R
A		3R
B		1R
C		6R
A		3R
C	B	2R
A		7R
B		16R
C		2R
B	A	7R
C		1R
A		3R
C		1R
A	B	5R
C		14R
A		2R
B		1R
A	C	7R
B		2R
C		1R
A		5R
C	B	14R
A		2R
B		3R
C		2R
B	A	5R
C		2R
A		20R
B		2R

Marker
Back

Color key
A *Ash*
B *Plum*
C *Bubblegum*

A *Deep Eggplant*
B *Burnt Rust*
C *Magenta*

Chart key
2 R = 2 rows

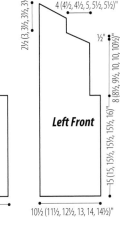

Back

4½ (5, 5½, 6, 6, 6½)"
12 (13, 14, 15, 16, 18)"
18 (19½, 21, 22½, 24, 25½)"

Left Front

4 (4½, 4½, 5, 5½, 5½)"
2½ (3, 3½, 3¼, 3½, 3½)"
½"
8 (8¾, 9½, 10, 10, 10½)"
15 (15, 15½, 15½, 16)"
10½ (11½, 12½, 13, 14, 14½)"

Button Band 2
1X, 2X, 3X

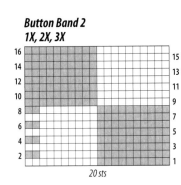

20 sts

Button Band 1
1X, 2X, 3X

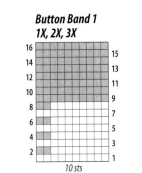

10 sts

Button Band 2
S, M, L

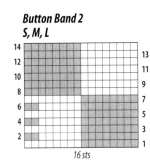

16 sts

Button Band 1
S, M, L

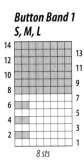

8 sts

Stitch key
☐ Knit on RS, purl on WS
▨ Purl on RS, knit on WS

Shape collar

Short row 1 (WS) Work 17 (17, 19, 19, 21, 21) stitches, wrap next stitch and turn work (W&T). **All RS rows** Work in pattern to end. **Short row 2** Work 14 (14, 15, 15, 17, 17) stitches, W&T. **Short row 3** Work 11 stitches, W&T. **Next WS row** Bind off 8 (10) stitches, complete row hiding wraps; place remaining stitches on hold.

Right Front

Work as Left Front to armhole shaping EXCEPT use Garter Border 2, Right Stripe Sequence AND work Buttonhole Band Chart at beginning of RS and end of WS rows. AT THE SAME TIME make buttonholes in the middle of the 1st, 2nd, 4th, 5th, and 7th stockinette sections of Buttonhole Band. To work buttonhole on WS rows, work to last 6 (7) stitches, bind off 3 stitches, knit to end. On the following row, k3 (4), cable cast on 3 stitches, finish row.

Shape armhole, shoulder, & collar

Work as Left Front EXCEPT bind off stitches at beginning of WS rows AND work short rows on RS rows.

Left (Right) Sleeve

With A (B) and smaller needles, cast on 38 (42, 44, 44, 46, 46) stitches, work Garter Border 2 (1). Change to larger needles. Work in stockinette stitch, following Stripe Sequence for Left (Right) sleeve for 2 rows. Work 2 rows continue, increasing 1 stitch each end of next (RS) row, then every 6 rows 15 (17, 18, 20, 21, 23) times — 70 (78, 82, 86, 90, 94) stitches. Work even until sleeve measures 19 (19½, 20, 20, 20½, 21½)" from cast-on.

Shape cap

Bind off 4 stitches at the beginning of the next 4 rows, then 2 stitches every row 12 (16, 18, 20, 22, 24) times — 30 stitches remain. Bind off 3 stitches at the beginning of the next 4 rows. Bind off remaining stitches.

Finishing

Join shoulder seams. With collar stitches on 2 needles and right sides facing, join collar with 3-needle bind off. Sew side of collar extension to back of neck, easing any excess into neck. Join side seams. Sew sleeves into armhole openings, sew sleeve seams. Sew on buttons.

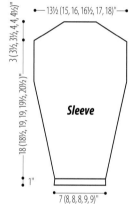

Sleeve

13½ (15, 16, 16½, 17, 18)"

3 (3½, 3½, 4, 4, 4½)"

18 (18½, 19, 19, 19½, 20½)"

1"

7 (8, 8, 8, 9, 9)"

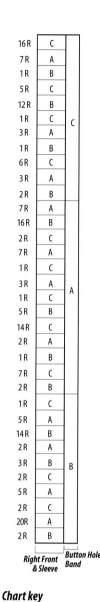

16R	C	
7R	A	
1R	B	
5R	C	
12R	B	
1R	C	C
3R	A	
1R	B	
6R	C	
3R	A	
2R	B	
7R	A	
16R	B	
2R	C	
7R	A	
1R	C	
3R	A	A
1R	C	
5R	B	
14R	C	
2R	A	
1R	B	
7R	C	
2R	B	
1R	C	
5R	A	
14R	B	
2R	A	
3R	B	B
2R	C	
5R	A	
2R	C	
20R	A	
2R	B	

Right Front & Sleeve | **Button Hole Band**

Color key
A Ash
B Plum
C Bubblegum

A Deep Eggplant
B Burnt Rust
C Magenta

Chart key
2 R = 2 rows

Stitch key
☐ Knit on RS, purl on WS
▧ Purl on RS, knit on WS
— 3-stitch buttonhole; place as directed in text

Buttonhole Band 2
1X, 2X, 3X

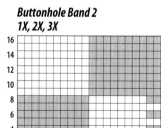

20 sts

Buttonhole Band 1
1X, 2X, 3X

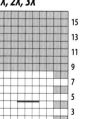

10 sts

Buttonhole Band 2
S, M, L

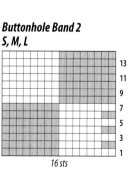

16 sts

Buttonhole Band 1
S, M, L

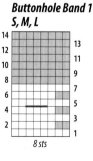

8 sts

Miters

29

Harlequin

What could be more addictive? Miters are just so easy and so rewarding, plus great fun to knit. They allow me to create stunning jackets and coats. Even simple designs like the Coco Vee Cape and Miter Vee Capelet never fail to turn heads.

Harlequin Swagger

How miters have evolved! After
making the Harlequin A-line Vest
with progressively smaller miters,
my next step was this fabulous
Swagger. Stripes of stockinette
and garter worked on larger
needles open the fabric, allowing
the skirt to flare, drape, and move.

Harlequin Swing

One design has so many possibilities. The skirt of the Swagger—knit from waist to hem—was just too inviting: I had to create this Swing Coat. The tapered fit of the upper body and sleeves accentuate the flare in the skirt. Miters make it so easy to refine the shape of a seamless garment, so easy to be dramatic.

34

Basic Miters

Work all shapes as follows, working colors, stitch numbers, and stitches (garter and stockinette) as key indicates.

Full Miter

Row 1 (RS) Cable cast on, or pick up and knit stitches along completed miter edges. *Row 2* Knit—1 garter ridge. *All RS rows* Change color, knit to 1 stitch before center stitch, SK2P, knit to end—2 stitches decreased. *Row 4* Purl—1 stockinette stripe. *Row 6* Knit. Repeat Rows 3–6. When 3 stitches remain, turn work to wrong side (WS); SK2P. Cut yarns not needed for next shape. Do not fasten off.

Right-half Miter

Row 1 (RS) Turn and slip stitch to right needle (counts as first stitch), pick up and knit required stitches along completed miter. *Row 2* Knit—1 garter ridge. *All RS rows* Change color, knit to last 2 stitches, SSK—1 stitch decreased. *Row 4* Purl—1 stockinette stripe. *Row 6* Knit. Repeat Rows 3–6. When 2 stitches remain, turn work to WS, k2tog. Cut yarns and fasten off.

Left-half Miter

Work as Right-half Miter EXCEPT on RS rows, k2tog at beginning of row.

Getting started with the
Harlequin Coat

First, work the Gauge Miter on page 38.
Use the Swagger Skirt Diagram as a map as you knit your way from Miter 1 through Miter 28.

1 Begin at the lower left corner with Miter 1.
*Its diamond shape tells us it is a full miter: its color helps locate the diamond in the Harlequin Key. The key tells us the number of stitches, whether they are picked up or cast on, the colors to use, and color order: **BA** means start with B, the first color. Refer to the Basic Full Miter instructions and the key for specifics, then work Miter 1 as follows:*

Row 1 (RS) With B and 4.5mm/US 7 needles, cable cast on 45 stitches for S/M (49 for L/1X). *Row 2* Knit—1 ridge in B. *Row 3* Change to A, knit to 1 stitch before center stitch, SK2P, knit to end—2 stitches decreased. *Row 4* Purl—1 stockinette stripe in A. *Row 5* Change to B, work as Row 3. *Row 6* Knit. Repeat Rows 3–6 until 3 stitches remain; turn work to WS, SK2P—1 stitch remains on needle. Do not cut yarns; the key shows both A and B will be used in Miter 2.

2 Now you're ready to work Miter 2.
The shape is not a diamond but a half diamond. We will follow the Basic Right-half Miter instructions; the color tells us that it is part of the second tier. All the miters within a tier share size, color, and stripe sequence.

Row 1 (RS) Turn and slip stitch from left needle to right; this counts as your first stitch. With A, pick up and knit 27 (29) stitches along Miter 1—28 (30) stitches. *Row 2* Knit—1 garter ridge in A. *All RS rows* Change to B, knit to last 2 stitches, SSK—1 stitch decreased. *Row 4* Knit—1 garter ridge in B. *Row 5* With A, work as Row 3 *Row 6* Purl—1 stockinette stripe in A. Repeat Rows 3–6 until 6 B garter ridges are complete (**A6B** in the Key). Change A to C and work until 2 stitches remain (for 2-color version continue with A and B) turn work to WS, k2tog. Cut yarns and fasten off (the next shape, Miter 3, does not build from Miter 2).

Swagger Skirt

Color key for Harlequin Coat

Swagger – 3-color	Swagger – 2-color	Swing Coat – 3-color
A Hunter Green	**A** Charcoal	**A** Dark Plum
B Citrus	**B** Camel	**B** Rose
C Lime		**C** Plum

3 **Now you're ready to work** Miter 3.

Miter 3 is exactly like Miter 1: in the same tier, in the same color and shape. Work it as for Miter 1.

4 Miter 4 **connects Miter 3 to Miter 1.**

The shape tells us to follow Basic Full Miter instructions; the color, that it is part of the second tier and will stripe like Right-half Miter 2:

Row 1 (RS) Turn and slip stitch from Miter 3 to right needle (first stitch). With A, pick up 26 (28) stitches along Miter 3, 1 stitch in its cast-on edge, and 27 (29) stitches along Miter 1 — 55 (59) stitches. Continue as for Miter 1, EXCEPT knit Row 4 AND work until there are 6 B ridges (**A6B**). Change A to C (for 2 colors, do not change) and complete Miter. Cut C; B will be used for Miter 5.

5 **For** Miter 5, **follow Basic Full Miter instructions with new specifics.**

Miter 5 is in a new tier with new color and stitch count.

Row 1 (RS) Turn and slip stitch from Miter 4 (first stitch). With A, pick up 30 (32) stitches along Miter 4, 1 stitch from point of Miter 1, and 31 (33) stitches along Miter 2 — 63 (67) stitches. Continue as for Miter 4 EXCEPT work 7 B ridges (**A7B**). Fasten off. For the longer swing coat, do not fasten off; follow instructions, diagram, and key on next page for Right-half Miter 5a.

6 **Miters 6–8 are worked as for Miters 3–5. For Swagger only, begin pickup for small Miter 9 along side of Miter 8, 15 (16) stripes above tip of Miter 4.**

Continue working Miters 10–28 for Swagger Skirt or Miters 8a–28c for Swing Skirt. For Swing, do not work miters 9, 13, 17, 21, 25, or 28.

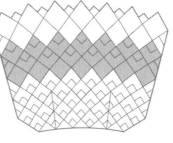

Chart key
— *Cast on*
-- *pick up and knit*
→ *Direction of work*

CO 45 (49)

Full 1, 3, 6, 10, 14, 18, 22

With 4.5 mm/US 7 needle, cast on with B. Work B in garter, A in stockinette.

Right-half 2   Left-half 26
Full 4, 7, 11, 15, 19, 23

Work as Basic Miters EXCEPT work 1 A ridge and 1 B ridge. Then work A in stockinette and B in garter until 6 B ridges. Change A to C (for 2 colors, do not change) and continue.

Full 5, 8, 12, 16, 20, 24, 27

Work as Basic Full Miter EXCEPT work 1 A ridge and 1 B ridge. Then work A in stockinette and B in garter until 7 B ridges. Change A to C (for 2 colors, do not change) and continue. Fasten off.

Full 9, 13, 17, 21, 25, 28

Shape as Basic Full Miter EXCEPT work in all garter. After 6 A ridges, alternate B and A. Fasten off.

STANDARD FIT

S (M, L, 1X)

A 36 (39, 42, 44)"

B SWAGGER 28 (30, 32, 34)"
SWING 38 (40, 42, 44)"

C 13½ (14¼, 15, 15¾)"

D SWAGGER 56 (56, 59½, 59½)"
SWING 77 (77, 82, 82)"

10cm/4"

42

23

over garter stitch (knit every row), using 4mm/US 6 needles

gauge miter measures 5" from point to point

1 2 **3** 4 5 6

Light weight

A 1100 (1200, 1375, 1500) yds
B 850 (925, 1050, 1150) yds
C 350 (375, 425, 475) yds

A 1250 (1375, 1575, 1725) yds
B 1050 (1125, 1275, 1400) yds

A 1650 (1800, 2050, 2250) yds
B 1275 (1375, 1575, 1725) yds
C 525 (575, 625, 675) yds

3.25mm/US 3, 4mm/US 6, and 4.5mm/US 7, or size to obtain gauge

3.75mm/US 5, 73cm (29") or longer

&

Stitch markers

Small 9 balls TRENDSETTER YARNS Merino VI in 81 Hunter Green (A), 7 balls in 329 Citrus (B), and 3 balls in 328 Lime (C); page 31

Medium 11 balls TRENDSETTER YARNS Merino VI in 305 Charcoal (A) and 9 balls in 9905 Camel (B); page 33

Large 15 balls SIGNATUR Pure New Wool DK in 738 Dark Plum (A), 12 balls in 627 Rose (B), and 5 balls in 626 Plum (C); page 35

Harlequin Coat

Notes

1 See *Techniques*, page 160, for k2tog, SSK, SK2P, M1, and cable cast-on. *2* Work each miter in the number order shown on diagrams. *3* Work skirt section first, then rotate it 180° and work bodice section by picking up stitches along original cast-on edges of squares. *4* 'Pick up' means 'pick up and knit'; see *Miter Tips* on page 141 for using dpn. *5* Instructions are given for 3-color version. For 2-color version as shown on cover, do not change to C, continue with A; special instructions are in parentheses.

⬦ Gauge Miter

Row 1 (RS) With A and 4mm/US 6 needle, cable cast on 37 sts. *All WS rows* Knit *All RS rows* Knit to 1 stitch before center stitch; slip 1, knit 2 together, pass slip stitch over (SK2P), knit to end—2 stitches decreased. When 3 stitches remain, turn work to wrong side; SK2P. Fasten off. From point to point, miter should measure 5". If you change needle size to get gauge, adjust other needle sizes accordingly.

Skirt Section

Note 1 Skirt section is worked in 2 sizes: S/M (L/1X) and 2 lengths: swagger (hip length) and swing (knee length).

Follow *Getting Started* on pages 36–37 for Miters 1–28 to complete the swagger jacket's skirt section or start the swing coat's skirt section. For the swing coat, work the additional skirt miters shown on this page: after Miter 5, work 5a; after 8, work 8a and 8b; continue following the Swing Skirt diagram.

77 (77, 82, 82)"

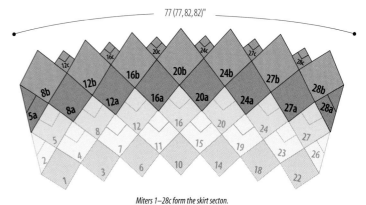

Miters 1–28c form the skirt secton.

Swing Skirt

Right-half 5a   Left-half 28a
Full 8a, 12a, 16a, 20a, 24a, 27a

Work B in garter, C (A) in stockinette until 7 B ridges. Change B to A (for 2 colors, do not change) and continue.

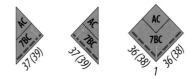

Full 8b, 12b, 16b, 20b, 24b, 27b, 28b

Work C (B) in garter, A in stockinette until 10 C (B) ridges. Change A to B (for 2 colors, do not change) and continue. Fasten off.

Mini 12c, 16c, 20c, 24c, 27c, 28c

Shape as Basic Miter EXCEPT work in all garter. After 6 A ridges, alternate B and A. Fasten off.

Bodice

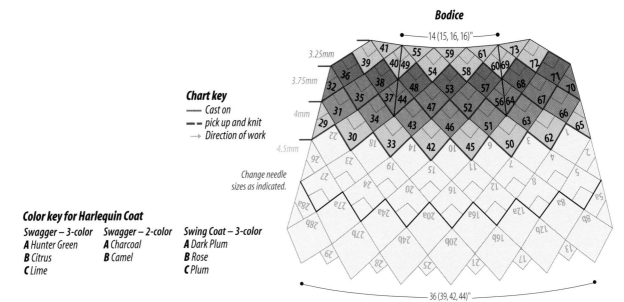

Chart key
— Cast on
– – pick up and knit
→ Direction of work

14 (15, 16, 16)"

3.25mm

3.75mm

4mm

4.5mm

Change needle sizes as indicated.

Color key for Harlequin Coat

Swagger – 3-color	Swagger – 2-color	Swing Coat – 3-color
A Hunter Green	**A** Charcoal	**A** Dark Plum
B Citrus	**B** Camel	**B** Rose
C Lime		**C** Plum

36 (39, 42, 44)"

Beginning with Miter 29, work bodice from cast-on edge of skirt.

Bodice Section

Notes 1 Bodice section is worked in four sizes:
S (M, L, 1X). **2** All bodice miters are worked in
garter stitch; 2 knit rows form one garter ridge.
3 Change needle sizes as indicated on diagram.

Miter 29

Row 1 (RS) With 4.5mm/US 7 needles and A, pick
up 20 (21, 22, 23) stitches along cast-on edge
of Miter 22. **Row 2 and all WS rows** Knit. **All RS rows**
Change color, knit to 2 last stitches, SSK.

Continue Miters 30–73, referring to Basic Full,
Right-half, and Left-half Miters on page 36
EXCEPT knit all WS rows AND change color on
RS rows only when indicated.

Right-half 29 Left-half 65
Full 30, 33, 42, 45, 50, 62

With 4mm/US 6 needles, alternate A and B
until 4 B ridges. Change A to C (B)
and continue.

Right-half 32, 44, 64 Left-half 37, 56, 70
Full 35, 47, 52, 67

Change to 3.75mm/US 5 needles. Work 7 B
ridges, then alternate A and B.

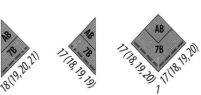

Right-half 49, 69 Left-half 40, 60
Full 39, 54, 58, 72

Change to 3.25mm/US 3 needles, work 6 C
(B) ridges, then alternate A and C (B) ridges.

Full 31, 34, 43, 46, 51, 63, 66

Alternate A and B until 4 B ridges. Change A
to C (B) and continue.

Full 36, 38, 48, 53, 57, 68, 71

Work 6 A ridges, then alternate B and A.

Bottom-half 41, 55, 59, 61, 73

Alternate B and C (A) ridges. Work same
as Full Miter EXCEPT knit all WS rows AND
k2tog at beginning and SSK at end of all RS
rows until 5 stitches remain, turn work to
WS, k2tog, k1, SSK. Bind off.

Sleeves

Notes *1* Work sleeves with 4mm/US 6 needles. *2* Center panel is worked first, then shaping is worked along sides of panel. Work miters in number order on diagram. *3* Center panel is worked in two sizes: S/M (L/1X). *4* If a shorter sleeve is desired, work Miter 24 as a Bottom-half miter.

Center panel

Work Miters 1–24, following Full Miter, Left-half Miter, Right-half Miter and Bottom-half Miter instructions on page 36. Rotate sleeve 180° and work Quarter Miters at cuff edge to complete center panel.

Sides of sleeve panel

Right side

Row 1 With RS facing and B, pick up and k105 (118) stitches along edge, beginning at Miter 17 and ending at Miter 25. **Row 2** Knit. Cut B. **Row 3** With A, knit. **Row 4** Bind off 10, purl to end. **Row 5** Bind off 2, knit to end. Repeat last 2 rows 5 (7) times more—33 (22) stitches. **Next row** (WS) Bind off 10, work to end. **Next row** Knit. **Sizes M and 1X only: Next row** (WS) Bind off 10 (6). **Next row** Knit. **All sizes** Bind off remaining stitches.

Left side

Work as for right side, picking up stitches along edge, beginning at Miter 26 and ending at Miter 22, and reverse shaping by binding off 10 at beginning of RS rows and 2 at beginning of WS rows.

Finishing

Join shoulders.

Front and neckband

Mark the top of Miter 32 (left front) and Miter 70 (right front). Measuring from these markers, mark every 4", down to hem and around the neck. **Row 1** With size 3.75mm/US 5 circular needle, RS facing, and B, begin at lower right front edge of skirt, and pick up and knit 23 stitches for every 4" EXCEPT pick up and knit 3 extra stitches at Miter 70 and Miter 32 markers (1 before, 1 at, and 1 after marker). **Row 2** Knit, removing all markers except at Miters 32 and 70. **Row 3** *Knit to marker, remove marker, M1, k1, M1; repeat from *, knit to end. **Row 4** Knit. Bind off loosely.

Set in sleeves. Sew sleeve seams.

27 (31) sts   13 (15)   13 (15)   13 (15)   13 (15)

Full 1   Full 2   Full 4

Work 5 A ridges then alternate C (B) and A.

14 (16)   14 (16)

Right-half 3   Left-half 8

Work 6 A ridges then alternate C (B) and A.

14 (16)   14 (16)

Full 5

Work 5 A ridges then alternate B and A.

15 (17)   15 (17)   14 (16)   14 (16)

Right-half 7   Left-half 13
Full 6, 9

Work 1 B ridge, 5 A ridges, then alternate B and A.

15 (17)   15 (17)

Full 10, 11, 14

Work 1 B ridge, 5 A ridges, then alternate C (B) and A.

16 (18)   16 (18)   16 (18)   16 (18)

Right-half 12   Left-half 18
Full 15, 16, 19

Work 2 B ridges, 5 A ridges, then alternate B and A.

17 (19)   17 (19)   17 (18)   17 (18)

Right-half 17   Left-half 22
Full 20

Work 2 B ridges, 5 A ridges, then alternate B and A.

17 (18)   17 (18)

Full 21, 23, 24*

Work 2 B ridges, 5 A ridges, then alternate C (B) and A ridges.

17 (18)   17 (18)

* For a shorter sleeve, work Miter 24 as a Bottom-half Miter.

Bottom-half 24*

Work 2 B ridges, 5 A ridges same as Full Miter EXCEPT knit all WS rows AND k2tog at beginning and SSK at end of RS rows until 5 stitches remain, turn work, k2tog, k1, SSK. Bind off.

14 (16) sts   14 (16) sts

Quarter 25, 26

Work in A, same as Miter 24 until 2 stitches remain, turn work, SSK. Bind off.

Center Panel

13½ (14¼, 15¾, 16¼)"

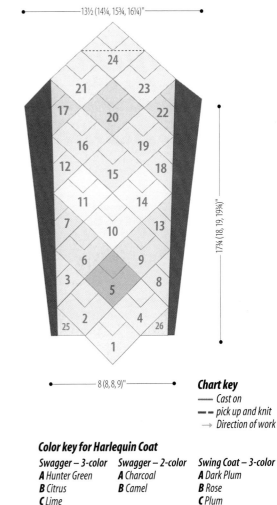

8 (8, 8, 9)"

17¾ (18, 19, 19¾)"

Chart key
—— Cast on
– – pick up and knit
→ Direction of work

Color key for Harlequin Coat

Swagger – 3-color	Swagger – 2-color	Swing Coat – 3-color
A Hunter Green	**A** Charcoal	**A** Dark Plum
B Citrus	**B** Camel	**B** Rose
C Lime		**C** Plum

Harlequin Vest

INTERMEDIATE

XS (S, M, L, 1X, 2X)

A 35 (37½, 40, 42½, 45, 50)"
B 27½ (29½, 31¼, 33¼, 35, 37)"
C 10 (12, 14, 16, 17, 18)
D 40 (42½, 45, 47½, 50, 52½)

10cm/4"

44 ▦ 21

*over garter stitch (knit every row),
using 4mm/6 US needles*

*gauge miter measures 4"
from point to point*

1 2 **3** 4 5 6

Light weight

MC 650 (725, 800, 925, 1050, 1175) yds
A 275 (325, 350, 400, 450, 500) yds
B & C 275 (300, 325, 375, 425, 475) yds each

MC 400 (450, 500, 575, 650, 725) yds
A 275 (325, 350, 400, 450, 500) yds
B & C 275 (300, 325, 375, 425, 475) yds each
D 250 (275, 300, 350, 400, 450) yds

3.5 mm/US 4, 3.75 mm/US 5, 4 mm/US 6,
or size to obtain gauge

Optional: Small double-pointed needle (dpn)
for pick up.

Medium 6 balls TRENDSETTER YARNS Merino
VI in 9509 Marine (MC), 3 balls each in 7440
Dark Teal (A), 8964 Royal Blue (B),
and 222 Turquoise (C)

Medium 4 balls TRENDSETTER YARNS MONDIAL
Superwool in 317 Olive (MC), 3 balls each in
400 Brown Heather (A), 300 Beige (B), 500
Brown (C), and 529 Chocolate (D); page 28

Notes
1 See *Techniques*, page 160, for k2tog, SSK, SK2P, and cable cast-on. **2** Change needle sizes as indicated on vest diagram. **3** Work each miter in order of numbers shown on diagram. **4** 'Pick up' means 'pick up and knit'; see *Miter Tips*, page 144, for using dpn. **5** Instructions are given for 5-color version. Changes for 4-color version are shown in parentheses.

Gauge Miter
Row 1 (RS) With A and 3.75mm/US 5 needle, cast on 29 sts. *Row 2* Knit. *All RS rows* Change to MC and knit to 1 stitch before center stitch; slip 1, knit 2 together, pass slip stitch over (SK2P); knit to end—2 stitches decreased. *Row 4* Purl. *Row 6* Knit. Repeat Rows 3–6 until 3 stitches remain. Turn work to wrong side; SK2P. Fasten off. From point to point, miter should measure 4". If you change needle size to get gauge, adjust the other needle sizes accordingly.

Vest
Follow *Getting Started* on pages 44–45.

Finishing
Join shoulders.

I first created the blue combination in four colors. Always wanting to add more, I played with neutrals and was compelled to add a fifth color! My next step would be to play with length, but I'll let you do that.

Basic Miters

Work the shapes as follows, working colors, stitch numbers, and stitches (garter and stockinette) as key indicates.

Full Miter

Row 1 (RS) Cable cast on or pick up and knit stitches along completed miter edges. *Row 2* Knit — 1 garter ridge. *All RS rows* Change color, knit to 1 stitch before center stitch, SK2P, knit to end — 2 stitches decreased. *Row 4* Purl — 1 stockinette stripe. *Row 6* Knit. Repeat Rows 3–6 until required number of stripes are completed. Continue in garter (knit every row) decreasing RS rows until 3 stitches remain, turn work to WS, SK2P. Cut yarns not needed for next shape. Do not fasten off.

Right-half Miter

Row 1 (RS) Turn and slip stitch to right needle (counts as first stitch), pick up and knit required stitches along completed miter. *Row 2* Knit — 1 garter ridge. *All RS rows* Change color, knit to last 2 stitches, SSK — 1 stitch decreased. *Row 4* Purl — 1 stockinette stripe. *Row 6* Knit. Repeat Rows 3–6 until required number of stripes are completed. Continue in garter, decreasing on RS rows until 2 stitches remain, turn work to WS, k2tog. Cut yarns not needed for next shape and fasten off.

Left-half Miter

Work as Right-half Miter EXCEPT on RS rows, k2tog at beginning of row.

Getting started with the
Harlequin Vest

First, work the Gauge Miter on page 42.
Use the portion of the vest diagram shown here as a map and work the miters in order.

1 **Begin with** Miter 1 **at lower left corner of the diagram.**
Its diamond shape tells us it is a full miter; its color helps locate the diamond in the Harlequin Key. The key tells us the number of stitches, whether they are picked up or cast on, and the contrast color to use. Refer to the Basic Full Miter instructions and the key for specifics, and work Miter 1 as follows:

Row 1 (RS) With MC and 4mm/US 6 needle, cable cast on 31 (33, 35, 37 39, 41) stitches. *Row 2* Knit — 1 ridge in MC. *Row 3* Change to A, knit to 1 stitch before center stitch, SK2P, knit to end — 2 stitches decreased. *Row 4* Knit — 1 garter ridge in A. *Row 5* With MC, work as Row 3. *Row 6* Purl — 1 stockinette stripe. Repeat Rows 3–6 until 5 (5, 6, 6, 7, 7) A garter ridges are completed. Cut A. *Center* With MC, continue in garter until 3 stitches remain. Turn work to WS, SK2P — 1 stitch remains. Cut colors not needed in next miter.

2 **Now you're ready to work** Miter 2.
The shape is not a diamond but a half diamond. We will follow the Basic Right-half Miter instructions; the color tells us that it is part of the second tier. All miters in a tier share size and stripe sequence.

Row 1 (RS) Turn and slip stitch from left needle to right; this counts as your first stitch. With B, pick up 15 (16, 17, 18, 19, 20) stitches along Miter 1 — 16 (17, 18, 19, 20, 21) stitches. *Row 2* Knit — 1 garter ridge. *Row 3* With D for 5-color version (MC for 4-color version), knit to last 2 stitches, SSK — 1 stitch decreased. *Row 4* Purl — 1 stockinette stripe in D (MC). *Row 5* With B, knit to last 2 stitches, SSK. *Row 6* Knit. Repeat Rows 3–6 until 5 (5, 6, 6, 7, 7) stripes in D (MC) are completed. Cut D. *Center* With B, repeat Rows 5–6 until 2 stitches remain. Turn work to WS, k2tog. The next shape, Miter 3, does not build from Miter 2, so cut B and fasten off.

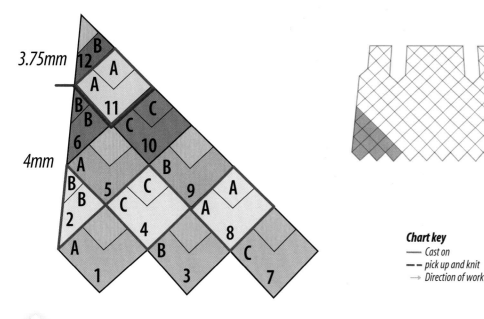

3.75mm

4mm

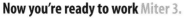

Chart key
—— Cast on
– – pick up and knit
→ Direction of work

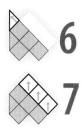

3 **Now you're ready to work** Miter 3.
Miter 3 is in the same tier as Miter 1. Work as for Miter 1 EXCEPT use B instead of A as contrast color.

4 Miter 4 **connects Miter 3 to Miter 1.**
The shape tells us to follow the Basic Full Miter instructions; the color, that it is a part of the second tier and shares specifics with Right-half Miter 2.

Row 1 (RS) Turn and slip stitch from Miter 3 to right needle (first stitch). With C, pick up 14 (15, 16, 17, 18, 19) stitches along Miter 3, 1 stitch in cast-on edge, and 15 (16, 17, 18, 19, 20) stitches along Miter 1—31 (33, 35, 37, 39, 41) stitches. Continue as for Miter 1, alternating C with D (MC), until there are 5 (5, 6, 6, 7, 7) stockinette stripes in D (MC). Cut D. *Center* Continue in garter with C until 3 stitches remain. Turn work to WS, SK2P. Cut C but do not fasten off.

5 **For** Miter 5, **follow Basic Full Miter instructions with new specifics.**
Miter 5 is in a new tier with a new stitch count.

Row 1 (RS) Turn and slip stitch from Miter 4. With A, pick up 14 (15, 16, 17, 18 19) stitches along Miter 4, 1 stitch from point of Miter 1, and 15 (16, 17, 18, 19, 20) stitches along Miter 2—31 (33, 35, 37, 39, 41) stitches. Continue as for Miter 4 alternating A with MC EXCEPT work 4 (4, 5, 5, 6, 6) garter stripes in A. Cut A and complete Center with MC.

6 **Work Miter 6 as Miter 2 EXCEPT use MC instead of D AND work 4 (4, 5, 5, 6, 7) stockinette stripes in MC before cutting MC.**

7 **Work Miters 7–10 as for Miters 3–6 EXCEPT use contrast color indicated on map. Turn to next pages and work miters in order in vest diagram shown on page 47.**

Turn to next pages and work miters in order in vest diagram shown on page 47.

Harlequin Key

CO 31 (33, 35, 37, 39, 41)

Full 1, 3, 7

With 4mm/US 6 needles, cast on with MC. Work 5 (5, 6, 6, 7, 7) garter ridges in A, B, or C. Work center in MC (shaded area on chart).

Right-half 2 Full 4, 8

Work 5 (5, 6, 6, 7, 7) stockinette stripes in D (MC). Work center in A, B, or C.

Full 5, 9

Work 4 (4, 5, 5, 6, 6) garter ridges in A, B, or C. Work center in MC.

Right-half 6 Full 10

Work 4 (4, 5, 5, 6, 7) stockinette stripes in MC. Work center in A, B, or C.

Full 11

Change to 3.75mm/US 5 needles, work 4 (4, 5, 5, 6, 6) stockinette stripes in D (MC). Work center in A, B, or C.

Right-half 12

Work 4 (4, 5, 5, 6, 6) garter ridges in A, B, or C. Work center in MC.

CO 31 (33, 35, 37, 39, 41)

Full 13, 21, 31, 42, 61, 71, 83

With 4mm/US 6 needles, cast on with MC. Work 5 (5, 6, 6, 7, 7) garter ridges in A, B, or C. Work center in MC (shaded area on chart).

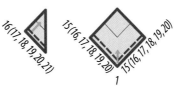

Left-half 97
Full 14, 22, 32, 43, 62, 72, 84

Work 5 (5, 6, 6, 7, 7) stockinette stripes in D (MC). Work center in A, B, or C.

Full 15, 23, 33, 44, 63, 73, 85, 98

Work 4 (4, 5, 5, 6, 6) garter ridges in A, B, or C. Work center in MC.

Left-half 111
Full 16, 24, 34, 45, 64, 74, 86, 99

Work 4 (4, 5, 5, 6, 7) stockinette stripes in MC. Work center in A, B, or C.

Full 17, 25, 35, 46, 65, 75, 87, 100, 112

Change to 3.75mm/US 5 needles, work 4 (4, 5, 5, 6, 6) stockinette stripes in D (MC). Work center in A, B, or C.

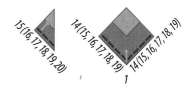

Left-half 129
Full 18, 26, 36, 47, 66, 76, 88, 101, 113

Work 4 (4, 5, 5, 6, 6) garter ridges in A, B, or C. Work center in MC.

Full 19, 27, 37, 48, 67, 77, 89, 102, 114, 130

Work 3 (3, 4, 4, 5, 5) stockinette stripes in MC. Work center in A, B, or C.

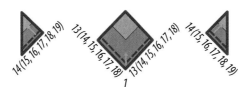

Right-half 20   Left-half 134
Full 28, 38, 49, 68, 78, 90, 103, 115, 131

Work 3 (3, 4, 4, 5, 5) garter ridges in A, B, or C. Work center in D (MC).

Full 29, 39, 50, 69, 79, 91, 104, 116, 132, 135

Work 3 (3, 4, 4, 5, 5) garter ridges in A, B, or C. Work center in MC.

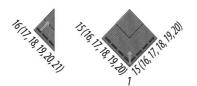

Right-half 30   Left-half 139
Full 40, 51, 70, 80, 92, 105, 117, 133, 136

Work 3 (3, 4, 4, 5, 5) stockinette stripes in MC. Work center in A, B, or C.

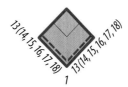

Full 41, 52, 81, 93, 106, 118, 137, 140

Change to 3.5mm/US 4 needles, and work 3 (3, 4, 4, 5, 5) garter ridges in A, B, or C. Work center in D (MC).

Right-half 55, 123   Left-half 138, 82
Full 53, 94, 107, 119, 141

Work 2 (2, 3, 3, 4, 4) stockinette stripes in MC. Work center in A, B, or C.

The Key

Chart key
— Cast on
–– pick up and knit
→ Direction of work

◇ Use D instead of MC

Color key for Harlequin Vest

MC Marine	**MC** Olive
A Dark Teal	**A** Brown Heather
B Royal Blue	**B** Beige
C Turquoise	**C** Brown
	D Chocolate

Change needle sizes as indicated.

35 (37½, 40, 42½, 45, 50)"

3.5mm

3.75mm

4mm

27½ (29½, 31¼, 33¼, 35, 37)"

40 (42½, 45, 47½, 50, 52½)"

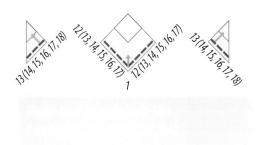

Work 2 (2, 3, 3, 4, 4) stockinette stripes in MC.
Work center in A, B, or C.

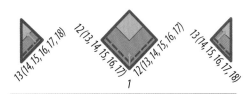

Right-half 96, 143 Left-half 59, 127
Full 57, 109, 121, 125, 145

Work 2 (2, 3, 3, 4, 4) garter ridges in A, B or C.
Work center in D (MC).

Work 2 (2, 3, 3, 4, 4) garter ridges in A, B or C.
Bottom-half: Work same as Full Miter EXCEPT k2tog at beginning and SSK at end until 5 stitches remain, turn, k2tog, k1, SSK. Bind off.
Quarters: Work as Bottom Half Miter until 2 stitches remain, turn, k2tog. Bind off.

CocoVee

Now I am not a pink girl, but I can't help but love this. The variegated yarn does all the work. When selecting the solid color for this combination, be aware that you'll lose the stripes if it matches too closely. Imagine wearing it over jeans.

CoCo Vee

EASY+

A
B

A 13½ (18)"
B 31½ (36)"

10cm/4"

40 ░░░░░░
17

**over garter stitch
(knit all rows)**

**Miter 1 measures approximately 6"
from point to point, 4½" along a side**

1 2 3 **4** 5 6

Medium weight

MC 450 (650) yds
CC 400 (600) yds

5mm/US 8, or size to obtain gauge

Optional Small dpn for pick-up

4 balls TRENDSETTER YARNS Merino VIII
in 335 Deep Eggplant (MC)
and 4 balls Tonalita in 2348 Sunset (CC);
page 51

7 balls TRENDSETTER YARNS Merino Otto
Shadow in 1787 Smoke and Ash (MC), and
6 balls Tonalita in 2374 Desert Valley (CC);
page 49

Notes
1 See *Techniques*, page 160, for SK2P and cable cast-on. **2** Work miters in order shown on Miter Order diagram. **3** 'Pick up' means 'pick up and knit'; see *Miter Tips*, page 144, for using dpn. **4** Always pick up stitches with right side (RS) facing and using MC. **5** Use cable cast-on throughout. **6** When 2 sets of numbers are shown, the capelet is blue, the cape is red; black numbers refer to both. For the smaller capelet, work only the miters shown in white on Miter Order diagram; for the larger cape, work all miters.

Miter 1
Row 1 (RS) With MC, cast on 39 stitches. Mark center stitch.
Row 2 Knit.
Row 3 With CC, knit to 1 stitch before center stitch, SK2P, knit to end — 2 stitches decreased.
Row 4 Knit.
Row 5 With MC, knit to 1 stitch before center stitch, SK2P, knit to end — 2 stitches decreased.
Row 6 Purl.
Repeat Rows 3–6 until 3 stitches remain, ending last repeat with Row 5.
Next row (WS) SK2P — 1 stitch remains. Do not fasten off and do not cut yarns.
Miter measures approximately 6" from point to point.

Miters 2–7, 16, 8, 17, 27
Row 1 (RS) Turn and slip the remaining stitch from last miter to right needle, pick up 19 stitches from left edge of last miter, cast on 19 stitches — 39 stitches. Continue and complete as for Miter 1, EXCEPT cut yarns and fasten off on Miters 7, 16, 8, 17, 27.

Miters 9, 18, 28, 38, 42, 46, 51, 50, 54, 57
Row 1 (RS) With MC, cast on 20 stitches, pick up 19 stitches from edge of miter to the left — 39 stitches. Continue and complete as for Miter 1.

Miters 10–15, 19–25, 29–30, 39–40, 43–44, 47–48, 52, 16, 26, 31–37, 41, 45, 49, 51, 53, 55–56, 58
Row 1 (RS) Turn and slip the remaining stitch from last miter to right needle, pick up 18 stitches from left edge of last miter, pick up 1 stitch in point of miter below, pick up 19 stitches from right edge of miter to the left — 39 stitches. Continue and complete as for Miter 1 EXCEPT cut yarns and fasten off on Miters 25, 30, 40, 44, 48, 52, 37, 41, 45, 49, 53, 56, 58.

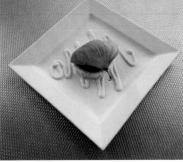

Designer Treat

1 Allowing color gradation to do the work: use a variegated yarn for the (CC) garter ridges and a solid for the (MC) stockinette stripes.

2 Control color: eliminate sections of the variegated yarn that match the solid color.

3 Use DK weight or lighter yarn and more miters to make a scarf.

CoCo Vee Capelet (Cape)
Miter Order

Chart key

— Cast on
- - Pick up and knit
— Cast on for capelet; pick up for cape
→ Direction of work
▢ For cape only

Panel Miter Order

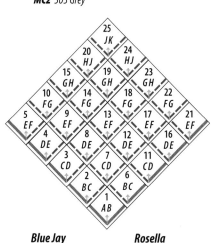

Currawong
- **A** 305 Charcoal
- **B** 42000 Ash
- **C** 303 Grey
- **D** 7800 Ecru
- **MC1** 200 Black
- **MC2** 303 Grey

Blue Jay
- **A** 667 Ensign
- **B** 672 Midnight
- **C** 625 Aegean
- **D** 631 Steel
- **E** 626 Plum
- **F** 657 Purple
- **G** 704 Blueberry
- **H** 663 Peacock
- **J** 671 Jacaranda
- **K** 704 Blueberry
- **MC1 & MC2** 731 Turkish

Rosella
- **A** 664 Cranberry
- **B** 672 Midnight
- **C** 612 Claret
- **D** 611 Ink
- **E** 664 Cranberry
- **F** 657 Purple
- **G** 627 Rose
- **H** 626 Plum
- **J** 705 Sweet Pea
- **K** 704 Blueberry
- **MC1** 612 Claret
- **MC2** 664 Cranberry

Owl
- **A** 716 Chocolate
- **B** 613 Black
- **C** 673 Fox
- **D** 681 Mid-Grey
- **E** 690 Mulga
- **F** 629 Sand
- **G** 630 Mocca
- **H** 608 Cream
- **J** 680 Pale Grey
- **K** 603 Raffia
- **MC1** 690 Mulga
- **MC2** 630 Mocca

Peahen
- **A** 613 Black
- **B** 631 Steel
- **C** 667 Ensign
- **D** 663 Peacock
- **E** 657 Purple
- **F** 697 Dark Olive
- **G** 626 Plum
- **H** 645 Khaki
- **J** 704 Blueberry
- **K** 662 Moss
- **MC1** 730 Aubergine
- **MC2** 645 Khaki

Miter Vee

Notes
1 See *Techniques*, page 160, for SK2P, and cable cast-on.
2 Work each miter in order of numbers shown on Panel Miter Order diagram. **3** 'Pick up' means 'pick up and knit' with right side (RS) facing; see *Miter Tips*, page 137, for using dpn. **4** Refer to one of the miter order diagrams for color placement. **5** When 2 sets of numbers are shown, the first is for the short capelet, the second is for the long capelet. **6** Use cable cast-on throughout.

Miter Panel
Miter 1
Row 1 (RS) With A, cast on 39 stitches. Mark center stitch.
Row 2 and all WS rows Knit.
Row 3 With B, knit to 1 stitch before center stitch, SK2P, knit to end —2 stitches decreased.
Row 5 With A, knit to 1 stitch before center stitch, SK2P, knit to end. Repeat Rows 3–6 until there are 7 ridges of A. Cut A, continue with B until 3 stitches remain. **Next row** (WS) SK2P — 1 stitch remains. Do not fasten off and do not cut yarn.

Miters 2–5
Row 1 Turn and slip the remaining stitch from last miter to right needle; with first color listed (B for Miter 2), pick up 19 stitches from left edge of last miter, and cast on 19 stitches — 39 stitches. Continue and complete as for Miter 1, EXCEPT alternate the 2 colors in the diagram (B and C for Miter 2, for example). Cut yarn and fasten off at end of Miter 5.

Miters 6, 11, 16, 21
Row 1 With first color listed, cast on 20 stitches, pick up 19 stitches from edge of miter to the left — 39 stitches. Continue and complete as for Miter 1, using colors listed.

Miters 7–10, 12–15, 17–20, 22–25
Row 1 Turn and slip the remaining stitch from last miter to right needle; with first color listed pick up 18 stitches from left edge of last miter, 1 stitch in point of miter below, 19 stitches from edge of miter to the left — 39 stitches. Continue and complete as for Miters 2–5.

EASY+

A 22"
B 36 (40)"

10cm/4"

28 | |
23

**over stockinette stitch
(knit on RS, purl on WS)**

Miter 1 measures approximately 5"

1 2 **3** 4 5 6

Light weight
Currawong
MC1, MC2 625 (675) yds each
A, C, D 200 yds each
B 100 yds

Blue Jay, Rosella, Owl, Peahen
MC1, MC2 625 (675) yds
A, K 15 yds each
B, J 45 yds each
C, H 105 yds each
D, G 165 yds each
E, F 195 yds each

4mm/US 6, or size to obtain gauge

Optional Small dpn for pick-up

Currawong
5 balls each TRENDSETTER YARNS Merino VI for MC1 and MC2; 2 balls each for A, C, and D; 1 ball for B; page 52

Blue Jay, Rosella, Owl, Peahen
7 balls each SIGNATUR Pure New Wool DK 8 ply for MC1 and MC2; 2 balls each for D, E, F, and G; 1 ball each for A, B, C, H, J, and K; page 55

Corrugated Garter ANY NUMBER OF STITCHES

Row 1 (RS) Purl.
Row 2 Knit.
Row 3 Knit.
Row 4 Purl.
Repeat Rows 1–4 for Corrugated Garter.

Large Basket Stitch MULTIPLE OF 42 + 21

Rows 1–27: RS rows * P21, k21; repeat from * end, p21.
WS rows * K21, p21; repeat from * end, k21.
Rows 28–54: WS rows * P21, k21; repeat from * end, p21.
RS rows * K21, p21; repeat from * end, k21.
Repeat Rows 1–54.

Small Basket Stitch MULTIPLE OF 14 + 7

Rows 1–9: RS rows * P7, k7; repeat from * across row, p7.
WS rows * K7, p7; repeat from * across row, k7.
Rows 10–18: WS rows * P7, k7; repeat from * across row, p7.
RS rows * K7, p7; repeat from * across row, k7.
Repeat Rows 1–18.

Fronts
Notes

1 Stitches are picked up from two adjoining sides of the Miter Panel. For four of the colorways, the left front is picked up from Miters 25, 20, 15, 10, and 5; the right front from Miters 21 — 25. For the black and white colorway, the left front is picked up from Miters 5–1; the right front from Miters 25, 20, 15, 10, and 5. **2** When worn, the right front wraps over the left. If the fronts are worked in different colors, select color accordingly.

Left Front

With MC1, cast on 20 stitches for collar, place marker (pm); then with RS of Miter Panel facing, pick up and knit 21 stitches from each miter along side of panel as shown in diagram — 125 stitches. **Establish patterns:** Beginning with Row 2 (WS), work Large Basket Stitch to marker, then Corrugated Garter over next 20 stitches (collar). Work in established patterns for 2 (2½) repeats of Large Basket Stitch — 108 (135) rows.
Stepped Edge Next block begins on Row 1 or 28. * **If Row 1, a RS row,** work to last 21 stitches, place them on hold. **If Row 28, a WS row,** work first 21 stitches, place them on hold, complete row. Work 26 more rows to complete block. Repeat from * 3 more times, EXCEPT on last repeat, place 42 stitches on hold. Continue with Corrugated Garter for 27 rows. Bind off.
Miter Trim

Miter 26 Following diagram for color, pick up 20 stitches from last 27 rows of collar, continue across 21 of 42 stitches on hold, decreasing from 21 to 19 stitches — 39 stitches. Continue and complete as for Miter 1 in colors listed.
Miter 27 Row 1 Turn and slip remaining stitch from last miter to right needle; pick up 19 stitches from Miter 26, work remaining 21 stitches on hold, decreasing 2 stitches to 19 stitches — 39 stitches. Continue and complete as for Miter 1 in colors listed. Fasten off.
Miters 28–30 Row 1 With first color listed, pick up 20 stitches along sides of stepped edge, continue across 21 stitches on hold decreasing 2 stitches to 19 stitches — 39 stitches, continue and complete as for Miter 27.

Right Front

With MC2, pick up and knit across Miter Panel and along collar cast-on as shown in diagram. Work as for Left Front EXCEPT work Small Basket Stitch instead of Large Basket Stitch AND reverse Stepped Edge Shaping as follows:
If Row 1, work first 21 stitches, place them on hold. **If Row 10,** work to last 21 stitches, place them on hold. Follow diagram for working Miters 31–35.

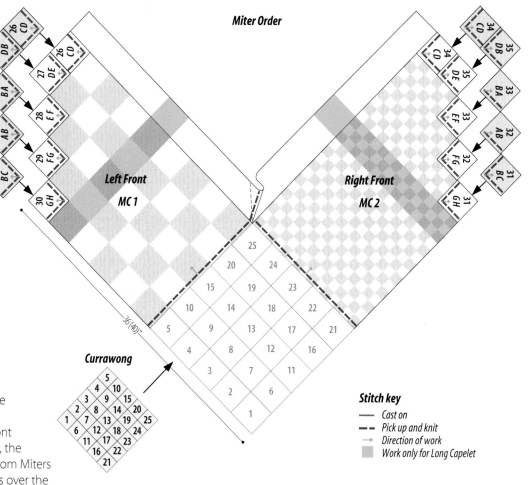

Miter Order

Left Front MC 1

Right Front MC 2

Currawong

36 (40)"

Stitch key
~~~~ Cast on
– – – Pick up and knit
→ Direction of work
▨ Work only for Long Capelet

Miter Vee in Peahen colorway (above);
below from left to right: Owl, Bluejay, and Rosella colorways.

Texture

increase for collar → direction of knitting

Basket St creates
reversible folds

increase
for hemline

wrapped creates a
collar of rib—
corrugated garter
turn back to
form collar

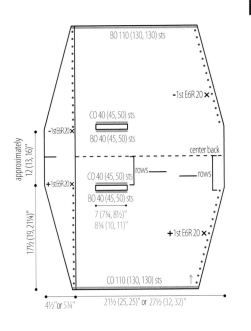

BO 110 (130, 130) sts

-1st E6R 20 ×

CO 40 (45, 50) sts
BO 40 (45, 50) sts

-1st E6R 20 ×

center back

approximately 12 (13, 16)"

CO 40 (45, 50) sts — rows — rows
+1st E6R 20 ×
BO 40 (45, 50) sts

7 (7¾, 8½)"
8¾ (10, 11)"

+1st E6R 20 ×

17½ (19, 21¼)"

CO 110 (130, 130) sts

4½" or 5¾"   21½ (25, 25)" or 27½ (32, 32)"

Boxes Drape

EASY +

A
B

S (M–L, 1X)
A Cross back width 12 (13, 16)"
B Center back length 21½ (25, 25)"
27½ (32, 32)"

10cm/4"
26/33
18/23
over Basket Stitch

1 2 **3** 4 5 6
Light weight
1,200 (1,500, 1,700) yds

1 2 3 **4** 5 6
Medium weight
1,100 (1,300, 1,550) yds

4mm/US 6 5mm/US 8
or size to obtain gauge,
60cm (24") or longer

&
Stitch markers

Medium: 12 balls TRENDSETTER YARN
Merino VI in Deep Eggplant 335; page 60

Medium: 13 balls TRENDSETTER YARN
Tonalita in Mossy Tree 2371; page 58

Notes

1 See *Techniques*, page 160, for k2tog, SSK, p2tog, M1, cable cast-on, wrap and turn for short rows, and bind off in pattern. **2** Vest is worked in one piece from left center front to right center front. **3** The pattern can be worked at 2 gauges, resulting in 2 lengths. Numbers for the solid-colored drape are blue and for the variegated drape are green. Shared numbers are black.

Corrugated Garter *ANY NUMBER OF STITCHES*

Row 1 (RS) Purl.
Row 2 Knit.
Row 3 Knit.
Row 4 Purl.
Repeat Rows 1–4.

Basket Stitch *MULTIPLE OF 20 STITCHES*

Rows 1–12 *K10, p10; repeat from *.
Rows 13–24 *P10, k10; repeat from *.
Repeat Rows 1–24.

K2, P2 Rib *MULTIPLE OF 4 + 2*

RS rows * K2, p2; repeat from *, end k2.
WS rows * P2, k2; repeat from *, end p2.

Left Front to Center Back

Cast on 110 (130, 130) stitches. Work 4 rows of K2, P2 Rib.

Establish patterns: *Chart A*, *Row 1* (RS) P4 for bottom edge, place marker (pm), [k10, p10] 5 (6, 6) times for body, pm, p6 for collar. *Row 2* (WS) Knit to marker, [k10, p10] 5 (6, 6) times, k4. Work 4 rows as established: Basket Stitch between markers, Corrugated Garter at each edge, as shown in Chart A. *Row 7: Increase row* (RS) Work to first marker, M1, work to second marker, M1, work to end. Continue, working Increase Row every 6 rows 19 more times — 150 (170, 170) stitches. AT SAME TIME, when work measures 17½ (19, 21¼)" from cast-on and ending with a RS row, begin armhole shaping.

Stitch key

☐ K on RS, p on WS
▨ P on RS, k on WS
Ⓜ Make 1

Chart key

→ Direction of knitting
· Increase or decrease
Refer to instructions for specific increase or decrease placement for each size.

Chart A

6 to 26-st collar   20-st repeat for body   4-st edge
marker   marker

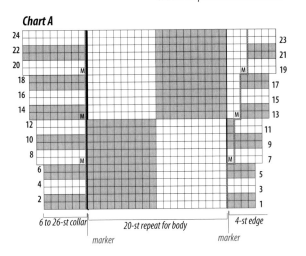

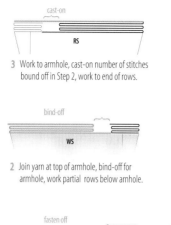

3 Work to armhole, cast-on number of stitches bound off in Step 2, work to end of rows.

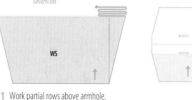

2 Join yarn at top of armhole, bind-off for armhole, work partial rows below armhole.

1 Work partial rows above armhole.

→ *Direction of knitting*

Shape armhole

Continue patterns and increases while working partial rows to shape armhole:

Partial row (WS) Work to first marker, then work 15 stitches, turn. Work 6 more partial rows across stitches just worked, do not turn work; cut yarn, leaving stitches on hold. With WS facing, join yarn at beginning of armhole (see illustration 2), bind off 40 (45, 50) stitches in pattern, and work to end. **Next 6 rows** Work stitches below armhole in established patterns. **Next row** (RS) Work to armhole, cable cast on 40 (45, 50) stitches, work stitches from holder (see illustration 3).

Back

Continue working in established patterns to 20th increase row; mark row. Work even on 150 (170, 170) stitches to approximately 6 (6½, 8)" from armhole cast-on, end with a Row 5 (11, 17, 23) of Basket Stitch pattern. Mark row for center back. Count rows from left armhole cast-on to center back and rows from last increase to center back; record both on schematic on previous page.

Shape Collar

Note Hide wraps when working across Short Rows 4, 5, 6, and last row.

Short row 1 (WS) Work 26 stitches of collar, wrap next stitch and turn (W&T). **All RS rows** Work to end in pattern. **Short row 2** Work 21 stitches, W&T. **Short row 3** Work 16 stitches, W&T. **Short row 4** Bind off 10 stitches, work 15 stitches, W&T. **Short row 5** Using cable cast-on, cast on 10 stitches, work 16 stitches, W&T. **Short row 6** Work 21 stitches, W&T, work to end. **Next WS row** Work across all stitches.

Center Back to Right Front

Note Work decreases as either k2tog or p2tog to stay in established pattern.

Work number of rows recorded from armhole cast-on to center back; repeat armhole shaping. **AT SAME TIME**, when number of rows recorded from last increase to center back has been worked, begin decreases as follows:

Decrease row (RS) Work to first marker, decrease, work to second marker, decrease. Work Decrease Row every 6 rows a total of 20 times — 110 (130, 130) stitches.

Work 6 rows even. Work 4 rows in K2, P2 Rib. Bind off loosely in pattern.

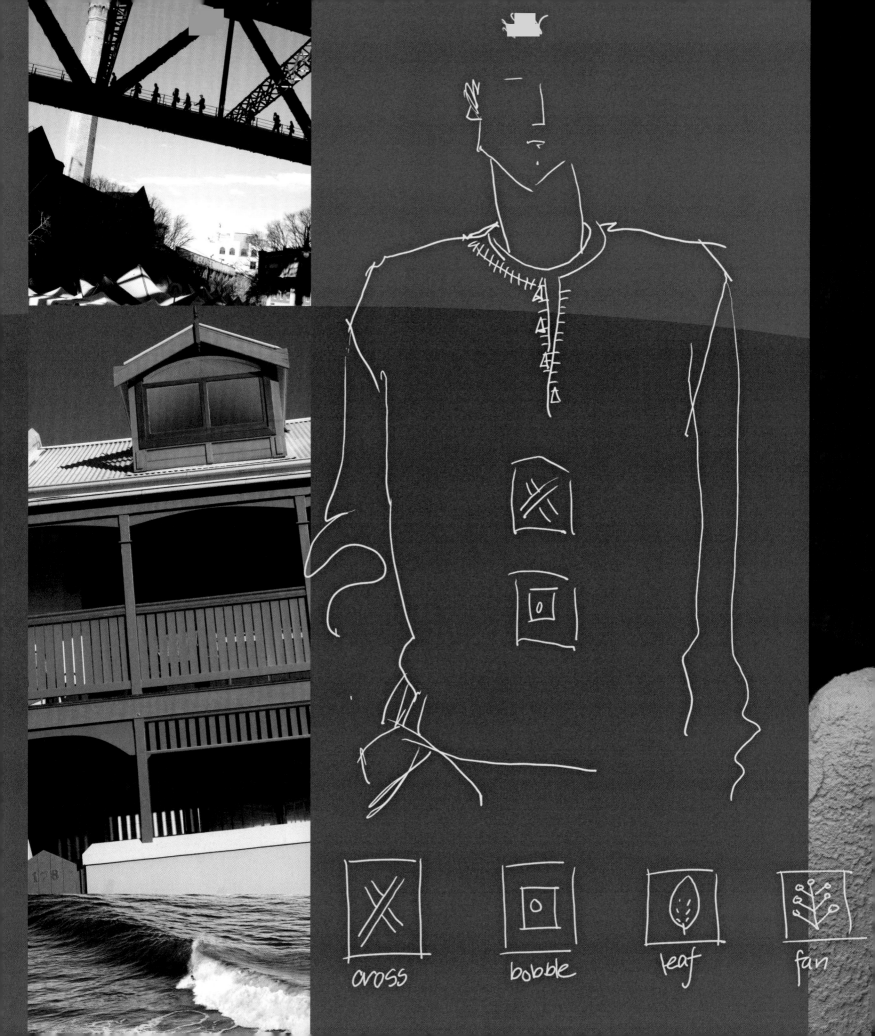

cross

bobble

leaf

fan

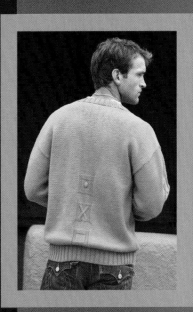

Dice

Kick back with this simple sweater design—the drop shoulder—and make it interesting with texture, color, and collar treatments.

Dice

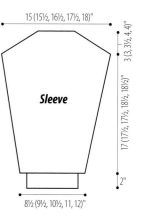

15 (15½, 16½, 17½, 18)"

3 (3, 3½, 4, 4)"

Sleeve

17 (17½, 17½, 18½, 18½)"

2"

8½ (9½, 10½, 11, 12)"

Note

See *Techniques*, page 160, for working from charts, S2KP2, M1, yo, k2tog, p2tog, SSK, pf&b, wrap and turn for short rows, 3-needle bind-off, and bind off in pattern.

K2, P2 Rib *MULTIPLE of 4 + 2*	**Corrugated Garter (CG)**	**Buttonhole (BH)**
Row 1 (RS) * K2, p2; repeat from *, end k2.	*Row 1* (WS) Knit.	On Row 4 of CG or WS row of rib, k2, yo, k2tog, k2. **Next row** Knit into yarn-over.
Row 2 P2, * k2, p2, repeat from *.	*Row 2* Purl.	
Repeat Rows 1–2	*Row 3* Purl.	
	Row 4 Knit.	
	Repeat Rows 1–4.	

Her (His) sleeves

With size 4mm/US 6 needles, cast on 46 (50, 54, 58, 62) stitches.
Work K2, P2 Rib until piece measures 2", increase 1 stitch on last row — 47 (51, 55, 59, 63) stitches.
Change to size 5mm/US 8 needles. Work 2 rows stockinette stitch, placing marker (pm) after first 16 (18, 20, 22, 24) stitches on each row. Increase 1 stitch at each end on next row, then every 8 rows 11 times — 71 (75, 79, 83, 87) stitches.
AT SAME TIME, beginning with Row 1, work Pattern Panel for sleeves over stitches between markers, working chart patterns in order shown. Work even in stockinette stitch until piece measures 19 (19½, 19½, 20 ½, 20½)" from cast-on.
Shape cap
Bind off 3 stitches at the beginning of every row until 17 (15, 19, 17, 15) stitches remain. Bind off.

Her (His) back

With 4.5mm/US 7 needles, cast on 94 (102, 114, 122, 134) stitches.
Work 2/2 Rib until piece measures 2½", increase 1 stitch on last row — 95 (103, 115, 123, 135) stitches.
Change to 5 mm/US 8 needles. Work 10 rows stockinette stitch, pm after first 40 (44, 50, 54, 60) stitches on first 2 rows. Beginning with Row 1, work Pattern Panel

Pattern Panel

Her sleeve and Back

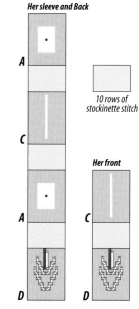

A

C

A

D

10 rows of stockinette stitch

Her front

C

D

INTERMEDIATE

B — A — C

S (M, L, 1X, 2X)

A 38 (42, 46, 50, 54)"
B 25 (25, 26, 27½, 28)"
C 32 (32, 34, 34½, 36½)"

10cm/4"

27

19

over stockinette stitch (knit on RS, purl on WS), using size 5mm/US8 needles

1 2 3 **4** 5 6

Medium weight
1450 (1550, 1725, 1925, 2125) yds

4mm/US6, 4.5mm/US7 and 5mm/US8, or size to obtain gauge

Her (His) Two (Three) • 16mm (5/8")

&

Stitch markers
Stitch holders
Cable needle (cn)

Small: 15 balls TRENDSETTER YARNS Merino VIII in 86276 Pink page 67

Large: 18 balls TRENDSETTER YARNS Merino VIII in 222 Turquoise page 63

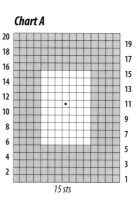

Chart A

20 18 16 14 12 10 8 6 4 2

19 17 15 13 11 9 7 5 3 1

15 sts

Chart B

20 18 16 14 12 10 8 6 4 2

19 17 15 13 11 9 7 5 3 1

15 to 16 to 15 sts

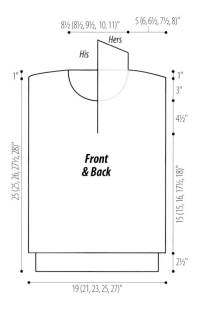

8½ (8½, 9½, 10, 11)"

5 (6, 6½, 7½, 8)"

Hers

His

1"

1"

3"

4½"

25 (25, 26, 27½, 28)"

15 (15, 16, 17½, 18)"

Front & Back

2½"

19 (21, 23, 25, 27)"

for back over stitches between markers. Work even in stockinette stitch until piece measures 24 (24, 25, 26½, 27)" from cast-on.

Shape shoulders

Her shawl collar At beginning of every row bind off 12 (13, 15, 15, 17) stitches twice, then 11 (13, 14, 16, 17) stitches 4 times. Bind off remaining stitches.

His Henley neckline At beginning of every row bind off 9 (11, 13, 13, 14) stitches twice, then 9 (10, 11, 12, 14) stitches 4 times. Bind off remaining stitches.

HER FRONT

Work as for Back EXCEPT work Her Pattern Panel, decreasing 1 stitch on last row of Chart C — 94 (102, 114, 122, 134) stitches. Work 14 rows even.

Left Front

Next row (RS) K34 (38, 44, 48, 54), pm, k10, pm, k6. Place remaining stitches on hold. **Establish collar pattern: Next row** (WS) Work Row 1 of Corrugated Garter (CG) to first marker, Row 1 of Basket Stitch to second marker and stockinette stitch to end. Continuing as established for approximately 1", work 2 buttonholes (BH). Work even for 2". Continue in pattern to same length as Back to shoulder.

His sleeve

B

A

B

His back

A

B

A

His front

B

A

Stitch key

☐ Knit on RS, purl on WS
▨ Purl on RS, knit on WS
⊙ Yarn over
▐ Pf&b
✔ K2tog
✔ P2tog
◥ SSK
▲ S2KP2
• *Bobble* (K1, p1, k1) into stitch, turn; p3, turn; SK2P
• *Optional bobble* (K1, p1, k1, p1, k1) into stitch, turn; p5, turn; k5, turn; p2tog, p1, p2tog, turn; SK2P
▦ *Stitches do not exist in these areas of chart*
⧄ **2/1 RPC** Slip 1 to cn, hold to back, k2; p1 from cn
⧅ **2/1 LPC** Slip 2 to cn, hold to front, p1; k2 from cn
⧄ **2/2 RC** Slip 2 to cn, hold to back, k2; k2 from cn
⧄ **1/1 RPC** Slip 1 to cn, hold to back, k1; p1 from cn
⧅ **1/1 LPC** Slip 1 to cn, hold to front, p1; k1 from cn

Chart C

20 19
18 17
16 15
14 13
12 LEAF INSERT 11
10 9
8 7
6 5
4 3
2 1

15 to 23 to 15 sts

LEAF INSERT

19
18
16 17
14 15
12 13
10 11
8 9
6 7
4 5
3
1 to 9 to 1 sts

Chart D

20 19
18 17
16 15
14 13
12 11
10 9
8 7
6 5
4 3
2 1

15 to 16 to 15 sts

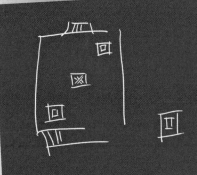

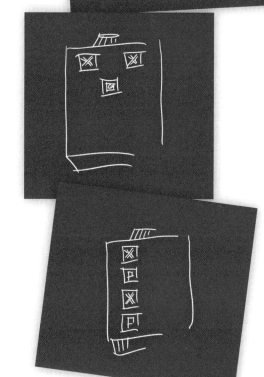

mix & match stitch pattern

Shape shoulder At beginning of next RS row, bind off 12 (13, 15, 15, 17) stitches once, then 11 (13, 14, 16, 17) stitches twice.

Collar extension Continue in established patterns on remaining 16 (15, 17, 17, 19) stitches until collar measures half the width of the back neck plus ½", end with a RS row.

Shape collar: Short row 1 (WS) Work 11 (10, 12, 12, 14) stitches, wrap next stitch and turn work (W&T). **All RS rows** Work to end in pattern. **Short row 2** Work 6 (5, 5, 5, 5) stitches, W&T.

Next WS row Bind off 6 stitches, complete row, hiding wraps; place remaining 10 (9, 11, 11, 13) stitches on hold.

Right Front

Next row (RS) Cast on 6 stitches, pm, k10 from holder, pm, knit remaining stitches — 50 (54, 60, 64, 70) stitches on needle. **Establish collar pattern: Next row** (WS) Work stockinette stitch to first marker, Row 1 of Basket Stitch to second marker and Row 1 of CG to end of row. Work as for Left Front to same length as shoulder shaping EXCEPT do not work buttonhole.

Shape shoulder and collar Work as for Left Front EXCEPT bind off stitches at beginning of WS rows AND work short rows on RS rows.

HIS FRONT

Work as for Back to end of panel EXCEPT work His Front Pattern Panel, decreasing 1 stitch on last row of Chart B — 94 (102, 114, 122, 134) stitches. Work 14 rows even.

Left Front

Next row (RS) K44 (48, 54, 58, 64), pm, k6. Place remaining stitches on holder. **Next row** (WS) Work Row 1 of CG to marker, stockinette stitch to end of row. Continue as established for 1", work 3 buttonholes. Continue to 5" less than beginning of shoulder shaping on Back.

Shape neck: Next RS row Work to last 12 (12, 13, 13, 14) stitches, place them on hold. At beginning of every WS row, bind off 3 stitches once, 2 stitches 2 (2, 2, 3, 3) times; decrease 1 stitch 2 times, then 1 stitch every other WS row 2 (2, 3, 3, 3) times — 27 (31, 35, 37, 42) stitches. Work even to same length as Back to shoulder shaping.

Shape shoulders At beginning of next RS row, bind off 9 (11, 13, 13, 14) stitches once, then 9 (10, 11, 12, 14) stitches twice.

Right Front

Next row (RS) Cast on 6 stitches, pm, knit stitches from holder — 50 (54, 60, 64, 70) stitches. **Next row** (WS) Work stockinette stitch to marker, work Row 1 of CG to end of row. Work as Left Front to neck shaping EXCEPT do not work buttonholes. Shape neck and shoulder as for Left Front EXCEPT place stitches on hold at end of WS row AND bind off at beginning of RS rows.

Finishing

Sew shoulder seams.

For shawl collar With collar stitches on 2 needles and RS facing, join collar with 3-needle bind-off. Sew side of collar extension to back of neck, easing excess into neck. Sew buttonband cast-on to inside of sweater.

For Henley neckline With 4.5mm/US 7 needles, RS facing, and beginning at center right front neck edge, k12 (12, 13, 13, 14) stitches from holder, pick up and k20 (20, 23, 25, 25) stitches up right front, k41 (41, 45, 49, 51) stitches from back neck, pick up and k21 (21, 24, 26, 26) stitches down left front, and k12 (12, 13, 13, 14) stitches from holder — 106 (106, 118, 126, 130) stitches. Work K2, P2 Rib for 1½", working buttonhole after 4 rows. Bind off loosely in pattern.

For both Measure down side from shoulder and mark distance equal to half sleeve width + ¾". Center sleeve between markers, stretching sleeve slightly. Sew sleeve to armhole. Sew underarm and side seams. Sew on buttons.

Basket Stitch

Basket Stitch

Rows 1–8 P5, k5.
Rows 9–16 K5, p5.
Repeat Rows 1–16.

Stitch key
☐ Knit on RS, purl on WS
▨ Purl on RS, knit on WS

Corrugated Garter

Row 1 (WS) Knit.
Row 2 Purl.
Row 3 Purl.
Row 4 Knit.
Repeat Rows 1–4.

Greta

Let's play with length and a little illusion. The Swagger skims loosely over the hips. The A-line appears fuller but is actually only longer. It meets the body at a narrower point making the hemline appear wider. Tempting style, beautiful texture.

Greta Swagger and Greta A-line

S (M, L, 1X, 2X, 3X)

A 39 (41, 45½, 50, 54, 58)"
B Swagger 23 (23½, 24, 24½, 25½, 26)"
A-line 29 (29½, 30, 30½, 31½, 32)"
C 27½ (28, 29, 29½, 32, 33½)"

10cm/4"

28

20

**over stockinette stitch (St st)
(knit on RS, purl on WS)
using larger needles**

1 2 3 **4** 5 6

Medium weight

Swagger
1450 (1550, 1625, 1750, 1950, 2100) yds

A-line
1925 (2050, 2175, 2350, 2600, 2775) yds

4mm/US 6 & 4.5mm/US 7,
or size to obtain gauge
For standard cuff only, 3.75mm/US 5

☺

2 (3) • 16mm (5/8")

&

Cable needle (cn), stitch holders

Swagger
Medium 16 balls in TRENDSETTER'S
Merino VIII 2029 Wine

A-line
Medium 21 balls in TRENDSETTER'S Merino
Otto Shadow 1822 Sands of Time

Notes

1 See *Techniques*, page 160, for p2tog, SSP, wrap and turn for short rows, and 3-needle bind-off. **2** The jacket is given in two lengths: Swagger (hip length) and A-line (mid-thigh length), with 2 cuff options. Both are worked the same EXCEPT A-line has 40 additional rows before decreases begin. **3** The number of sts increased or decreased in a row or section is abbreviated: 4-st inc or 2-st inc. **4** See *Chart Tips*, page 147.

Decreases

Dec A P2tog, * work to first 2 sts of diamond panel, p2tog, repeat from *, work to last 2 sts of row, SSP — 4-st dec.
Work 7 rows.
Dec B * Work to last 2 sts of diamond panel, SSP, repeat from *, work to end of row — 2-st dec. Work 7 rows.
Dec C P2tog, work to first 2 sts of diamond panel, p2tog, work to end of row — 2-st dec. Work 7 rows.
Dec D Work to last 2 sts of diamond panel, SSP, work to end of row — 1-st dec. Work 7 rows.
Dec E Work to first 2 sts of diamond panel, p2tog, work to last 2 sts of row, SSP — 2-st dec. Work 7 rows.

Back

With larger needles, cast on 124 (130, 138, 146, 156, 160) sts. Work in k1, p1 rib for 4 rows.
Establish patterns: Row 1 (R1) (RS) P12 (15, 18, 22, 26, 26), work R1 of Chart A over next 42 sts, p16 (16, 18, 18, 20, 24), work R1 of Chart A over next 42 sts, p12 (15, 18, 22, 26, 26). *Row 2 (R2)* K12 (15, 18, 22, 26, 26), work R2 of Chart A over 42 sts, k16 (16, 18, 18, 20, 24), work R2 of Chart A over 42 sts, k12 (15, 18, 22, 26, 26). Continue working, following chart, to end of R28 (28, 28, 28, 44, 44).
For A-line only Work through R68 (68, 68, 68, 84, 84) without any decreases, continuing diamond pattern as already established and beginning dec as directed on R29 (29, 29, 29, 45, 45).

Shape body

Notes

1 Decreases in chart are made on different rows for different sizes, but always occur on same rows as 3/3 RC. **2** Decreases are made in the diamond panel of the chart, either after the first or before the last cable. The shaded area of the chart does not show the resulting change in st counts. **3** Beginning with R84, center panel is worked in reverse stockinette. Rows between end of Chart A and beginning of Chart B are worked in established 3/3 cable and reverse stockinette patterns.

SMALL

R29, R45, R61 *Work to first 2 sts of diamond panel in Chart A, p2tog, repeat from *, work to end of row — 2-st dec. Work 7 rows. **R37, R53, R69** Dec B. **R77** Dec A EXCEPT work 5 rows. **R83** End diamond motif in Chart A — 4-st dec. Work 1 row.
R85 Dec B. **R93** Dec A. AT SAME TIME begin diamond motif in Chart B — 4-st dec, 4-st inc. Work 7 rows. **R101** Dec B EXCEPT work 3 rows.

MEDIUM

R29 *Work as for Small through R60, **R61** Dec A. **R69** Dec B. **R77** Dec A EXCEPT work 5 rows. **R83** End diamond motif in Chart A — 4-st dec. Work 1 row. **R85** Dec B. **R93** Dec A. AT SAME TIME begin diamond motif in Chart B — 4-st dec, 4-st inc. **R101** *Work to last 2 sts of diamond panel, SSP, repeat from *, work to end of row — 2-st dec. Work 3 rows.

LARGE, 1X

R29 *Work to the first 2 sts of diamond panel in Chart A, p2tog, repeat from *, work to end of row — 2-st dec. Work 7 rows. **R37** Dec B. **R45** Dec A. **R53** Dec B.
R61 Dec A. **R69** Dec B. **R77** Dec A EXCEPT work 5 rows. **R83** End diamond motif in Chart A — 4-st dec. Work 1 row. **R85** Dec B. **R93** Dec A. **R101** Dec B EXCEPT work 3 rows to underarm, begin diamond motif in Chart B — 2-st dec, 4-st inc.

2X

R45 Dec A. **R53** Dec B. **R61** Dec A. **R69** Dec B. **R77** Dec A EXCEPT work 5 rows. **R83** End diamond motif in Chart A — 4-st dec. Work 1 row. **R85** Dec B. **R93** Dec A. **R101** Dec B EXCEPT work 3 rows to underarm.

3X

R45 P2tog, work to last 2 sts, SSP — 2-st dec. Work 7 rows. **R53** Work across — 0 sts dec. Work 7 rows. **R61** Dec A. **R69** Dec B. **R77** Dec A EXCEPT work 5 rows. **R83** End diamond motif in Chart A — 4-st dec. Work 1 row. **R85** Dec B. **R93** Dec A. **R101** Dec B EXCEPT work 3 rows.

Back

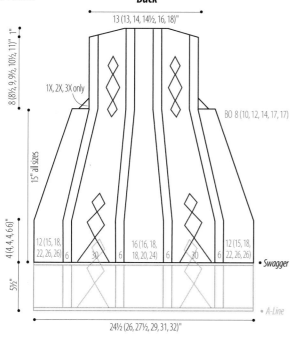

Chart A

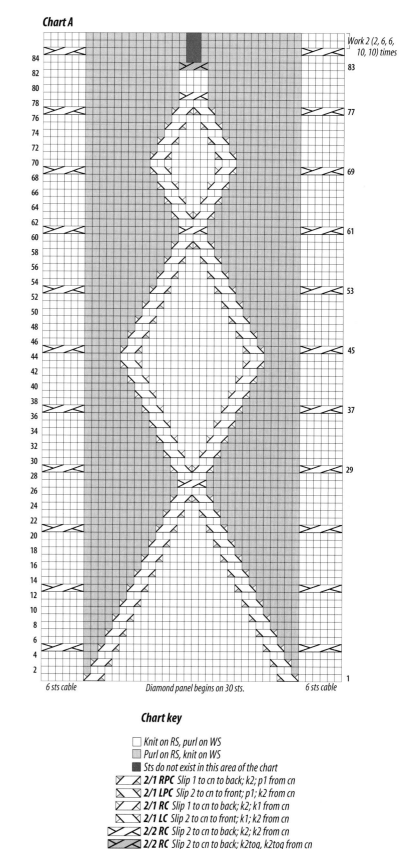

Work 2 (2, 6, 6, 10, 10) times

6 sts cable   Diamond panel begins on 30 sts.   6 sts cable

Chart key

☐ Knit on RS, purl on WS
▨ Purl on RS, knit on WS
■ Sts do not exist in this area of the chart
⊠ **2/1 RPC** *Slip 1 to cn to back; k2; p1 from cn*
⊠ **2/1 LPC** *Slip 2 to cn to front; p1; k2 from cn*
⊠ **2/1 RC** *Slip 1 to cn to back; k2; k1 from cn*
⊠ **2/1 LC** *Slip 2 to cn to front; k1; k2 from cn*
⊠ **2/2 RC** *Slip 2 to cn to back; k2; k2 from cn*
⊠ **2/2 RC** *Slip 2 to cn to back; k2tog, k2tog from cn*
⊠ **3/3 RC** *Slip 3 to cn to back; k3; k3 from cn*

Chart B

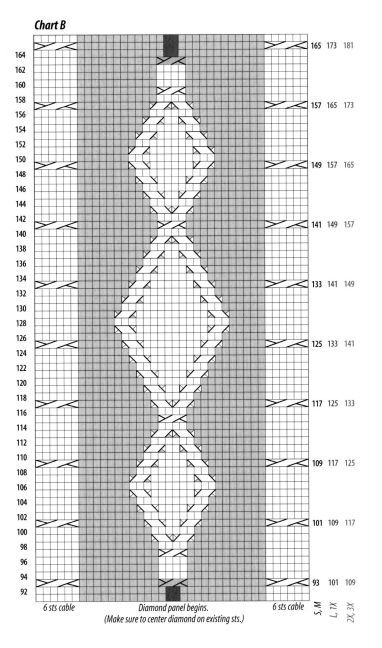

164 162 160 158 156 154 152 150 148 146 144 142 140 138 136 134 132 130 128 126 124 122 120 118 116 114 112 110 108 106 104 102 100 98 96 94 92

165 173 181
157 165 173
149 157 165
141 149 157
133 141 149
125 133 141
117 125 133
109 117 125
101 109 117
93 101 109

S, M
L, 1X
2X, 3X

6 sts cable   *Diamond panel begins.*   6 sts cable
(Make sure to center diamond on existing sts.)

Chart key

☐ *Knit on RS, purl on WS*
▨ *Purl on RS, knit on WS*
■ *Sts do not exist in this area of the chart*
2/1 RPC *Slip 1 to cn to back, k2; p1 from cn*
2/1 LPC *Slip 2 to cn to front, p1; k2 from cn*
2/1 RC *Slip 1 to cn to back, k2; k1 from cn*
2/1 LC *Slip 2 to cn to front, k1; k2 from cn*
2/2 RC *Slip 2 to cn to back, k2; k2 from cn*
2/2 RC *Slip 2 to cn to back, k2tog, k2tog from cn*
2/2 RC *Slip 1 to cn to back, k1, M1, (k1, M1) from cn*
3/3 RC *Slip 3 to cn to back, k3; k3 from cn*

Notes
1 100 (104, 110, 118, 128, 136) sts on needles: the two larger sizes reflect the lower diamond dec not yet replaced by upper diamond inc — Diamond panels contain 20 (20, 20, 20, 20, 22) sts **2** Smaller needles are used for the remaining rows. **3** After armhole bind off (and armhole decrease for 1X, 2X, 3X), continue to k2 at beginning and end of every row for garter st edge. **4** Only the Small and Medium sizes have Center panel decreases made in the center panel not the diamond panel.

Shape armholes
Change to smaller needles for remainder of pattern.
ALL SIZES
R105 Bind off 8 (10, 12, 14, 17, 17), work across. **R106** Bind off 8 (10, 12, 14, 17, 17), work across — 84 (84, 86, 90, 94, 102) sts.

SMALL
R107, R108 K2, work across, k2. **R109, R125** K2, *work to the first 2 sts of diamond panel in chart B, p2tog, repeat from *, work to last 2 sts, k2 — 2-st dec. Work 7 rows. **R117, R133** K2, *work to last 2 sts of diamond panel, SSP, repeat from *, work to last 2 sts of row, k2 — 2-st dec. Work 7 rows. **R141, R157** K2, work to the first 2 sts of Center panel, p2tog, work to last 2 sts, k2 — 1-st dec. Work 7 rows. **R149** K2, work to the last 2 sts of Center panel, SSP, work to last 2 sts, k2 — 1-st dec. Work 7 rows. **R165** K2, work to the last 2 sts of Center panel B, SSP, work to last 2 sts, k2 — 5-st dec and diamond panel in Chart B is completed. Work 3 rows. **R167** Begin shoulder shaping on 68 sts.

MEDIUM
R107, R108 K2, work across, k2. Work as for Small through Row 164. **R165** K2, work to the last 2 sts of Center panel, SSP, work to last 2 sts, k2 —5-st dec and diamond panel in Chart B is completed. Work 5 rows. **R171** Begin shoulder shaping on 68 sts.

LARGE
R107, R108 K2, work across, k2 — 84 (84, 86, 90, 94, 102) sts. **R109** K2, *work to the first 2 sts of diamond panel in Chart B, p2tog, repeat from *, work to last 2 sts, k2 — 2-st dec. Work 7 rows. **R117** K2, *work to last 2 sts of diamond panel, SSP, repeat from *, work to last 2 sts of row, k2 — 2-st dec. Work 55 rows. **R173** K2, work to the last 2 sts, k2 — 4-st dec and diamond panel in Chart B is completed. Work 3 rows. **R175** Begin shoulder shaping on 78 sts.

1X
R107, R108 K2, work across, k2. **R109** P1, p2tog *work to last 3 sts of row, SSP, p1 — 2-st dec. Work 3 rows. **R113** Repeat R109. Work 59 rows. **R173** K2, *work to the last 2 sts, k2 — 4-st dec and diamond panel in Chart B is completed. Work 7 rows. **R179** Begin shoulder shaping on 82 sts.

2X
R107, R108 K2, work across, k2. **R109** P1, p2tog, work to last 3 sts, SSP, p1, AT SAME TIME begin diamond motif in Chart B — 2-st dec, 4-st inc. Work 3 rows. **R113** P1, p2tog, work to last 3 sts, SSP, p1 — 2-st dec. Work 3 rows. **117** Work as R113. Work 63 rows. **R181** K2, work across and completing diamond panel in Chart B, k2 — 4-st dec. Work 1 row. **R183** Begin shoulder shaping on 88 sts.

3X
Work as for 2X through Row 181. Work 5 rows. **R187** Begin shoulder shaping on 96 sts.

Shape shoulders
Bind off 7 (7, 7, 9, 9, 9) sts at the beginning of the next 2 rows, 7 (7, 8, 8, 9, 10) sts at the beginning of the next 4 rows, bind off remaining sts.

Left Front

With larger needles, cast on 74 (77, 80, 84, 93, 93) sts. Work in k1, p1 rib for 4 rows.

Establish patterns: R1 (RS) P12 (15, 18, 22, 26, 26), work R1 of diamond panel in Chart A over 42 sts, (p5, k5) twice, p0 (0, 0, 0, 5, 5). **R2** K0 (0, 0, 0, 5, 5), (p5, k5) twice, work R2 of diamond panel over 42 sts, k12 (15, 18, 22, 26, 26). Continue reverse stockinette, diamond panel, and Basket Stitch as established, following charts until R28 (28, 28, 28, 44, 44) is complete.

For A-line only Work through R68 (68, 68, 68, 84, 84) without any decreases, continuing diamond pattern as established and beginning dec on R29 (29, 29, 29, 45, 45).

SMALL

R29, R45, R61 Work to the first 2 sts of diamond panel in Chart A, p2tog, work to end of row — 1-st dec. Work 7 rows. **R37, R53, R69** Dec D. **R77** Dec C EXCEPT work 5 rows. **R83** End diamond motif in Chart A — 2-st dec. Work 1 row. **R85** Dec D. **R93** Dec C AT SAME TIME begin diamond motif in Chart B — 2-st dec, 2-st inc. **R101** Dec D EXCEPT work 3 rows.

MEDIUM

R29 Work as for small through Row 60. **R61** Dec C. **R69** Dec D. **R77** Dec C EXCEPT work 5 rows. **R83** End diamond motif in Chart A — 2-st dec. Work 1 row. **R85** Dec D. **R93** Dec C AT SAME TIME begin diamond motif in Chart B — 2-st dec, 2-st inc. **R101** Dec D EXCEPT work 3 rows.

LARGE, 1X

R29 Work to the first 2 sts of diamond panel in Chart A, p2tog, work to end of row — 1-st dec. Work 7 rows. **R37** Dec D. **R45** Dec C. **R53** Dec D. **R61** Dec C. **R69** Dec D. **R77** Dec C EXCEPT work 5 rows. **R83** End diamond motif in Chart A — 2-st dec. Work 1 row. **R85** Dec D. **R93** Dec C. **R101** Dec D EXCEPT work 3 rows AT SAME TIME begin diamond motif in Chart B — 1-st dec, 2-st inc.

2X

R45 Dec C. **R53** Dec D. **R61** Dec C. **R69** Dec D. **R77** Dec C EXCEPT work 5 rows. **R83** End diamond motif in Chart A — 2-st dec. Work 1 row. **R85** Dec D. **R93** Dec C. **R101** Dec D EXCEPT work 3 rows.

3X

R45 Dec 1, work to end of row — 1-st dec. Work 7 rows. **R53** Work across — 0 sts dec. Work 7 rows. **R61** Dec C. **R69** Dec D. **R77** Dec C EXCEPT work 5 rows. **R83** End diamond motif in Chart A — 2-st dec. Work 1 row. **R85** Dec D. **93** Dec C. **R101** Dec D EXCEPT work 3 rows.

Note 62 (64, 66, 70, 79, 81) sts on needles because you ended diamond panel in Chart A (dec 2) and started diamond panel in Chart B (inc 2) in the 4 smaller sizes — 20 (20, 20, 20, 20, 22) sts in diamond panel.

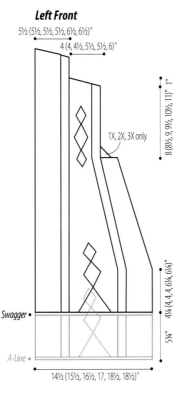

Left Front

5½ (5½, 5½, 5½, 6½, 6½)"

4 (4, 4½, 5½, 5½, 6)"

8 (8½, 9, 9½, 10½, 11)" 1"

1X, 2X, 3X only

4¼ (4, 4, 4, 6¼, 6¼)"

5¾"

Swagger •

A-Line •

14½ (15½, 16½, 17, 18½, 18½)"

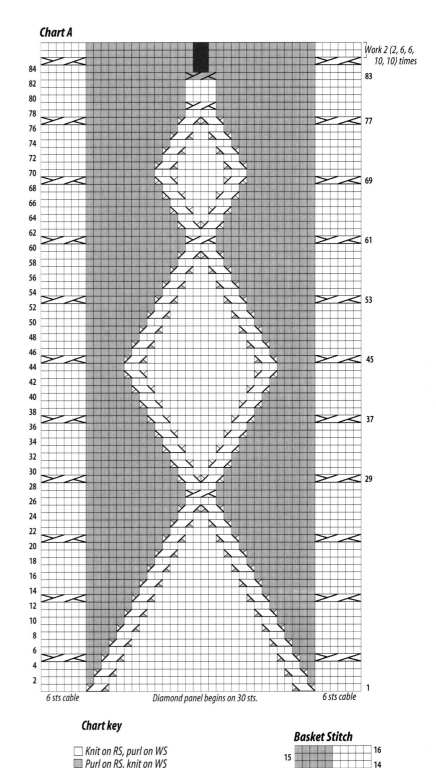

Chart A

Work 2 (2, 6, 6, 10, 10) times

6 sts cable   Diamond panel begins on 30 sts.   6 sts cable

Chart key

- ☐ Knit on RS, purl on WS
- ▨ Purl on RS, knit on WS
- ■ Sts do not exist in this area of the chart
- **2/1 RPC** Slip 1 to cn to back; k2; p1 from cn
- **2/1 LPC** Slip 2 to cn to front; p1; k2 from cn
- **2/1 RC** Slip 1 to cn to back; k2; k1 from cn
- **2/1 LC** Slip 2 to cn to front; k1; k2 from cn
- **2/2 RC** Slip 2 to cn to back; k2; k2 from cn
- **2/2 RC** Slip 2 to cn to back; k2tog, k2tog from cn
- **3/3 RC** Slip 3 to cn to back; k3; k3 from cn

Basket Stitch

10 sts

Note After armhole bind-off (and decreases for 1X, 2X, 3X), k2 sts at beginning of every RS row, and k2 sts at end of every WS row for garter st edge.

Shape armholes
ALL SIZES
Change to smaller needles for remainder of pattern. **R105** Bind off 8 (10, 12, 14, 17, 17) sts, work to end of row — 54 (54, 54, 56, 62, 64) sts. **R106** Work across.
SMALL
R107 K2, work across. **R108** Work across, k2. **R109** K2, work to the first 2 sts of diamond panel in Chart B, p2tog, work to end of row — 1-st dec. Work 7 rows. **R117** K2, work to last 2 sts of diamond panel, SSP, work to end of row — 1-st dec. Work 7 rows. **R125–140** Repeat last 16 rows once. Work 25 rows even. **R165** K2, work across, diamond panel in Chart B is completed — 2-st dec. Work 1 row — 48 sts. **R167** Begin shoulder shaping.
MEDIUM
R107 K2, work across. **R108** Work across, k2. **R109** Work as for small through row 164. **R165** K2, work across, diamond panel in Chart B is completed — 2-st dec. Work 5 rows — 48 sts. **R171** Begin shoulder shaping.
LARGE
R107 K2, work across. **R108** Work across, k2. **R109** K2, work to the first 2 sts of diamond panel in Chart B, p2tog, work to end of row. Work 7 rows — 1-st dec. **R117** K2, work to last 2 sts of diamond panel, SSP, work to end of row — 1-st dec. Work 55 rows. **R173** K2, work across, diamond panel in Chart B is completed — 2-st dec. Work 1 row — 50 sts. **R175** Begin shoulder shaping.
1X
R107 K2, work across. **R108** Work across, k2. **R109** P1, p2tog, work to end of row — 1-st dec. Work 3 rows even. **Row 113** Work as Row 109. Work 59 rows. **R173** K2, work across, diamond panel in Chart B is completed — 2-st dec. Work 5 rows — 52 sts. **R179** Begin shoulder shaping.
2X
R107 K2, work across. **R108** Work across, k2. **R109** P1, p2tog, work to end of row, AT SAME TIME begin diamond panel in Chart B — 1-st dec, 2 st inc. Work 3 rows. **R113** P1, p2tog, work to end of row — 1-st dec. Work 3 rows. **R117** Work as R113. Work 63 rows. **R181** K2, work across, diamond panel in Chart B is completed — 2-st dec. Work 1 row — 59 sts. **R183** Begin shoulder shaping.
3X
R109 Work as for 2X through Row 181. Work 5 rows — 61 sts. **R187** Begin shoulder shaping. Armhole depth 8½ (9, 10, 10½, 11, 11½)" from armhole bind-off.

Shape shoulders
Bind off 7 (7, 7, 9, 9, 9) sts at the beginning of the next RS row, 7 (7, 8, 8, 9, 10) sts at the beginning of the next 2 RS rows — 27 (27, 27, 27, 32, 32) sts remain. Continue pattern (Basket Stitch, cable, garter selvedge st) until half the width of the back neck plus ½" is reached, ending with a RS row.
Shape collar
Short row 1 (WS) Work 20 (20, 20, 20, 25, 25) sts, wrap next stitch and turn work (W&T). **All RS rows** Work to end. **Short row 2** 17 (17, 17, 17, 22, 22) sts, W&T. **Short row 3** Work 14 (14, 14, 14, 19, 19) sts, W&T. **Short row 4** Work 11 (11, 11, 11, 16, 16) sts, W&T. **WS** Bind off 8 sts, complete row, hiding wraps; place remaining sts on hold.

Right Front
With larger needles, cast on 74 (77, 80, 84, 93, 93) sts. Work in k1, p1 rib for 4 rows.
Establish patterns: Row 1 (RS) K0 (0, 0, 0, 5, 5), (p5, k5) twice, work Row 1 of diamond panel Chart A over next 42 sts, p12 (15, 18, 22, 26, 26). **Row 2** (WS) K12 (15, 18, 22, 26), work Row 2 of diamond panel Chart A over next 42 sts, (p5, k5) twice, p 0 (0, 0, 0, 5, 5). Continue as estab-

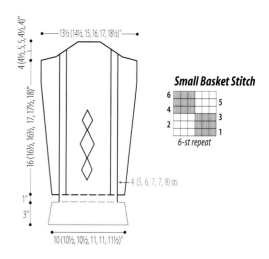

Small Basket Stitch

6-st repeat

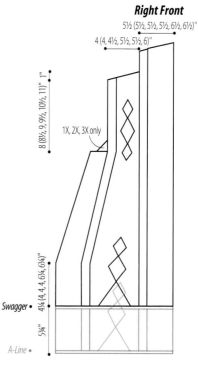

Right Front

5½ (5½, 5½, 5½, 6½, 6½)"

4 (4, 4½, 5½, 5½, 6)"

8 (8½, 9, 9½, 10½, 11)"

1X, 2X, 3X only

1"

4¼ (4, 4, 4, 6¼, 6¼)"

5¾"

Swagger •

A-Line •

Basket Stitch

10 sts

Chart key

☐ Knit on RS, purl on WS
▦ Purl on RS, knit on WS

lished in Basket Stitch, diamond panel, and reverse stockinette until Row 28 (28, 28, 28, 44, 44) is complete.

Work as for Left Front EXCEPT reverse shaping by working Dec E instead of Dec C. AT SAME TIME, work buttonholes 7 and 10½" (10, 13½, and 17" for longer version) from cast on as follows:

Next RS row Work 5 stitches in Basket Stitch, bind off 2 sts, complete row. **Next row** cast on 2 sts over bind-off. Bind off for armhole on WS rows and work short rows for collar on RS rows.

Sleeves

With larger needles, cast-on 54 (54, 54, 60, 60, 60) sts.

Turn-back cuff: Establish Small Basket Stitch Chart: Rows 1–4 Place marker. *K3, p3; repeat from*. **Rows 5–8** *P3, k3; repeat from*, AT SAME TIME decrease 1 st each side on Row 7. **Rows 9–20** Repeat Rows 1–8, then 1–4, decreasing every other RS row 1 (0, 0, 1, 1, 0) time — 48 (50, 52, 54, 54, 56) sts. Mark row and begin sleeve patterns.

Standard cuff Place marker. With smaller needles, cast on 46 (48, 50, 52, 52, 54) sts. Work 8 rows of k1, p1 rib, increasing 4 sts evenly across last row—50 (52, 54, 56, 56, 58) sts. Mark row.

Establish sleeve patterns: Row 1 (RS) With larger needles, p4 (5, 6, 7, 7, 8), pm, k6, p30, k6, pm, purl to end. **Row 2** Knit to marker, p6, k30, p6, knit to end. **Row 3** Inc 1, purl to marker, work Chart B to next marker, purl to last st, inc 1. Continue working reverse St st and chart pattern as established, AT SAME TIME increase 1 st at each end of Row 5. then every 6 rows 7 (9, 10, 11, 14, 17) times — 66 (72, 76, 80, 86, 94) sts. Work even until sleeve measures 17 (17½, 17½, 18, 18½, 19)" from marker or standard cuff cast-on.

Cap shaping

Bind off at beginning of rows: 5 sts 4 times, 2 sts 6 (6, 6, 6, 26, 26) times, 1 st 10 (8, 16, 10, 0, 0) times, 2 sts 6 (10, 8, 12, 0, 0) times. Bind off remaining sts.

Finishing

Block. Join shoulder seams, sew collar to back neck, set in sleeves, sew sleeve and side seams. With RS facing, join front bands with 3-needle bind off. Attach buttons.

Chart B

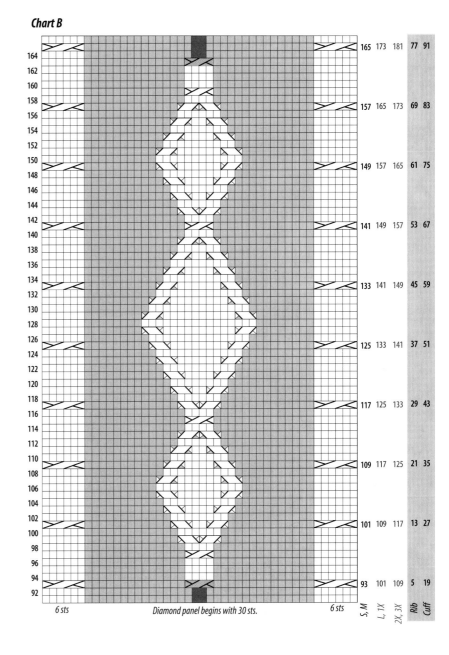

Diamond panel begins with 30 sts.

6 sts   6 sts

Chart key

☐ Knit on RS, purl on WS
▨ Purl on RS, knit on WS
■ Sts do not exist in this area of the chart
2/1 RPC Slip 1 to cn to back, k2; p1 from cn
2/1 LPC Slip 2 to cn to front, p1; k2 from cn
2/1 RC Slip 1 to cn to back, k2; k1 from cn
2/1 LC Slip 2 to cn to front, k1; k2 from cn
2/2 RC Slip 2 to cn to back, k2; k2 from cn
2/2 RC Slip 2 to cn to back, k2tog, k2tog from cn
2/2 RC Slip 1 to cn to back, k1, M1, (k1, M1) from cn
3/3 RC Slip 3 to cn to back, k3; k3 from cn

KNIT THE COLORS OF AUSTRALIA   SPRING SWAGGER DRAPE

Greta Vest

Get out your cable needle! If I am knitting in a single color, then I am cabling. This design combines cables and diamonds with short-rows at the hemline. Just for fun, I added a second option for intarsia lovers—cabled fronts with an Orbit back!

Greta Vest

Notes

1 See *Techniques*, page 160, for k2tog, wrap and turn (W&T) for short rows, M1, and 3-needle bind-off. *2* See Adding a rib, page 149 for *Finishing Tips*.

Double Moss (DM)

Row 1 *K2, p2; repeat from *.
Row 2 Knit the knits, purl the purls.
Row 3 *P2, k2; repeat from *.
Row 4 Purl the purls, knit the knits.
Repeat Rows 1–4 for pattern.

Left Front

Cast on 59 (63, 67, 73) sts. **Rows 1, 3, and 5** (RS) Knit to last 20 (22, 23, 24) sts, k2tog, knit to end. **Rows 2, 4, and 6** Knit. Garter stitch border completed — 56 (60, 64, 70) sts.
Begin pattern and short rows: Row 7 K39 (41, 44, 49), wrap next stitch and turn work (W&T). **Row 8** Slip 1, p7, W&T. **Row 9** Slip 1, k9, W&T. **Row 10** Slip 1, p14, W&T. **Row 11** Slip 1, k16, W&T. **Row 12** Slip 1, p17 (17, 18, 21), k1 (1, 1, 0), p3 (3, 2, 0), W&T.
Note For Left and Right Front, continue shaping points with W&T at end of each row, slip 1 at beginning of each row until you are working full width of piece. (No more W&T or slip at beginning of row.)
Continue working Chart Left Front as established to Row 27, (29, 31, 31), then center Chart A in St st panel.

Shape neck

When work measures 10 (10, 11, 12)" from cast-on at side, begin neck shaping by decreasing in the St st section and AT SAME TIME increasing in the DM button bands as follows: on RS row, work to 3 sts before last cable, k2tog, p1, work cable, M1, DM 8. Work shaping every 8 rows 7 (8, 9, 11) times — 15 (16, 17, 19) sts in DM section. Work to 12 (13, 14, 15)" and begin shaping armhole.

Shape armhole

Bind off 10 sts at the beginning of the next RS row, then 2 sts at the beginning of the following 4 (5, 5, 6) RS rows — 2 (2, 4, 4) sts remain at the DM armhole edge. Continue shaping collar in DM section at neck 3 (2, 3, 1) times — 18 (18, 20, 20) sts in DM section. Work even to 8½ (9, 9½, 10)".

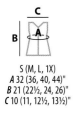

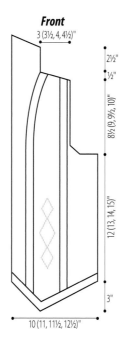

Front

3 (3½, 4, 4½)"
2½"
½"
8½ (9, 9½, 10)"
12 (13, 14, 15)"
3"
10 (11, 11½, 12½)"

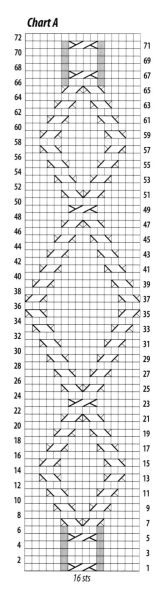

Chart A

16 sts

Chart key

☐ *Knit on RS, purl on WS*
▨ *Purl on RS, knit on WS*
2/1 RC Slip 1 to cn to back; k2; k1 from cn
2/1 LC Slip 2 to cn to front; k1; k2 from cn
2/2 RC Slip 2 to cn to back; k2; k2 from cn

Chart Left Front, S

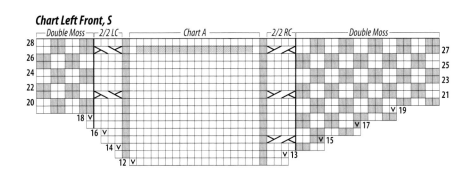

Chart Left Front, M

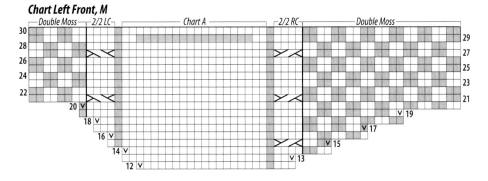

Chart Left Front, L

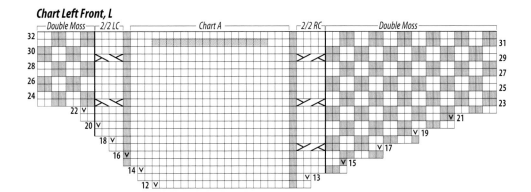

Chart Left Front, 1X

Shape shoulder

Bind off 6 (6, 7, 8) sts at the beginning of the next 2 RS rows, 6 (7, 8, 8) sts at the beginning of the next RS row — 23 (23, 25, 25) sts.

Collar extension

Continue pattern as established until collar height measures 2½, (2½, 3, 3)", ending with RS row.

Short-row collar shaping

Short row 1 (WS) Work to last 7 sts, W&T.

All RS rows Work across to end of row.

Short row 2 (WS) Work to last 9 sts, W&T.

Short row 3 (WS) Work to last 11 sts, W&T.

Short row 4 (WS) work to last 13 sts, W&T.

Short row 5 (WS) bind off 8 sts, place remaining 15 (15, 17, 17) sts on holder.

Chart key

☐ *Knit on RS, purl on WS*
▨ *Purl on RS, knit on WS*
▨ *Begin Chart A, Row 1*
Ⅴ *Sl 1 purlwise*
⧄ **2/2 RC** *Slip 2 to cn to back, k2, k2 from cn*
⧅ **2/2 LC** *Slip 2 to cn to front, k2, k2 from cn*

Right Front

Cast on 59 (63, 67, 73) sts.

Rows 1, 3, and 5 (RS) Knit 18 (20, 21, 22) sts, k2tog, knit to end. ***Rows 2, 4, and 6*** Knit. Garter stitch border completed — 56 (60, 64, 70) sts.

Next row (RS) Establish pattern and begin short rows to shape hemline. AT SAME TIME at 1½ (2, 2¼, 2¼)" begin buttonholes as follows: on RS row work 3 sts, bind off 2 sts, finish row. On next row cast on 2 sts over 2 sts that were bound off. Work 3 more buttonholes spaced 2¾" apart. ***Row 7*** K20 (21, 23, 24) sts, W&T. ***Row 8*** Slip 1, p2, W&T. ***Row 9*** Slip 1, k7, W&T. ***Row 10*** Slip 1, p9, W&T. ***Row 11*** Slip 1, k14, W&T. ***Row 12*** Slip 1, p16, W&T. Working from charts, continue as established until Row 27, (29, 31, 31). Begin Chart A centering in St st panel.

Shape neck

When work measures 10 (10, 11, 12)" from CO at side, begin shaping the neck by decreasing in the St st section and AT SAME TIME increasing in the DM center section as follows: on next RS row, DM 8, M1, work cable section, p1, SSK, work pattern to end. Work shaping every 8 rows 7 (8, 9, 11) times — 15 (16, 17, 19) sts in DM section. Work to 12 (13, 14, 15)" and begin shaping armhole.

Shape armhole

Bind off 10 sts at the beginning of the next WS row, then 2 sts at the beginning of the following 4 (5, 5, 6) WS rows — 2 (2, 4, 4) sts remain in the DM section before the cable section. Continue increasing in DM section at neck for collar 3 (2, 3, 1) times — 18 (18, 20, 20) sts in DM section. Work even to 8½ (9, 9½, 10)".

Shape shoulder

Bind off 6 (6, 7, 8) sts at the beginning of the next 2 WS rows, 6 (7, 8, 8) sts at the beginning of the next WS row — 23 (23, 25, 25) sts.

Collar extension

Continue pattern of DM and cable with p1 at seam edge as established. Work until collar height measures 2½ (2½, 3, 3)", ending with a WS row.

Short row collar shaping

Short row 1 (RS) Work to last 7 sts, W&T. ***All WS rows*** Work across to end. ***Short row 2*** (RS) Work to last 9 sts, W&T. ***Short row 3*** (RS) Work to last 11 sts, W&T. ***Short row 5*** (RS) Work to last 13 sts, W&T. ***Short row 7*** (RS) Bind off 8 sts, place remaining 15 (15, 17, 17) sts on holder.

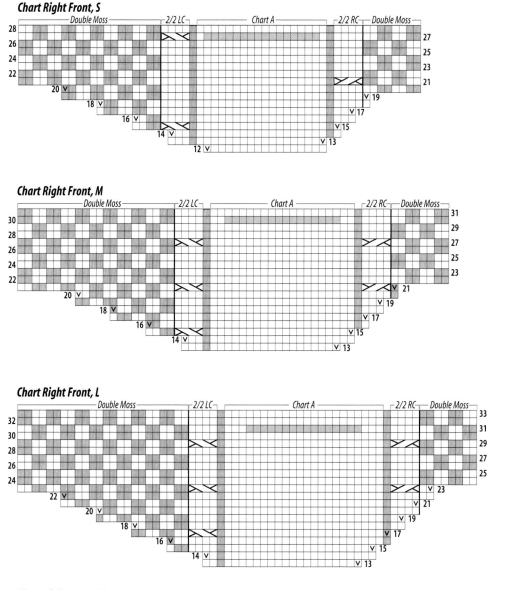

Chart Right Front, S

Chart Right Front, M

Chart Right Front, L

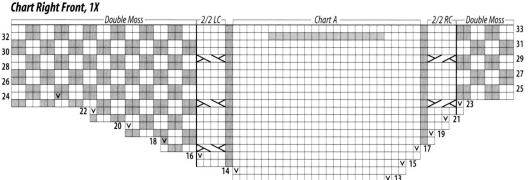

Chart Right Front, 1X

Left Back

Note: For Left and Right Back continue shaping points with W&T at end of each WS row, slip 1 at beginning of each RS row until you are working full width of piece. (No more W&T or slip at beginning of row.) With 4mm/US size 6 needles, cast on 47 (52, 57, 62) sts. **Rows 1 and 3** (RS) P1, k4, p1, knit to end. **Rows 2, 4, and 6** Knit to last 6 sts, p6. **Row 5** P1, 2/2 RC, p1, knit to end. Garter stitch border with cable completed.

Next row (RS) establish pattern and begin short rows to shape hemline. Row 7 P1, k4, p1, k2, W&T. **Row 8** Slip 1, p7. **Row 9** P1, k4, p1, k10, W&T. **Row 10** Slip 1, p15. Working from charts, continue as established through Row 20, k2tog at beginning of last row as shown on chart. Break yarn and place stitches on hold.

Chart Left Back, S

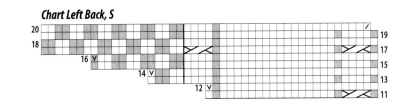

Chart Left Back, M

Chart Left Back, L, 1X

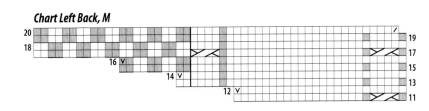

Chart Right Back, S

Chart Right Back, M

Chart Right Back, L, 1X

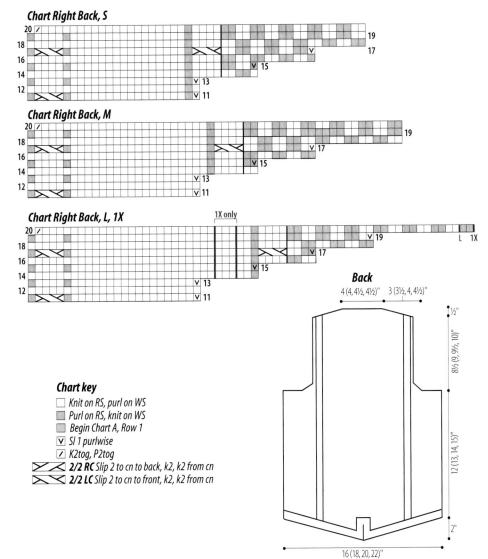

Chart key
- ☐ Knit on RS, purl on WS
- ▨ Purl on RS, knit on WS
- ▦ Begin Chart A, Row 1
- ⍌ Sl 1 purlwise
- ⁄ K2tog, P2tog
- ⧅ **2/2 RC** Slip 2 to cn to back, k2, k2 from cn
- ⧄ **2/2 LC** Slip 2 to cn to front, k2, k2 from cn

Back

4 (4, 4½, 4½)" 3 (3½, 4, 4½)"

½"

8½ (9, 9½, 10)"

12 (13, 14, 15)"

2"

16 (18, 20, 22)"

Right Back

Cast on 47 (52, 57, 62) sts. **Rows 1 and 3** (RS) Knit to the last 6 sts, p1, k4, p1. **Rows 2, 4, and 6** P6, knit to end. **Row 5** Knit to last 6 sts, p1, 2/2 LC, p1. Garter stitch border with cable completed.

Next row (RS) Establish pattern and begin short rows to shape hemline. Row 7 Knit to last 6 sts, p1, k4, p1. **Row 8** P8, W&T. **Row 9** Slip 1, k1, p1, k4, p1. **Row 10** P16, W&T. Working from charts, continue as established through Row 20. **Row 21** Work across Right AND Left Back by working in pattern across right back to cable, p1, k8, p1 over center 10 sts, work Left Back to end — 92 (102, 112, 122) sts. **Row 22** Work to center 10 sts, k1, p8, k1, work to end. **Row 23** Work to center 10 sts, p1, 2/2 LC, 2/2 RC, p1, work to end. **Rows 24–27** Work to center 10 sts, k10, work to end. **Row 28** Work to center 10 sts, p10, work to end. Continue in pattern as established. When piece measures 11 (12, 13, 14)", begin Chart B in center 4 sts of stockinette panel, begin shaping armhole at 12 (13, 14, 15)".

Shape armholes

Bind off 10 sts at the beginning of the next 2 rows, then 2 sts at the beginning of the following 8 (10, 10, 12) rows — 2 (2, 4, 4) sts remain in the DM section before the cable section — 56 (62, 72, 78) st. Work even to 9 (9½, 10, 11)".

Shape shoulders

Bind off 6 (6, 7, 8) sts at the beginning of the next 4 rows, 6 (7, 8, 8) sts at the beginning of the next 2 rows, bind off remaining 20 (24, 28, 30) sts.

Finishing

Block. Sew shoulder seams and side seams. Sew on buttons.

Orbit Chart

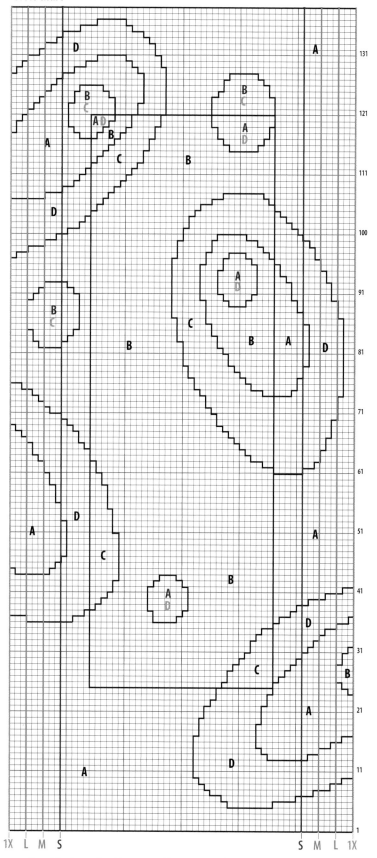

131
121
111
100
91
81
71
61
51
41
31
21
11
1

1X L M S ⋯ S M L 1X

Note *If 2 colors are listed for an area of the chart, the Red is for S, M; the Green is for L, 1X, 2X.*

Work Orbit Vest following Greta instructions for Fronts and Back to 4 rows above join of left and right backs. Work Orbit chart over center 42 (48, 54, 60) sts.

Color key Grey (Rust)

A *Mid Grey (Rust)*
B *Pale Grey (Orange)*
C *Rust (Light Grey)*
D *Brick (Chocolate)*

Chart B

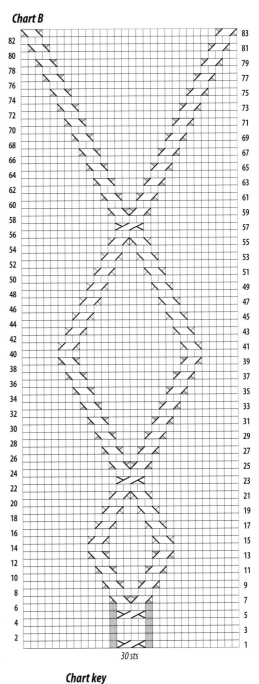

30 sts

Chart key

☐ Knit on RS, purl on WS
▨ Purl on RS, knit on WS
2/1 RPC *Slip 1 to cn to back; k2; p1 from cn*
2/1 LPC *Slip 2 to cn to front; p1; k2 from cn*
2/1 RC *Slip 1 to cn to back; k2; k1 from cn*
2/1 LC *Slip 2 to cn to front; k1; k2 from cn*
2/2 RC *Slip 2 to cn to back; k2; k2 from cn*

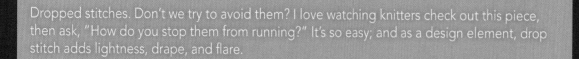

Dropped stitches. Don't we try to avoid them? I love watching knitters check out this piece, then ask, "How do you stop them from running?" It's so easy; and as a design element, drop stitch adds lightness, drape, and flare.

Drop Stitch

Drop Stitch Jacket

Drop and ladder to great effect, adding flare and air to the Drop Stitch Jacket. Cast on and swatch to learn to drop on purpose. Then drop over and over again for very simple, very stylish results.

Drop Stitch Jacket

INTERMEDIATE

C
B | A
D

XS (S, M, L, 1X)
A 34 (38, 41, 45, 49)"
B 26 (26½, 27, 27½, 28)"
C 27 (28½, 28, 28½, 29)"
D 50 (53½, 57, 61, 63)"

10cm/4"

28

22

**over stockinette stitch
(knit on RS, purl on RS)**

1 2 3 **4** 5 6

Medium weight
1300 (1400, 1550, 1700, 1800) yds

4.5 mm/US 7
or size to obtain gauge

&

Cable needle
Stitch markers
Stitch holder

Medium: 15 balls TRENDSETTER YARNS/
MONDIAL Prima in 114 Coral; page 87

Notes
1 See *Techniques*, page 160 for long-tail cast-on, k2tog, SSK, SSP, M1, and wrap and turn for short rows. **2** See *Drop Stitch Tips*, page 148. **3** Schematics show measurements before stitches are dropped.

Drop Stitch (D1) Drop stitch off left needle. Work 2 rounds, then unravel stitch down to M1 or cast-on.
3/3 RC Slip 3 stitches to cable needle (cn), hold to back, k3; k3 from cn.
3/3 LC Slip 3 stitches to cable needle (cn), hold to front, k3; k3 from cn.

Back
Using long tail cast-on, cast on 109 (119, 129, 139, 149) stitches.
Row 1 (RS) K4, * p1, k4; repeat from * to end. **Row 2** P4, * k1, p4; repeat from *, to end. Repeat last 2 rows 14 times.
Drop Stitch Section 1
Row 31 (RS) K4, * p1, k4, D1, k4; repeat from *, end p1, k4 — 99 (108, 117, 126, 135) sts. **Row 32** (WS) P4, * k1, p8; repeat from *, end k1, p4. **Row 33** K4, * p1, k8; repeat from *, end p1, k4. Repeat last 2 rows 10 times, then work Row 32 once.
Drop Stitch Section 2
Row 55 (RS) K4, * D1, k8; repeat from *, end D1, k4 — 88 (96, 104, 112, 120) sts. Work in stockinette st through Row 122.
Shape armholes
Row 123 and 124 Bind off 4 (5, 5, 7, 8) sts at the beginning of the next 2 rows.
Row 125 (RS) K1, SSK, work to last 3 sts, k2tog, k1. **Row 126** (WS) P1, p2tog, work to last 3 sts, SSP, p1. Repeat last 2 rows 3 (3, 4, 4, 5) times more — 64 (70, 74, 78, 80) sts.
Working 52 (56, 56, 60, 62) rows even — 184 (188, 190, 194, 198) rows total.
Shape shoulder and neck
Next row (RS) Bind off 7 (8, 8, 9, 9) sts, work 15 (17, 19, 19, 19) sts, bind off center 18 (18, 18, 20, 22) sts, work to end.
Continue working left shoulder only.
Next row (WS) Bind off 7 (8, 8, 9, 9) sts, purl to neck edge. **Next row** Bind off 2 sts at neck edge and work to end. Bind off 7 (8, 9, 9, 9) sts at the beginning of next 2 RS rows and fasten off.
With WS facing, rejoin yarn at right neck edge, bind off 2, and purl remaining 14 (16, 18, 18, 18) sts. Bind off 7 (8, 9, 9, 9) sts at the beginning of next 2 RS rows and fasten off.

4 (4, 4½, 4½, 5)"
11½ (13, 14, 14½, 14½)"
3½ (4½, 4½, 5, 4½)"
1"
8½ (9, 9½, 10, 10½)"

Back

17½"

16 (17½, 19, 20½, 22)"
23"
20 (21½, 23, 25, 27)"

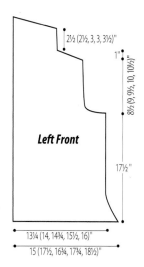

2½ (2½, 3, 3, 3½)"
1"
8½ (9, 9½, 10, 10½)"

Left Front

17½"

13¼ (14, 14¾, 15½, 16)"
15 (17½, 16¾, 17¾, 18½)"

Left Front Band

LF1 P1, 3/3 RC, p2, M1, p2, k2, D1, k2, p4, k2, M1, k2, p2, D1, p2, k2, p2.

LF2 P1, 3/3 RC, p2, D1, p2, k2, M1, k2, p4, k2, D1, k2, p2, M1, p2, k2, p2.

Left Front

Cast on 82 (87, 92, 97, 102) sts. **Establish pattern: Rows 1, 3, and 5** (RS) K4, * p1, k4; repeat from * to last 33 sts (front band), place marker (pm), p1, k6, p4, k2, p1, k2, p4, k4, p2, k1, p2, k2, p2. **Rows 2, 4, 6, and 8** P4, k2, p1, k2, p4, k4, p2, k1, p2, k4, p7, slip marker (sm) * p4, k1; repeat from *, end p4. **Row 7** Work to marker, p1, 3/3 RC [slip 3 stitches to cable needle (cn), hold to back, k3; k3 from cn], p4, k2, p1, k2, p4, k4, p2, k1, p2, k2, p2. Repeat Rows 1–8 twice, then work Rows 1–6 once.

Drop Stitch Section 1

Row 31 (RS) K4, * D1, k4, p1, k4; repeat from * 3 (4, 4, 5, 5) times, D1 (0, 1, 0, 1), k4 (0, 4, 0, 4), sm, work LF1 — 77 (82, 86, 91, 95) sts. **Rows 32, 34, 36, and 38** (WS) P4, k4, p2, k1, p2, k4, p4, k2, p1, k2, p7, sm, p8 (4, 8, 4, 8), *k1, p8; repeat from * to end. **Rows 33, 35, and 37** (RS) *K8, p1; repeat from * 3 (4, 4, 5, 5) times, k8 (4, 8, 4, 8), sm, p1, k6, p2, k1, p2, k4, p4, k2, p1, k2, p4, k2, p2. Repeat last 8 rows twice.

Drop Stitch Section 2

Row 55 (RS) * K8, D1; repeat from * 3 (4, 4, 5, 5) times, k8 (4, 8, 4, 8), sm, work LF2 — 73 (77, 81, 85, 89) sts. **Row 56** (WS) P4, k2, p1, k2, p4, k4, p2, k1, p2, k4, p7, sm, purl to end. **Row 57** (RS) Knit to marker, p1, k6, p4, k2, p1, k2, p4, k4, p2, k1, p2, k2, p2. Continue even as established through Row 78, working 3/3 RC on Rows 63 and 71.

Drop Stitch Section 3

Row 79 (RS) Knit to marker, work LF1—73 (77, 81, 85, 89) sts. **Row 80** (WS) P4, k4, p2, k1, p2, k4, p4, k2, p1, k2, p7, sm, purl to end. **Row 81** (RS) Knit to marker, p1, k6, p2, k1, p2, k4, p4, k2, p1, k2, p4, k2, p2. Continue even in established pattern through Row 102, working 3/3 RC on Rows 87, 95, and every following 8th row.

Drop Stitch Section 4

Row 103 (RS) Knit to marker, work LF2 — 73 (77, 81, 85, 89) sts. Continue even to Row 118.

Shape V-neck

Note Neck shaping is worked on RS rows by decreasing before marker every 8th (cable) row.

Row 119 Knit to 2 sts before marker, k2tog, work to end. Work 3 rows even.

Shape armhole

Row 123 (RS) Bind off 4 (5, 5, 7, 8) sts, work to end of row — 68 (71, 75, 77, 80) sts. **Row 124** Work even. **Row 125** K1, SSK, work to end. **Row 126** Work to last 3 sts, SSP, p1.

Drop Stitch Section 5

Row 127 K1, SSK, knit to 2 stitches before marker, k2tog, work LF1. Work 5 (7, 7, 7, 7) rows, decreasing at beginning of RS rows and end of WS rows as for Rows 125 and 126 — 59 (60, 64, 66, 69) sts. Work 2 (2, 0, 0, 0) rows even. **Row 135** (RS) K1, SSK 0 (0, 0, 1, 1) time, knit to 2 sts before marker, k2tog, p1, 3/3 RC, p2, k1, p2, k4, p4, k2, p1, k2, p4, k2, p2. **Row 136** (WS) Work to last 3 sts, SSP 0 (0, 0, 0, 1) time, p3 (3, 3, 3, 1) — 58 (59, 63, 64, 66) sts. Continue through Row 158, placing a decrease before marker on Rows 143 and 151. **Row 159** (RS) Knit to 2 sts before marker, k2tog, p1, 3/3 RC, p2, D1, p2, k4, p4, k2, D1, k2, p4, k2, p2. Continue working in pattern, placing decreases before marker on next 0 (1, 0, 1, 2) Cable rows. Work even through Row 182 (186, 190, 194, 198).

Shape shoulder

Next row (RS) Bind off 6 (6, 9, 9, 10) sts, then bind off 8 (8, 9, 9, 9) sts at the beginning of the next 2 RS rows. Continue cable and ribbing over remaining 31 front band sts. Work to half the width of the back neck plus ½".

Collar extension

Short row 1 (WS) Work in pattern across 24 sts, wrap next stitch and turn work (W&T). **All RS rows** Work to end. **Short row 2** (WS) Work in pattern across 20 sts, W&T. **Short row 3** (WS) Work in pattern across 16 sts, W&T. **Next WS row** Bind off first 10 sts, work across remaining 21 sts picking up wraps when you come to them. Place sts on holder and break yarn.

Right Front Band

RF1 P2, k2, p2, D1, p2, k2, M1, k2, p4, k2, D1, k2, p2, M1, p2, 3/3 RC, p1.
RF2 P2, k2, p2, M1, p2, k2, D1, k2, p4, k2, M1, k2, p2, D1, p2, 3/3 RC, p1.

Right Front

Cast on 82 (87, 92, 97, 102) sts. *Establish pattern: Rows 1, 3, and 5* (RS) P2, k2, p2, k1, p2, k4, p4, k2, p1, k2, p4, k6, p1, pm, *k4, p1; repeat from*, end k4. *Rows 2, 4, 6, and 8* (WS) P4, *k1, p4; repeat from* to marker, p7, k4, p2, k1, p2, k4, p4, k2, p1, k2, p4. *Row 7* P2, k2, p2, k1, p2, k4, p4, k2, p1, k2, p4, 3/3 RC, p1, sm, *k4, p1; repeat from*, end k4. Repeat Rows 1–8 twice, then work Rows 1–6 once.

Drop Stitch Section 1

Row 31 (RS) Work RF1, sm, k4 (0, 4, 0, 4), D1 (0, 1, 0, 1), k4, *p1, k4, D1, k4; repeat from* 3 (4, 4, 5, 5) times — 77 (82, 86, 91, 95) sts. **Rows 32, 34, 36, and 38** (WS) * P8, k1; repeat from * 3 (4, 4, 5, 5) times, p8 (4, 8, 4, 8), sm, p7, k2, p1, k2, p4, k4, p2, k1, p2, k4, p4. **Rows 33, 35, and 37** (RS) P2, k2, p4, k2, p1, k2, p4, k4, p2, k1, p2, k6, p1, sm, k8 (4, 8, 4, 8), *p1, k8; repeat from* 3 (4, 4, 5, 5) times. Repeat Rows 31–38 twice.

Drop Stitch Section 2

Row 55 (RS) Work RF2, sm, k8 (4, 8, 4, 8), *D1, k8; repeat from* 3 (4, 4, 5, 5) times. **Rows 56, 58, 60, and 62** (WS) Purl to marker, p7, k4, p2, k1, p2, k4, p4, k2, p1, k2, p4. **Rows 57, 59, and 61** (RS) P2, k2, p2, k1, p2, k4, p4, k2, p1, k2, p4, k6, p1, sm, knit 40 (44, 48, 52, 56) sts. Continue even through Row 78, working 3/3 RC on Rows 63 and 71.

Drop Stitch Section 3

Row 79 (RS) Work RF1, sm, knit to end—73 (77, 81, 85, 89) sts. **Row 80** (WS) Purl to marker, p7, k2, p1, k2, p4, k4, p2, k1, p2, k4, p4. **Row 81** (RS) P2, k2, p4, k2, p1, k2, p4, k4, p2, k1, p2, k6, p1, sm, knit to end. Continue even through Row 102, working 3/3 RC on Rows 87 and 95.

Drop Stitch Section 4

Row 103 (RS) Work RF2, sm, work to end. Continue even through Row 118, working 3/3 RC on Row 111.

Shape V-neck

Row 119 Work to marker, sm, SSK, work to end. Work 3 rows even.

Shape armhole

Row 123 (RS) Work even. **Row 124** (WS) Bind off 4 (5, 5, 7, 8) sts, work to end — 68 (71, 75, 77, 80) sts. **Row 125** Work to last 3 sts SSK, k1. **Row 126** P1, p2tog, work to end.

Drop Stitch Section 5

Row 127 Work RF1, sm, SSK, knit to 3 sts from end, SSK, k1. Work 5 (7, 7, 7, 7) rows decreasing at end of every RS row and beginning of every WS row — 59 (60, 64, 66, 69) sts. Work 2 (2, 0, 0, 0) rows even. **Row 135** (RS) P2, k2, p4, k2, p1, k2, p4, k4 p2, k1, p2, 3/3 RC, p1, sm, SSK, knit to last 3 sts, SSK 0 (0, 0, 1, 1) time, k3 (3, 3, 1, 1). **Row 136** (WS) P3 (3, 3, 3, 1), p2tog 0 (0, 0, 0 1) time, work across as established—58 (59, 63, 64, 66) sts. Continue through Row 158 placing a decrease before marker on Rows 143 and 151. **Row 159** (RS) P2, k2, p4, k2, D1, k2, p4, k4 p2, D1, p2, 3/3 RC, p1, sm, SSK, knit to end. Continue working in pattern, placing decreases after marker on next 0 (1, 0, 1, 2) cable rows. Work even to Row 182 (186, 190, 194, 198).

Shape shoulder

Next row (WS) Bind off 6 (6, 9, 9, 10) sts, then bind off 8 (8, 9, 9, 9) sts at beginning of next 2 WS rows. Continue cable and ribbing over remaining 31 front band stitches. Work to half the width of the back neck plus ½".

Collar extension

Short row 1 (RS) Work in pattern across 24 sts, wrap next stitch and turn work (W&T.) **All WS rows** Work to end. **Short row 2** (RS) Work in pattern across 20 sts, W&T. **Short row 3** (RS) Work in pattern across 16 sts, W&T. **Next short row** (RS) Bind off first 10 sts, work across remaining 21 sts picking up wraps when you come to them. Place stitches on holder and do not break yarn.

Sleeves

Cast on 47 (47, 51, 51, 55) sts. **Row 1** (RS) K3 (3, 5, 5, 7), *p1, k4; repeat from* 7 times, end p1, end k3 (3, 5, 5, 7). **Row 2** P3 (3, 5, 5, 7), *k1, p4; repeat from* 7 times, end k1, p3 (3, 5, 5, 7). Repeat last 2 rows 14 times more. **Row 31** (RS) K3 (3, 5, 5, 7), *p1, k4, D1, k4; repeat from* 3 times, end p1, k3 (3, 5, 5, 7) — 43 (43, 47, 47, 51) sts. **Rows 32, 34** (WS) P3 (3, 5, 5, 7), *k1, p8; repeat from* 3 times, end k1, p3 (3, 5, 5, 7). **Row 33** (RS) K3 (3, 5, 5, 7), *p1, k8; repeat from* 3 times, end p1, k3 (3, 5, 5, 7). Repeat last 2 rows 4 times more.

Drop Stitch Section 1

Row 43 (RS) K1, M1, k2 (2, 4, 4, 6), *D1, k4, M1, k4; repeat from* 3 times, end D1, k2 (2, 4, 4, 6), M1, k1 — 44 (44, 48, 48, 52) sts. **Rows 44, 46, and 48** (WS) P8 (8, 10, 10, 12) *k1, p8; repeat from* twice, k1, p8 (8, 10, 10, 12). **Rows 45, 47, and 49** (RS) Knit to first purl st, *p1, k8; repeat from* twice, p1, knit to end of row. **All following rows** Work stitches as they present themselves or as instructed below, AT SAME TIME increase at beginning and end of every 6 rows 4 (4, 6, 0, 0) times through Row 73 (73, 85, 49, 49), then every 4 rows 8 (8, 5, 17, 17) times until 105 (113, 117, 117, 117) rows — 66 (66, 67, 79, 83) sts.

Drop Stitch Section 2

Row 67 (RS) Knit to first purl st, *D1, k4, M1, k4; repeat from* twice, D1, knit to end of row. **Row 68** (WS) Purl to first M1 st, *k1, p8; repeat from* once, k1, purl to end.

Drop Stitch Section 3

Row 91 (RS) Knit to first purl st, *D1, k4, M1, k4; repeat from* once, D1, knit to end. **Row 92** (WS) Purl to first M1 st, k1, p8, k1, purl to end.

Drop Stitch Section 4

Row 115 (RS) Knit to first purl st, D1, k4, M1, k4, D1, knit to end. **Row 116** (WS) Purl to first M1 st, k1, purl to end.

Shape cap

Row 125, (125, 129, 129, 133) (RS) At beginning of row, bind off 5 (5, 5, 7, 8) sts twice, then 2 (2, 2, 3, 3) sts 4 times, AT SAME TIME on Row 139 (RS), knit to center purl st, D1, knit to end. Continue decreasing 1 st at beginning of next 16 (16, 22, 22, 22) rows. Bind off 2 sts at beginning of next 10 (10, 8, 8, 8) rows, bind off remaining 10 (10, 10, 14, 16) sts.

Finishing

Check to make sure all dropped sts are fully dropped. Join shoulder seams, sew collar to back neck, set in sleeves, sew sleeve and side seams. With RS facing, join front bands with 3-needle bind off.

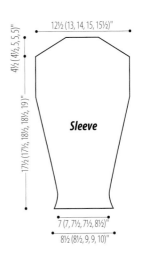

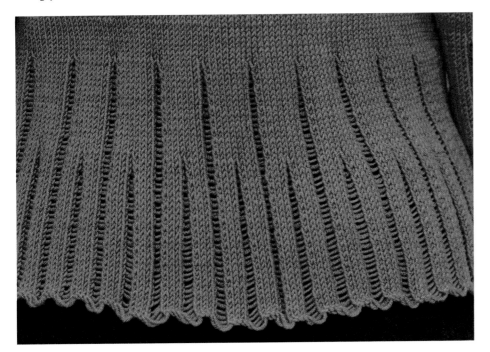

Drop Stitch Tunic and Skirt

I don't do cute, but on Lydia, the pink tunic is kinda cute. It's worked in tiers with extra stitches cast on, then dropped to create flare at the hemline. As the knitting unfolds, cables join in to keep the journey interesting.

Drop Stitch Tunic

XS (S, M, L, 1X)
A 34 (36, 38, 40, 42)"
Before drop 28 (30, 32, 33, 35)"
B 26 (27, 28, 28½, 29)"
C 10 (11, 12, 13, 14)"

10cm/4"

28

23

**over stockinette stitch
(knit on RS, purl on WS)**

1 2 3 **4** 5 6

Medium weight

625 (700, 775, 825, 925) yds

4 mm/US 6,
or size to obtain gauge, 60cm (24") or longer

&

Cable needle (cn)
Stitch marker

Medium 8 balls TRENDSETTER YARNS/
MONDIAL Solare in 68 Fuchsia; page 92

Notes
1 See *Techniques*, page 160, for knitting in rounds, long-tail cast-on, and M1. **2** Work tunic in rounds to armhole shaping, then work back and front separately in rows (back and forth). **3** See *Drop Stitch Tips*, page 148.

Drop Stitch (D1) Drop stitch off left needle. Work 2 rounds, then unravel stitch down to M1 or cast-on.
2/2 RC Slip 2 stitches to cable needle (cn), hold to back, k2; k2 from cn.
2/2 LC Slip 2 stitches to cable needle (cn), hold to front, k2; k2 from cn.

Tunic
With 4mm/US 6 needle and long-tail cast-on, cast on 204 (216, 228, 240, 252) stitches. Place marker (pm), join, and work in k2, p1 rib, for 3¼ (3¼, 3½, 3½, 4)".
Drop Stitch Section
Drop stitch round 1 * K2, D1, k2, p1; repeat from * around — 170 (180, 190, 200, 210) stitches.
Work in k4, p1 rib until piece measure 5½ (5½, 6½, 6½, 7½)".
Drop stitch round 2 * K2, M1, k2, D1; repeat from *.
Following rib rounds, k2, p1, * k4, p1; repeat from *, end k2.
Work in k4, p1 rib until piece measures 8½ (8½, 9¼, 10¼, 11)".
Drop stitch round 3 * K2, D1, k2, M1; repeat from *.
Work in k4, p1 rib until piece measures 12 (12, 13, 13, 14)".
Drop & Cable Section 1
Rnd 1 * K2, M1, k2, D1; repeat from *. *Rnds 2–6, 8–11* * P1, k4; repeat from *. *Rnds 7, 19* K2, * p1, 2/2LC, p1, k4; repeat from * to last 8 stitches, p1, 2/2LC, p1, k2. *Rnd 12* K2, * p1, k4; repeat from * around to last 3 stitches, p1, place 2 stitches on cn drop to back, remove marker, k2, replace marker. *Rnd 13* K2 from cn, * p1, k4, p1, 2/2 RC; repeat from * to last 8 stitches, p1, k4, p1, k2. *Rnds 14–18, 20* K2, p1, * k4, p1; repeat from * end k2.
Drop & Cable Section 2
Rnd 1 * K2, D1, k2, M1; repeat from *. *Rnds 2–8, 10-16, 18-23* * K4, p1; repeat from *. *Rnd 9 and 24* * K4, p1, 2/2 RC, p1; repeat from *, to last 8 stitches, p1, 2/2 RC, p1, k2. *Rnd 17* * 2/2 LC, p1, k4, p1; repeat from *.
Rnd 25 [K4, D1] twice, [k2, M1, k2, D1] 13 (14, 15, 16, 17) times, [k4, D1] 4 times, [k2, M1, k2, D1] 13 (14, 15, 16, 17) times, [k4, D1] twice. *Rnds 26–31* K10, [p1, k4] 12 (13, 14, 15, 16) times, p1, k20, [p1, k4] 12 (13, 14, 15, 16) times, p1, k10. *Rnd 32* K12, [p1, k4] 12 (13, 14, 15, 16) times, p1, k20, [p1, k4] 12 (13, 14, 15, 16) times, p1, k2, bind off 6.
Shape armholes
Next row Remove marker, bind off 10 sts, k2, [p1, k4] 12 (13, 14, 15, 16) times, p1, k2, bind off 16 sts, k2, [p1, k4] 12 (13, 14, 15, 16) times, p1, k2, bind off 6 sts — 65, 70, 75, 80, 85 stitches in Front and Back. Place Front stitches on hold.

Back

Row 1, 3, 5, 7, 9 (WS) K2, *k1, p4; repeat from *, k3. *Row 2* (RS) K2, *p1, 2/2LC; repeat from *, p1, k2. *Rows 4, 6, 8* (RS) K2, *p1, k4; repeat from *, p1, k2. *Row 10* (RS) K2, *D1, k2, M1, k2; repeat from* D1, k2 — 64 (69, 74, 79, 84) sts. *Rows 11, 13, 15* (WS) K2 p2,*k1, p4; repeat from * to last 5 stitches, k1, p2, k2. *Rows 12, 14, 16* (RS)* K4, p1; repeat from *, k4. *Rows 17, 19, 21, 23* (WS) K2, p2, *k1, p4; repeat from * to last 5 stitches, k1, p2, k2. *Row 18* (RS) K4, p1, *2/2 RC, p1; repeat from *, k4. *Rows 20, 22* (RS) *K4, p1; repeat from *, K4. *Row 24* (RS) *K4, p1, 2/2 LC, p1; repeat from * to last 4 sts, k4. *Rows 25–29, 31–35* Work k4, p1 rib as established. *Row 30* (K4, p1) twice, [2/2 RC, p1, k4, p1] 5 (5, 6, 6, 7), k4, [p1, k4] 0 (1, 0, 1, 0). Repeat Rows 24–35 once, then work in established rib until armhole measures 7½ (8, 8¼, 8½, 9)", end with a RS row.

Shape shoulders

Next 2 rows (RS) Bind off 7 (8, 8, 9, 9) stitches, work 11 (13, 13, 17, 17) stitches, work k1, p1 rib over center 26 (25, 30, 25, 30) stitches, pattern to end. *Next 4 rows* Bind off 6 (7, 7, 9, 9) stitches at beginning of each row, maintaining rib in center and pattern over remaining stitches. Bind off.

Front

Place stitches from holder on needle.
Work as for Back through Row 24.

Rows 25 and 27 (WS) K2, p2, [k1, p4] 2 (3, 3, 4, 4) times, k1, p2 (0, 0, 0, 0), k30 (29, 34, 29, 34), p2 (0, 0, 0, 0), k1, [p4, k1] 2 (3, 3, 4, 4) times, p2, k2. *Rows 26 and 28* (RS) [K4, p1] 3 (4, 4, 5, 5) times, k34 (29, 34, 29, 34), [p1, k4] 3 (4, 4, 5, 5) times. *Row 29* (WS) K2, p2, k1, [p4, k1] 2 (3, 3, 4, 4) times, p2 (0, 0, 0, 0), k2, bind off 26 (25, 30, 25, 30), k1, p2 (0, 0, 0, 0), [k1, p4] 2 (3, 3, 4, 4) times, k1, p2, k2.

Left Front

Continue over 19 (22, 22, 27, 27) stitches, placing Right Front on hold. *Row 30* (RS) [K4, p1] 3 (4, 4, 5, 5) times, k4 (2, 2, 2, 2). *Row 31* (WS) K2 (3, 3, 3, 3), p2 (4, 4, 4, 4), [K1, p4] 2 (2, 2, 3, 3) times, k1, p2, k2. Continue, working cables to match Back and keeping first and last 2 stitches in garter stitch.

Shape shoulder

Next WS row Bind off 7 (8, 8, 9, 9) stitches at arm edge, work to end. *All RS rows* Work in pattern to end. *Next 2 WS rows* bind off 6 (7, 7, 9, 9) stitches beginning of row work to end.

Right Front

Rejoin yarn at neck edge, and continue over 19 (22, 22, 27, 27) stitches. *Row 30* (RS) K4 (2, 2, 2, 2), [p1, k4] 3 (4, 4, 5, 5) times. *Row 31* (WS) K2, p2, [k1, p4] 2 (3, 3, 4, 4) times k1 (3, 3, 3, 3) p2 (0, 0, 0, 0), k2 (0, 0, 0, 0). Continue right front placing cables to match back making sure to keep first and last 2 stitches in garter.

Shape shoulder

Next RS row Bind off 7 (8, 8, 9, 9) stitches at arm edge work to end. *All WS rows* Work in pattern to end. *Next 2 RS rows* Bind off 6 (7, 7, 9, 9) stitches at beginning of row, work to end.

Finishing

Block pieces. Sew shoulder and side seams.

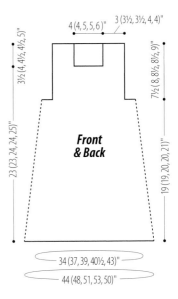

4 (4, 5, 5, 6)" 3 (3½, 3½, 4, 4)"

3½ (4, 4½, 4½, 5)"

7½ (8, 8¼, 8½, 9)"

23 (23, 24, 24, 25)"

Front & Back

19 (19, 20, 20, 21)"

34 (37, 39, 40½, 43)"

44 (48, 51, 53, 50)"

Drop Stitch Skirt

B [A] C

XS (S, M, L, 1X)
A 35 (38½, 42, 45½, 49)"
B 25½ (26, 27, 28, 28½)"
C 56 (62, 68, 74, 80)"

10cm/4"

27 [ ] 19

over stockinette stitch
(knit on RS, purl on WS)
with 4.5 mm/US 7 needle

1 2 3 **4** 5 6

Medium weight
925 (1000, 1150, 1300, 1425) yds

3.75 mm/US 5, 4 mm/US 6, 4.5 mm/US 7
or size to obtain gauge, 60cm (24") or longer

&

Cable needle (cn)
1" elastic (waist measurement + 2")

Extra Small: 10 balls TRENDSETTER YARNS
Merino VIII in 8964 Royal Blue

Notes

1 See *Techniques*, page 160 for knitting in rounds, M1, and long-tail cast-on.
2 Skirt is worked in rounds from hem to waist. **3** See *Drop Stitch Tips* page 148.

Drop Stitch (D1) Drop stitch off left needle. Work 2 rounds, then unravel stitch down to M1 or cast-on.
2/2 RC Slip 2 stitches to cable needle (cn), hold to back, k2; k2 from cn.
2/2 LC Slip 2 stitches to cable needle (cn), hold to front, k2; k2 from cn.

Skirt

With 4 mm/US 6 needle and using long-tail cast-on, cast on 240 (264, 288, 312, 336) stitches. Place marker, join, and work in k2, p1 rib for 3 (3, 3½, 3½, 4)".

Drop stitch section

Drop round 1 Change to 4.5 mm/US 7 needle, *k2, drop stitch (D1), k2, p1; repeat from* — 200 (220, 240, 260, 280) stitches. Work in k4, p1 rib until piece measures 5½ (5½, 6, 6, 7)".
Drop round 2 * K2, M1, k2, D1; repeat from* — 200 (220, 240, 260, 280) stitches
Next round K2, p1, *k4, p1; repeat from*, end k2. Repeat last round until piece measures 8½ (8½, 9, 10, 11)".

Drop and cable section

Round 1 * K2, D1, k2, M1; repeat from *.
Rounds 2–6 * K4, p1; repeat from *.
Round 7 * 2/2RC, p1, k4, p1; repeat from *.
Rounds 8–12 * K4, p1; repeat from *.
Round 13 * K4, p1, 2/2LC, p1; repeat from *.
Rounds 14–18 * K4, p1; repeat from *.
Round 19 * 2/2RC, p1, k4, p1; repeat from *.
Rounds 20–24 * K4, p1; repeat from *.
Round 25 * K2, M1, k2, D1; repeat from *.
Rounds 26–30 * K2, p1, k2; repeat from *.
Round 31 * K2, p1, 2/2LC, p1, k2; repeat from *.
Rounds 32–35 * K2, p1, k2; repeat from *.
Round 36 * K2, p1, k2; repeat to last 2 stitches; work 2/2RC with last 2 stitches of Round 36 and first 2 stitches of Round 37.
Round 37 * P1, k4, p1, 2/2RC; repeat from*, end p1, k4, p1, k2.
Rounds 38–42 * K2, p1, k2; repeat from *.
Round 43 * K2, p1, 2/2LC, p1, k2; repeat from *.
Rounds 44–48 * K2, p1, k2; repeat from *.
Repeat Rounds 1–24 once and Rounds 13–18 once.

Cable section

Round 1 * 2/2RC, p1; repeat from *.
Rounds 2–6 * K4, p1; repeat from *. Work Rounds 1–6, until piece measures approximately 24½ (25, 26, 27, 27½)".

Waistband

Decrease round Change to 3.75 mm/US 5 needle, *k3, k2tog; repeat from * — 160 (176, 192, 208, 224) stitches. Knit until work measures 2" from Decrease round. Bind off loosely.
Casing Sew bind-off to Decrease round, leaving last 2" open. Insert elastic; overlap ends and sew together. Sew opening closed.

35 (38½, 42, 45½, 49)"

Waist Band

1"

Cable

24½ (25, 26, 27, 27½)"

Drop & Cable

Drop stitch 2

Drop stitch 1

56 (62, 68, 74, 80)"

KNIT THE COLORS OF AUSTRALIA   S W I N G   S W A G G E R   D R A P E

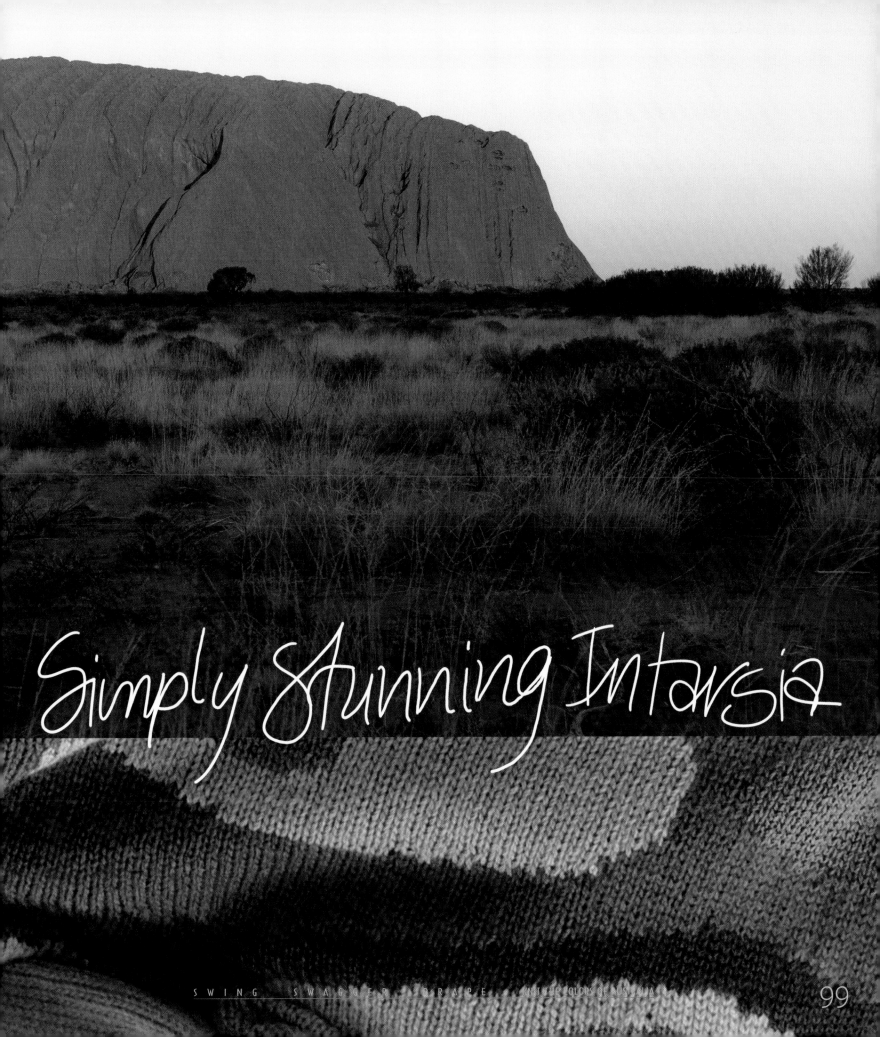

Simply Stunning Intarsia

Lava

How can you not want to knit intarsia?
Just look at the patterns and colors, it's
like unfolding a story as you knit.

MIX LAVA with
Stripes and blocks

lava

stripe

increase for collar

↑
Increase
for hemline

→ direction of knitting

use one graph for 3 styles.

wrapped creates
a collar of rib—

This is topography—dry river
beds, valleys and hills, pebbles and
stones—follow its flow.

The Lava Drape—I am presently
wearing mine as a vest while I knit the
sleeves! Create your own destination,
from desert floor to coral reef.

KNIT THE COLORS OF AUSTRALIA   S W I N G   S W A G G E R   D R A P E

Lava Jacket

S (M, L, 1X, 2X)

A 36 (39, 42, 45, 48)"
B 21½ (22, 23½, 24, 24)"
C 30½ (33, 33, 34, 35)"

10cm/4"

29

21

**over stockinette stitch
(knit on RS, purl on WS),
using smaller needles**

1 2 3 **4** 5 6

Medium weight

A 375 (425, 450, 500, 525) yds
B 155 (175, 190, 205, 215) yds
C 440 (500, 535, 590, 615) yds
D 220 (250, 270, 300, 310) yds

4mm/US 6 & 4.5mm/US 7,
or size to obtain gauge

&

Stitch markers

5 • 16mm (5/8")

Medium 5 balls TRENDSETTER YARNS
Merino VIII in Ash 42000 (A), 2 balls Citrus
2062 (B), 5 balls in Grey 303 (C), and 3 balls
Lime 328 (D); pages 100, 101

Notes

1 See *Techniques*, page 160, for intarsia, wrap and turn for short rows, and 3-needle bind-off. **2** If only 2 numbers are given, the first is for sizes S, M, L and the second in parentheses is for sizes 1X, 2X. **3** Use separate lengths of yarn for each block of color. Bring new color under old at color change to twist yarn and prevent holes. **4** See *Intarsia Tips*, page 141.

Left (Right) Sleeve

With C and smaller needles, cast on 38 (42, 44, 44, 46) stitches, knit 8 rows. Change to larger needles and begin Left (Right) Sleeve Chart with Row 1 (RS). Increase 1 stitch each end of Row 3, then every following 6 rows 15 (17, 18, 20, 21) times — 70 (78, 82, 86, 90) stitches. Work even until sleeve measures 19½ (20, 20, 20, 20)" from cast-on.

Shape cap

Bind off 4 stitches at beginning of next 4 rows, then 2 stitches every row 12 (16, 18, 20, 22) times — 30 stitches remain. Bind off 3 stitches at beginning of next 4 rows; bind off remaining stitches.

(continues on page 109)

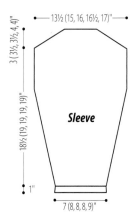

13½ (15, 16, 16½, 17)"

3 (3½, 3½, 4, 4)"

18½ (19, 19, 19, 19)"

Sleeve

1"

7 (8, 8, 8, 9)"

Stitch key

☐ Knit on RS, purl on WS
▨ Purl on RS, knit on WS
— 3-stitch buttonhole; place as directed in text

**Buttonhole Band 2
1X, 2X**

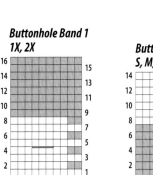

20 sts

**Buttonhole Band 1
1X, 2X**

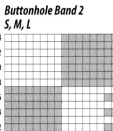

10 sts

**Buttonhole Band 2
S, M, L**

16 sts

**Buttonhole Band 1
S, M, L**

8 sts

**Button Band 2
1X, 2X**

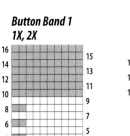

20 sts

**Button Band 1
1X, 2X**

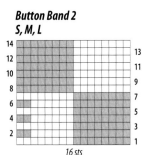

10 sts

**Button Band 2
S, M, L**

16 sts

**Button Band 1
S, M, L**

8 sts

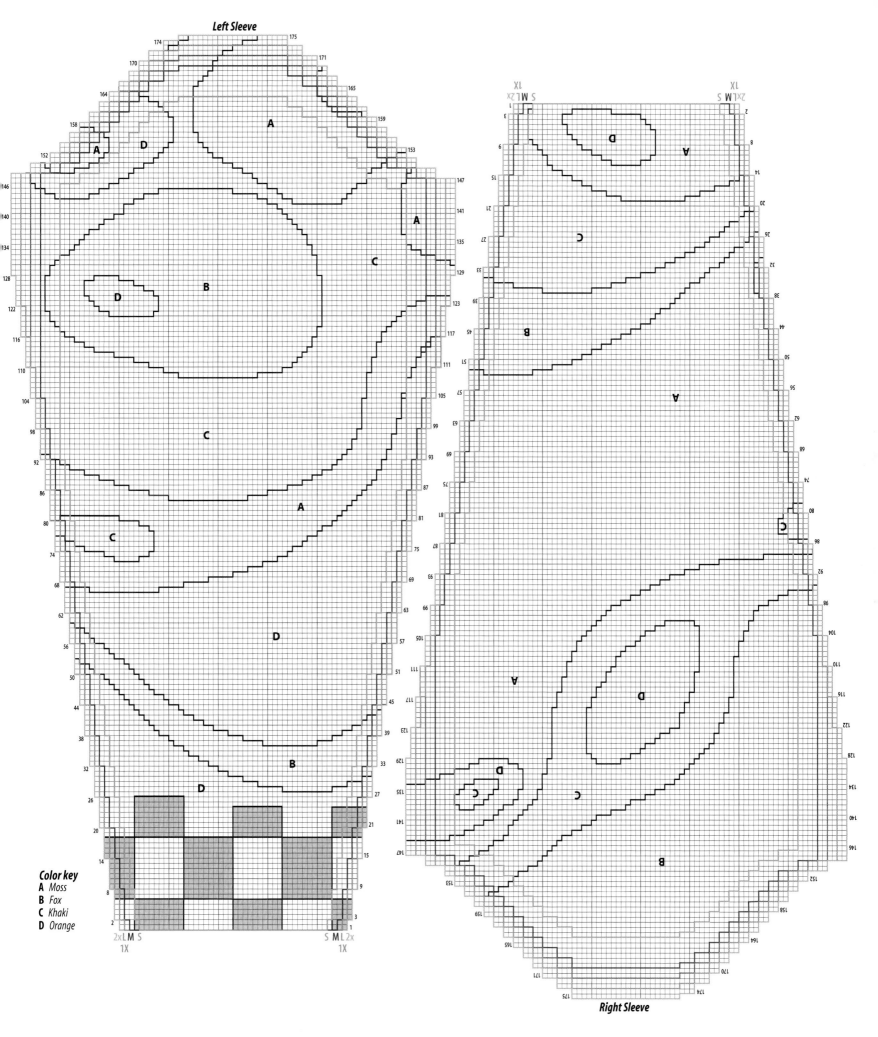

Left Sleeve

Right Sleeve

Color key
A *Moss*
B *Fox*
C *Khaki*
D *Orange*

Lava Drape

INTERMEDIATE+

S (M-L, 1X)
A 11 (12½, 15)"
B 28 (29½, 31½)"
C 32½ (34, 36½)"

10cm/4"

30

22

• over stockinette stitch
(knit on RS, purl on WS),
using larger needle

1 2 **3** 4 5 6

Light weight

A 575 (650, 750) yds
B 475 (525, 600) yds
C 375 (425, 475) yds
D 600 (675, 750) yds

3.25mm/US 3 and 4mm/US 6, or size to
obtain gauge, 60cm (24") or longer

&

Stitch markers

Medium-Large 6 balls SIGNATUR
Pure New Wool DK in 662 Moss (A),
5 balls 673 Fox (B), 4 balls 645 Khaki (C),
and 7 balls 665 Rust (D); pages 102, 103.

Notes

1 See *Techniques*, page 160, for intarsia, k2tog, SSK, p2tog, M1, cable cast-on, wrap and turn for short rows, and bind off in pattern. **2** Drape is worked in one piece from left center front to right center front. **3** Work increased stitches in Corrugated Garter for the collar and stockinette stitch at the hemline. **4** Row gauge is very important. **5** See *Intarsia Tips*, page 141.

Drape

Left Front to Center Back

With larger needle and D, cast on 110 (114, 124) stitches. Work 4 rows Corrugated Garter.

Establish pattern: Chart A

Size S, Row 13 (RS) K4 (bottom edge); place marker (pm), M1, k6, [p10, k10] 4 times, p10 (body), pm; k10 (collar) — 111 sts.
Size M–L, Row 1 (RS) K4 (bottom edge); place marker (pm), M1, [k10, p10] 5 times (body), pm; k10 (collar) — 115 sts.
Size 1X, Row 1 (RS) K4 (bottom edge); place marker (pm), M1, [k10, p10] 5 times, k10 (body), pm; k10 (collar) — 125 sts.
Row 14 (2, 2) (WS) Work Corrugated Rib to first marker, Basket Stitch to second marker, and Corrugated Rib to end of row.
Continue as established through Row 24, increasing 1 stitch after first marker every RS row for body and 1 stitch after second marker on 5th (9th, 9th) row, then every 8 rows for collar.
Begin Chart B: Row 25 (RS) Continue working in Corrugated Garter as established (at bottom and collar edges) and intarsia chart between markers, increasing as indicated every RS row through Row 120 — 150 (160, 170) stitches between markers. AT SAME TIME, continue to increase every 8 rows for collar until 26 (28, 30) collar stitches—180 (192, 204) stitches. Mark last collar increase.
(continues on page 110)

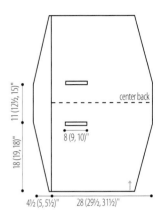

center back

8 (9, 10)"
18 (19, 18)"
11 (12½, 15)"
4½ (5, 5½)"
28 (29½, 31½)"

Corrugated Garter

ANY NUMBER OF STITCHES
Row 1 (RS) Knit.
Row 2 Purl.
Row 3 Purl.
Row 4 Knit.
Repeat Rows 1–4 for Corrugated Garter.

Basket Stitch

MULTIPLE OF 20 STITCHES
Rows 1–12 * K10, p10;
repeat from *.
Rows 13–24 * P10, k10;
repeat from *.
Repeat Rows 1–24.

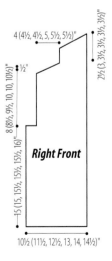

4 (4½, 4½, 5, 5½, 5½)"
2½ (3, 3½, 3½, 3½, 3½)"
8 (8½, 9½, 10, 10, 10½)"
½"
15 (15, 15½, 15½, 15½, 16)"

Right Front

10½ (11½, 12½, 13, 14, 14½)"

Chart A

24
22
20
18
16
14
12
10
8
6
4
2

23
21
19
17
15
13 *Begin S*
11
9
7
5
3
1 *Begin M-L, 1x*

10- to 26 (28, 30)-st collar | S, 1x only | 20-st repeat for body | 4-st edge

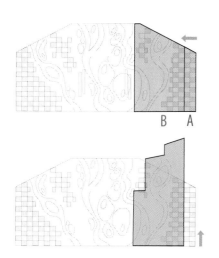

B A

Jacket

Right Front

With C and smaller needles, cast on 56 (60, 66, 70, 74) stitches. Knit 8 rows. Change to larger needles. **Establish patterns** Beginning with Row 1 (RS) and C, work Buttonhole Band Chart 1 across first 8 (10) stitches; place marker (pm); work Chart B over 48 (52, 58, 60, 64) stitches. **Row 2** Work Chart B to marker, Buttonhole Band Chart 1 (page 100) to end. Work as established for 6 (5) repeats of Buttonhole Band Chart 1. **Next RS row** Work Buttonhole Band Chart 2 over 16 (20) stitches, continuing to work first 8 (10) stitches in C and following Chart B for the additional 8 (10) stitches. AT SAME TIME make buttonholes in the 1st, 2nd, 4th, 6th and 7th stockinette sections. To work buttonhole on WS rows, work to last 6 (7) stitches, bind off 3 stitches, knit to end. On the following row, k3 (4), cast on 3 stitches, finish row. Continue until piece measures 15 (15, 15½, 15½, 15½, 16)" from cast-on.

Shape armhole

Bind off 15 (17, 18, 19, 20) stitches at beginning of next WS row — 41 (43, 48, 51, 54) stitches. Work even until piece measures 8 (8½, 9½, 10, 10)" from armhole bind-off.

Shape shoulder

Bind off 10 (11, 12, 13, 14) stitches at beginning of next WS row. **Next WS row** Bind off 10 (10, 11, 12, 13) stitches, work to end.

(continues on page 110)

Stitch key
☐ Knit on RS, purl on WS
▨ Purl on RS, knit on WS
Ⓜ Make 1

▨ For jacket, work in stockinette stitch.

— For 1X, 2X, jacket only, work C shape but not D shape.

Chart note
Charts B, C, D, and E show body stitches only.

Color key
A Moss
B Fox
C Khaki
D Rust

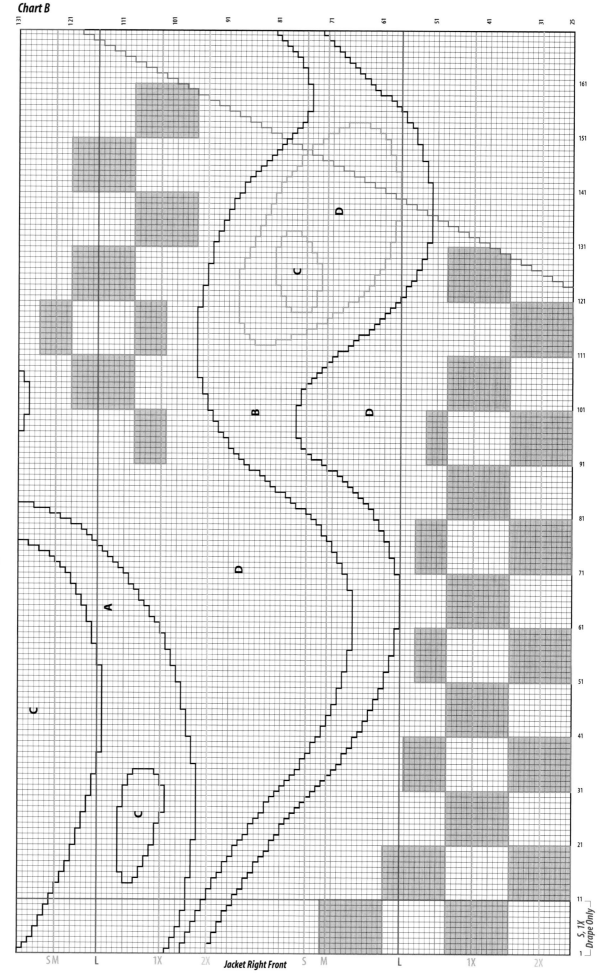

Chart B

Jacket Right Front

Jacket

(continued from page 109)

Collar extension

Continue on remaining 21 (22, 25, 26, 27) stitches, working the extra 5 (6, 9, 6, 7) stitches in Basket Stitch, until piece measures half the width of the back neck plus ½", end with a WS row.

Shape collar

Short row 1 (RS) Work 17 (17, 19, 19, 21) stitches, wrap next stitch and turn work (W&T). *All WS rows* Work to end. **Short row 2** Work 14 (14, 15, 15, 17) stitches, W&T. **Short row 3** Work 11 stitches, W&T. **Next RS row** Bind off 8 (10) stitches, complete row, hiding the wraps; place remaining stitches on hold.

Back

With B and smaller needles, cast on 94 (102, 110, 118, 126) stitches. Knit 8 rows. Change to larger needles and begin working Chart C with Row 1. Continue until piece measures same length as Left Front to armhole bind-off.

Shape armholes

Bind off 15 (17, 18, 19, 20) stitches at beginning of next 2 rows — 64 (68, 74, 80, 86) stitches. Work even until piece measures 8 (8½, 9½, 10, 10)" from bind-off.

Shape shoulders and neck

Next RS row K22 (23, 25, 27, 29) stitches, bind off center 20 (22, 24, 26, 28) stitches, knit to end. *Left shoulder:* **Next row** Bind off 10 (11, 12, 13, 14) stitches, purl to neck edge. **Next row** Bind off 2 stitches, knit to end. Bind off remaining stitches. *Right shoulder:* **Next row** (WS) Join yarn at neck edge, purl to end. **Next row** Bind off 10 (11, 12, 13, 14) stitches. **Next row** Bind off 2 stitches. **Next row** Bind off remaining stitches.

(continues on page 112)

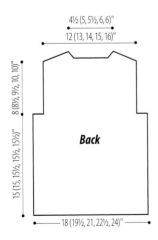

4½ (5, 5½, 6, 6)"
12 (13, 14, 15, 16)"

15 (15, 15½, 15½, 15½)"

8 (8½, 9½, 10, 10)"

Back

18 (19½, 21, 22½, 24)"

Drape

(continued from page 108)

Begin Chart C

Count rows from last collar increase marker to center back. Mark that same number of rows beyond the center back on the chart. On that row (a RS row), begin collar decreases: k2tog (or p2tog) after second marker; repeat every 8 rows until 10 collar stitches remain. AT SAME TIME, work to left armhole placement on chart.

Armhole shaping

Next partial row (RS) Work 115 (100, 105) stitches, turn. Work 4 more partial rows across stitches just worked, cut yarn, leaving stitches on hold, do not turn work. With RS facing, join yarn at beginning of armhole, bind off 45 (50, 55) stitches, work to end. **Next 4 partial rows** Work stitches above armhole. **Next row** (WS) Work to armhole, cable cast on 45 (50, 55) stitches, work stitches from holder.

(continues on page 113)

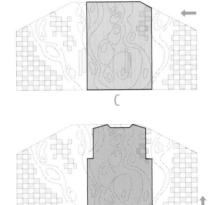

C

Stitch key

☐ Knit on RS, purl on WS
▨ Purl on RS, knit on WS
Ⓜ Make 1

▦ For jacket, work in stockinette stitch.

Color key

A Moss
B Fox
C Khaki
D Rust

Take time to check your cross back measurement and your row gauge. Then confirm that armhole placement on Chart C is correct for you. For help, see Fit and Style, page 152 .

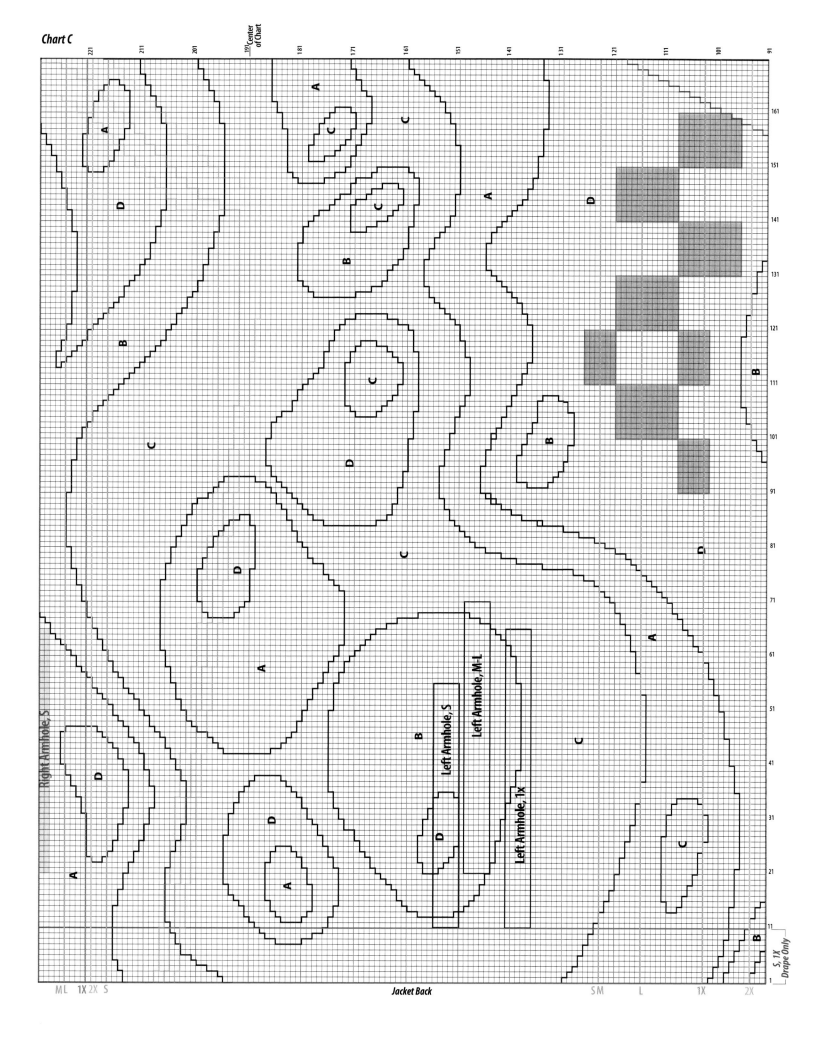

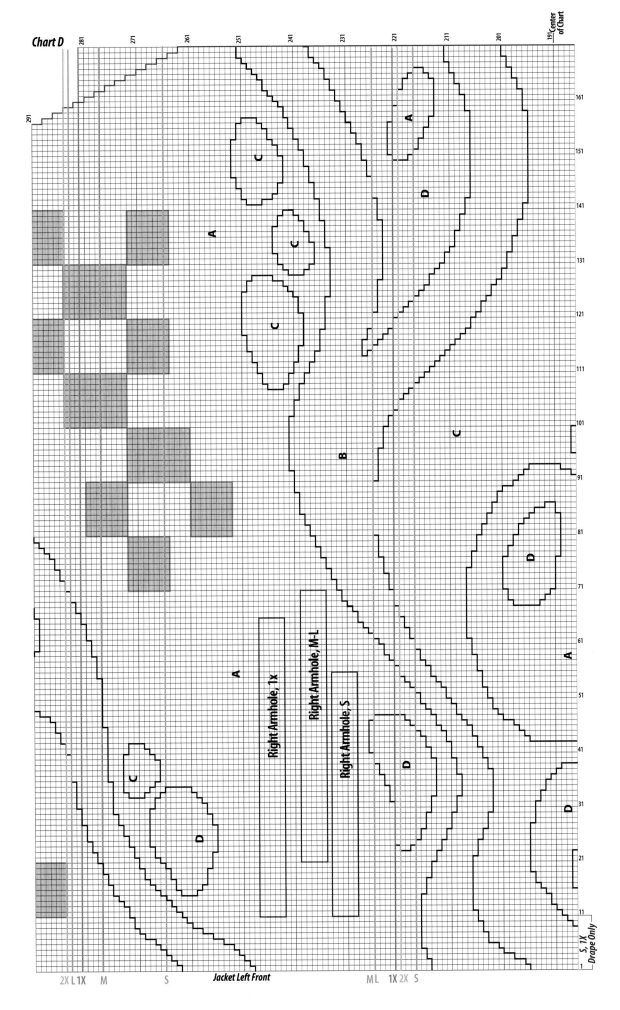

Chart D

Color key on chart:
A Moss
B Fox
C Khaki
D Rust

Right Armhole, 1x
Right Armhole, M-L
Right Armhole, S

Jacket Left Front

S, 1X Drape Only

Jacket
(continued from page 110)

Left Front

Work as Right Front to armhole shaping EXCEPT work Buttonband Chart 1 (page 106) at beginning of WS and end of RS rows.

Shape armhole, shoulder, & collar

Work as Right Front EXCEPT bind off stitches at beginning of RS rows AND work short rows on WS rows.

Finishing

Join shoulder seams. With collar stitches on 2 needles and right sides facing, join collar with 3-needle bind off. Sew sides of collar extension to back of neck, easing excess into neck. Sew sleeves into armhole. Join side and sleeve seams. Sew on buttons.

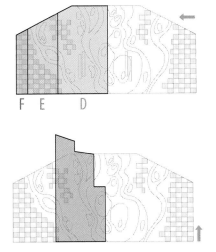

F E D

Color key
A Moss
B Fox
C Khaki
D Rust

Stitch key
☐ Knit on RS, purl on WS
▨ Purl on RS, knit on WS
Ⓜ Make 1
▨ For jacket, work in stockinette stitch.

Drape

(continued from page 110)

Collar and body shaping

Begin Chart D Work to right armhole placement and repeat armhole shaping. On Row 263 of Chart D, begin decreasing for body as follows: Work to first marker, k2tog. Work Charts E and F, continuing decreases to 110 (114, 124) stitches. Work 4 rows of Corrugated Garter. Bind off loosely in pattern.

(continues on page 114)

Chart F

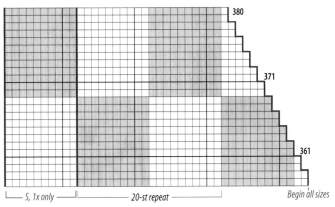

380
371
361

└─ S, 1x only ─┘└──── 20-st repeat ────┘ Begin all sizes

Chart E

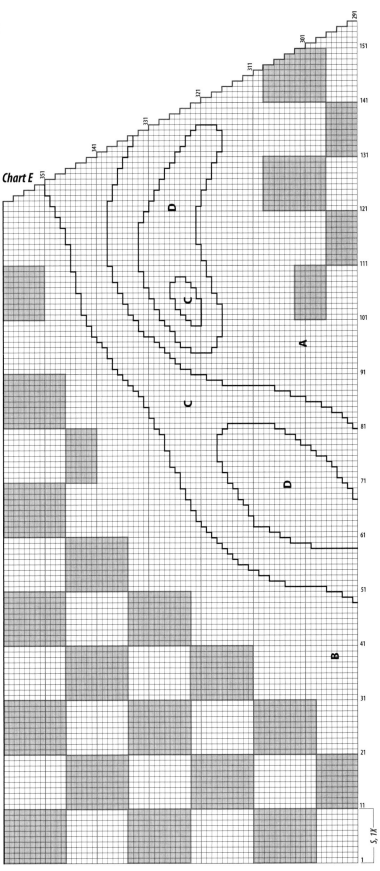

Drape

(continued from page 113)

Sleeves

With C and larger needle, cast on 60 (66, 66) stitches. Work 4 rows Corrugated Garter on all stitches: with D, work to first marker; with B, work to second marker; with D, work to end.

Establish Small Basket pattern: Rows 1–4 * P3, k3; repeat from *. ***Rows 5–8*** * K3, p3; repeat from *. Repeat last 8 rows, 2 more times. AT SAME TIME decrease on Row 7, then every RS row 5 more times—48 (54, 54) stitches remain. Work even to 2¾", change to smaller needles and work 8 rows of k1, p1 rib. On the last WS row, increase 2 (0, 4) stitches evenly across last row—50 (54, 58) stitches. ***Begin sleeve chart: Row 1*** Change to larger needles and begin working sleeve as marked on Chart D for your size. Increase 1 stitch each end of next RS row, then every 6 rows 11 (13, 15) times more—74 (82, 90) stitches. Work even until sleeve measures 21 (21½, 22)" from beginning of rib.

Shape cap

Bind off 4 stitches at the beginning of next 4 rows, then 2 stitches at beginning of every row 15 (19, 23) times—28 stitches remain. Bind off 3 stitches at beginning of next 4 rows. Bind off the remaining stitches.

Finishing

Sew sleeve seam, reversing seam halfway through cuff. Sew sleeves into armhole opening.

Stitch key
- ☐ Knit on RS, purl on WS
- ▨ Purl on RS, knit on WS
- Ⓜ Make 1

Color key
- **A** Moss
- **B** Fox
- **C** Khaki
- **D** Rust

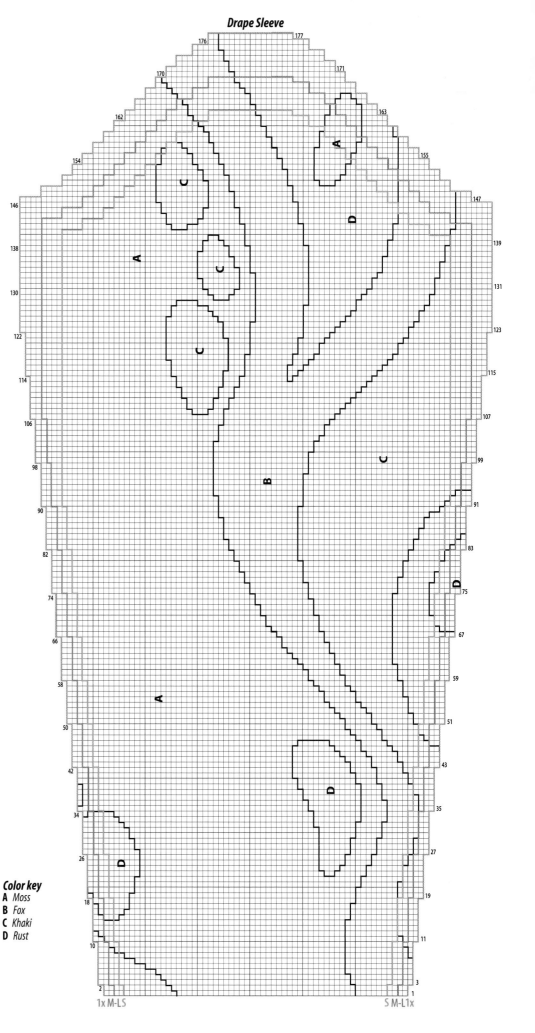

Drape Sleeve

Lava Sweater

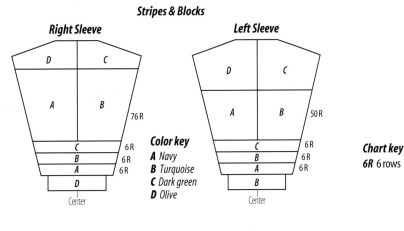

Notes

1 See *Techniques*, page 160, for intarsia knitting, p2tog, SSK, and bind-off in pattern. **2** Use separate lengths of yarn for each block of color. Bring new color under old at color change to twist yarn and prevent holes. **3** The Lava Chart and Sleeve Charts are worked in 4 colors; the Stripe Sequence is worked in 3. **4** See *Intarsia Tips*, page 141.

Left (Right) Sleeve

*With B (D) and size 4mm/US 6 needles, cast on 46 (50, 54, 58, 62) stitches, placing marker after 23 (25, 27, 29, 31) stitches. *Row 1* (RS) * K2, p2; repeat from*, end k2. *Row 2* P2, *k2, p2; repeat from*. Repeat Rows 1–2 until work measures 3", end with a WS row. Change to size 5mm/US 8 needles. *Begin Stripes & Blocks in stockinette stitch* Following diagram, work 6-row stripes across all stitches; work color blocks by changing colors at marker. AT SAME TIME increase 1 stitch each end of row 3, then every 8 rows 11 times — 70 (74, 78, 82, 86) stitches. Work even until sleeve measures 20 (19, 19½, 18½, 19)" from cast-on.

Shape cap
Bind off 3 stitches at the beginning of every row until 16 (14, 18, 16, 20) stitches remain. Bind off.

Back

With D and 4.5mm/US 7 needles, cast on 94 (102, 114, 122, 134) stitches, placing marker after 47 (51, 57, 61, 67) stitches.
Row 1 * K2, p2; repeat from*, k2. *Row 2* P2, *k2, p2; repeat from*. Repeat last 2 rows once. Change to A and continue in rib until piece measures 2½" from cast-on. Change to 5mm/US 8 needles.
Begin Stripe Sequence in stockinette stitch Follow diagram, working 2-color sections by changing colors at marker. Continue until piece measures 25 (25, 26, 27½, 28)" from cast-on, end with a WS row.

Shape shoulders
Bind off 9 (11, 11, 12, 14) stitches at the beginning of the next 2 rows, 9 (10, 12, 13, 14) stitches at the beginning of the next 4 rows. Bind off remaining 40 (40, 44, 46, 50) stitches.

Sleeve

15 (15½, 16½, 17, 18)"
2½ (3, 3½, 3½, 4)"
17 (16, 16½, 15½, 16)"
3"
8½ (9½, 10, 11, 12)"

Stripe Sequence

B	D	16R
A		7R
B		1R
D		5R
A	B	12R
D		1R
A		3R
B		1R
D		6R
A		3R
D	B	2R
A		7R
B		16R
D		2R
B	A	7R
D		1R
A		3R
D		1R
A	B	5R
D		14R
A		2R
B		1R
A	D	7R
B		2R
D		1R
A		5R
D	B	14R
A		2R
B		3R
D		2R
B	A	5R
D		2R
A		20R
B		2R

Center Back

Stripes & Blocks

Right Sleeve

D | C
A | B
76R
C 6R
B 6R
A 6R
D
Center

Left Sleeve

D | C
A | B
50R
C 6R
B 6R
A 6R
B
Center

Color key
A Navy
B Turquoise
C Dark green
D Olive

Chart key
6R 6 rows

EASY +

S (M, L, 1X, 2X)

A 38 (42, 46, 50, 54)"
B 26 (26, 27, 28½, 29)"
C 32 (32, 34, 34½, 36½)"

10cm/4"

27
19

over stockinette stitch (knit on RS, purl on WS), using size 5mm/US8 needles

1 2 3 **4** 5 6

Medium weight
A, B, D 325 (350, 375, 425, 475) yds each
C 475 (500, 550, 625, 675) yds

4mm/US6, 4.5mm/US7 and 5mm/US8, or size to obtain gauge

&
Stitch markers and stitch holders

Large: 4 balls each TRENDSETTER YARNS Merino VIII in 9509 Marine (A), 222 Turquoise (B), 329 Citrus (D), and 6 balls 81 Hunter Green (C); pages 104/105

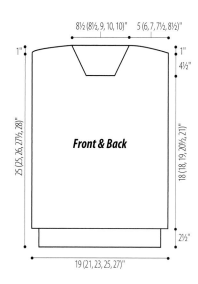

8½ (8½, 9, 10, 10)" — 5 (6, 7, 7½, 8½)"

1" — 1"

4½"

Front & Back

25 (25, 26, 27½, 28)"

18 (18, 19, 20½, 21)"

2½"

19 (21, 23, 25, 27)"

Front

Begin as for Back, EXCEPT cast on and work 4 rows with D, then complete rib with A. Change to 5mm/US 8 needles and work Lava Chart until piece measures 20½ (20½, 21½, 23, 23½)" from cast-on, end with a WS row.

Shape left neck and shoulder

Next row (RS) Work 38 (42, 48, 52, 56) stitches, place remaining stitches on hold. Turn and work 2 rows, slipping first stitch at neck edge. Bind off 3 stitches at beginning of every WS row once, then 2 stitches 2 (2, 3, 3, 3) times. P2tog at beginning of next 2 WS rows, then every other WS row 2 (2, 2, 3, 3) times — 27 (31, 35, 38, 42) stitches. Work even until piece measures same length as Back to shoulder, end with a WS row. **Shape shoulder** Bind off 9 (11, 11, 12, 14) stitches at beginning of next RS row, then 9 (10, 12, 13, 14) stitches at beginning of next 2 RS rows.

Shape right neck and shoulder

Leave center 18 (18, 18, 18, 22) stitches on hold. With RS facing, join yarn to remaining 38 (42, 48, 52, 56) stitches. Shape as for Left neck and shoulder EXCEPT work neck shaping at beginning of RS rows using SSK, AND work shoulder shaping at beginning of WS rows.

Finishing

Block. Join left shoulder seam.

Neckband

Row 1 (RS) Beginning at right shoulder, with C and using 4.5mm/US 7 needles, pick up and knit 42 (42, 44, 48, 52) back neck stitches, 25 (25, 26, 28, 28) stitches along left side, 18 (18, 18, 18, 22) front neck stitches, 25 (25, 26, 28, 28) stitches along right side — 110 (110, 114, 122, 130) stitches. **Row 2** (WS) P1, *k2, p2; repeat from * to end, p1. **Row 3** (RS) K1, *k2, p2: repeat from * to end, k1. **Row 4** With A, p1 [k2, p2] 12 times, k2; with B, [p2, k2] 9 (9, 10, 12, 14) times; with C, [p2, k2] 5 times, p3. **Row 5** With C, k1 [k2, p2] 5 times, k2; with B, [p2, k2] 9 (9, 11, 12, 14) times; with A, [p2, k2] 12 times, p2, k1. Repeat last 2 rows until collar measures 3". With D, work 2 rows in rib. Bind off in pattern.

Sew right shoulder and neck band seam. Measure down body side from shoulder and mark distance equal to half sleeve width + ¾". Center sleeve between markers, stretching sleeve slightly. Sew sleeve to armhole. Sew underarm and side seams.

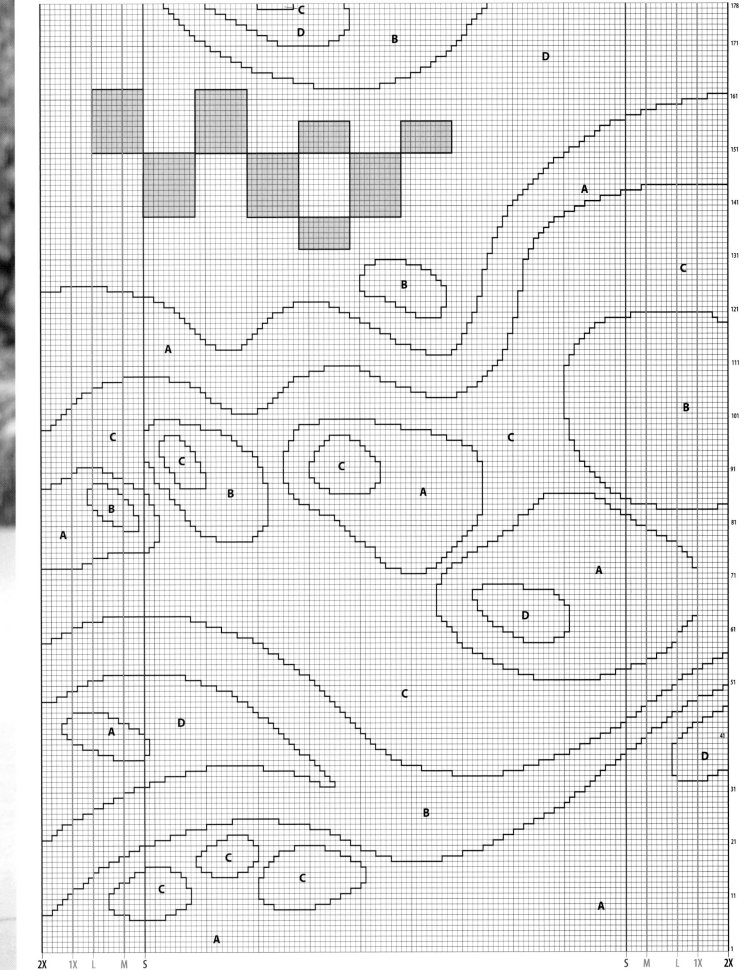

Lava Chart

Stitch key
- ☐ K on RS, p on WS
- ▨ P on RS, k on WS

Color key
- **A** Marine
- **B** Turquoise
- **C** Hunter Green
- **D** Citrus

Deco

The Deco design was first inspired by
an Art Deco tea service Clarice Cliff
designed in the 1930s. The highlights
in the trees were influenced by artworks
seen in Carmel. I took this California
coloration into the Drape style.

Deco Jacket

A simple color change cools the vivid greens of the Deco Drape to soft twilights for the Jacket.

121

Deco Drape & Jacket

Jacket

Jacket

INTERMEDIATE+

S (M, L, 1X, 2X)

A 39 (42, 44, 46, 48)"
B 22½ (22½, 23, 23, 23¼)"
C 30 (31, 32, 32½, 33)"

over stockinette stitch
(knit on RS, purl on WS)
using larger needles

Light weight

A, E, H 180 (200, 215, 235, 250) yds each
B, L 375 (425, 450, 500, 550) yds each
C, F, G, M 65 (70, 75, 85, 90) yds each
D, J, K 110 (125, 140, 150, 160) yds each

3.75mm/US 5 and 4mm/US 6, 60cm (24")
or longer

Seven 16mm (⅝")

&

Stitch markers
Cable needle (cn)

Small: 4 balls each SIGNATUR Pure New Wool
DK in 717 Charcoal (B), 602 Ivory (L),
2 balls each 612 Claret (A), 704 Blueberry (E),
631 Steel (H), 1 ball each 662 Moss (C),
655 Mid-green (D), 626 Plum (F),
657 Purple (G), 609 Aztec (J), 625 Aegean (K),
and 662 Moss (M); page 121

Jacket

Notes

1 See *Techniques*, page 160, for intarsia, SSK, long-tail cast-on, and 3-needle bind-off.
2 For casting on in colors, see *Intarsia Tips*, page 141.

Sleeves

With B and smaller needle, cast on 45 (49, 49, 51, 51) stitches. Knit 12 rows, increasing 6 (6, 6, 8, 8) stitches on the last row — 51 (55, 55, 59, 59) stitches. Change to 4mm/US 6 needles.
Work from Sleeve Chart, increasing 1 stitch each end of the 3rd, then every 8 rows 11 (13, 13, 15, 15) times more — 75 (83, 83, 91, 91) stitches. Work even until sleeve measures 18½ (19, 19½, 19½, 19½)" from cast-on.

Shape cap

At beginning of every row, bind off 4 stitches 4 times, 2 stitches 16 (18, 20, 22, 26) times, then 4 stitches 4 times. Bind off remaining stitches.

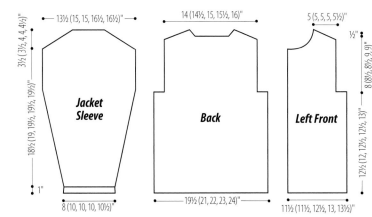

13½ (15, 15, 16½, 16½)"
3½ (3½, 4, 4, 4½)"
18½ (19, 19½, 19½, 19½)"
Jacket Sleeve
1"
8 (10, 10, 10, 10½)"

14 (14½, 15, 15½, 16)"
Back
19½ (21, 22, 23, 24)"

5 (5, 5, 5, 5½)"
½"
8 (8½, 8½, 9, 9)"
12½ (12, 12½, 12½, 13)"
Left Front
11½ (11½, 12½, 13, 13½)"

Drape

Drape

INTERMEDIATE+

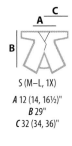

S (M–L, 1X)

A 12 (14, 16½)"
B 29"
C 32 (34, 36)"

over stockinette stitch
(knit on RS, purl on WS)
using larger needles

Light weight

A 325 (375, 425) yards
B, C, D, F, G, M 75 (85, 100) yards each
E, J, K 200 (225, 250) yards each
H, L 500 (575, 650) yards each

3.25 mm/US 3, 4 mm/US 6, or size to obtain
gauge, 60cm (24") or longer

Stitch markers

Medium-Large: 5 balls each SIGNATUR Pure
New Wool DK in 719 Sequoia (H),
731 Turkish (L), 3 balls 657 Purple (A),
2 balls each 671 Jacaranda (E), 660 Olive (J),
697 Dark Olive (K), 1 ball each 729 Oxblood (B),
673 Fox (C), 647 Brick (D), 704 Blueberry (F),
705 Sweet Pea (G), and 665 Rust (M); page 119

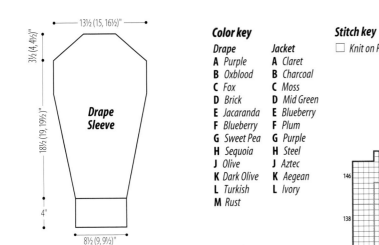

13½ (15, 16½)"

3½ (4, 4½)"

18½ (19, 19½)"

Drape Sleeve

4"

8½ (9, 9½)"

Color key

Drape
A Purple
B Oxblood
C Fox
D Brick
E Jacaranda
F Blueberry
G Sweet Pea
H Sequoia
J Olive
K Dark Olive
L Turkish
M Rust

Jacket
A Claret
B Charcoal
C Moss
D Mid Green
E Blueberry
F Plum
G Purple
H Steel
J Aztec
K Aegean
L Ivory

Stitch key

☐ Knit on RS, purl on WS

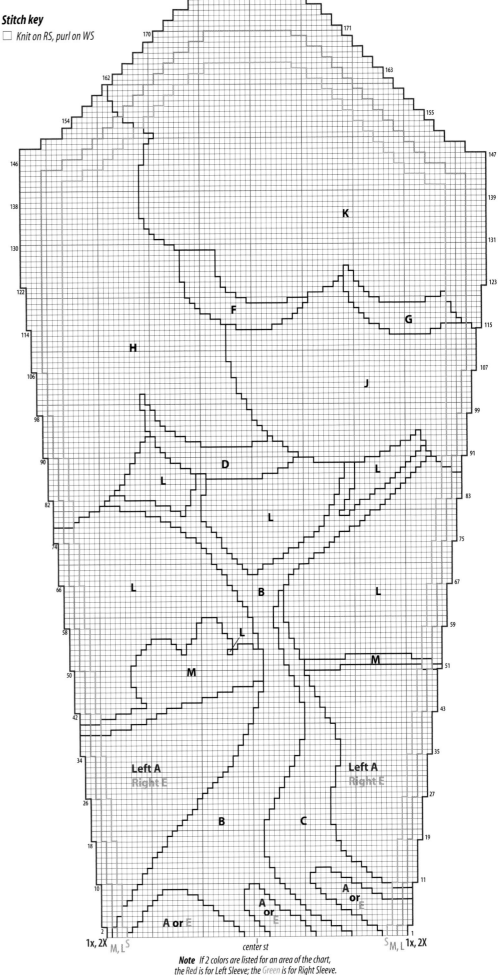

Sleeve Chart

Note If 2 colors are listed for an area of the chart, the *Red* is for Left Sleeve; the *Green* is for Right Sleeve.

Drape

Notes

1 See *Techniques*, page 160, for intarsia, k2tog, SSK, p2tog, M1, cable cast-on, wrapping stitches on short rows, and bind off in pattern. **2** Drape is worked in one piece from left center front to right center front. **3** Increased stitches will be worked in Corrugated Garter for the collar and stockinette stitch at the hemline. **4** Row gauge is very important. **5** Sleeves begin on different intarsia rows. Keep shaping the same, but begin Right Sleeve with R19 for intarsia.

Corrugated Garter *ANY NUMBER OF STITCHES*

Row 1 (RS) Purl.
Row 2 Knit.
Row 3 Knit.
Row 4 Purl.
Repeat Rows 1–4 for Corrugated Garter.

Basket Stitch *MULTIPLE OF 8 + 4*

Row 1 (RS) * K4, p4, repeat from * to last 4 stitches; k4.
Row 2 * P4, k4, repeat from * to last 4 stitches; p4.
Row 3 * P4, k4, repeat from * to last 4 stitches; p4.
Row 4 * K4, p4, repeat from * to last 4 stitches; k4.

Left (Right) Sleeve

Shaped cuff With smaller needle and D (E), cast on 63 (66, 69) stitches. **Row 1** * P3, k3; repeat from *, end p3 (0, 3). **Row 2** K3 (0, 3), * p3, k3; repeat from * to end. Repeat last 2 rows 2 more times. Continue in ribbing, decrease 1 stitch each end on every RS row 8 times — 47 (50, 53) stitches. Work even until piece measures 4" from cast-on, increasing 4 (5, 6) stitches evenly across row on last (WS) — 51 (55, 59) stitches. Change to larger needles and begin Sleeve Chart with Row 1 (R19 and E, centering chart pattern over 51, 55, 59 stitches). Increase 1 stitch each end of next RS row then every 8 rows 11 (13, 13, 15, 15) times — 75 (83, 83, 91, 91) stitches. Work even until sleeve measures 21¼ (21½, 22)".

Shape Cap

At beginning of every row, bind off 4 stitches 4 times, 2 stitches 15 (19, 23) times, then 3 stitches 4 times. Bind off remaining stitches.

Jacket

Left Front

With B and smaller needles, cast on 63 (66, 69, 72, 75) stitches. Knit 10 rows. Change to larger needles.

Establish patterns Beginning with Row 1 (RS), work Chart A over 54 (57, 60, 63, 66) stitches; place marker (pm); with B, p1, k6, p2 (front band).
WS rows Purl to marker, work Chart A to end. **Row 3** Work Chart A to marker; p1, k6, p2. **Row 5** Work Chart A to marker; p1, 3/3 RC, p2.
Continue patterns as established, crossing cable every 8 rows, until piece measures 12½ (12, 12½, 12½, 13)", end with a WS row.

Shape armhole

Note Chart A does not show armhole, neck or shoulder shaping. Maintain Chart A pattern over remaining stitches.
Bind off 15 (17, 19, 21, 23) stitches at beginning of next RS row. Work Chart A and front band over 48 (49, 50, 51, 52) stitches to 5½ (5½, 5½, 6¾, 6¾)" from bind-off, end with WS row. (Mark armhole shaping on Chart A to assist in knitting the Right Front and Back).

Shape neck

Next row (RS) Work to last 11 (11, 12, 13, 13) stitches and place on hold. Bind off 2 stitches at beginning of the next 2 WS rows, decrease 1 stitch at neck edge at beginning of next 3 WS rows, then decrease 1 stitch at beginning of every other WS row 2 times—28 (29, 29, 29, 30) stitches. Work even to 8½ (8½, 8½, 9, 9)" from armhole bind-off.

Shape shoulder

Bind off 9 (10, 10, 10, 10) stitches at beginning of next 2 RS rows. Bind off remaining 10 (9, 9, 9, 10) stitches on next RS row. Mark shoulder shaping on Chart A to assist in knitting the Right Front and Back.

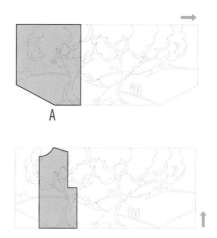

A

Drape

Left Front to Center Back

With larger needle, cast on 124 stitches following colors shown on the chart—color A 10 stitches, color B 92 stitches, color C 15 (18, 20) stitches, Color D 17 (14, 12) stitches. Work 4 rows of Basket Stitch maintaining colors as established.

Establish patterns: Beginning Chart with Row 13 (5, 1), (RS) P4 (bottom edge), place marker (pm), knit following chart over 110 stitches (body), pm, p10 (collar). **Row 2** (WS) K10, slip marker (sm), purl following chart over 110 stitches, sm, k4.

Work increase at collar beginning with row 19, then every 8 rows; at hemline beginning with row 14 (5, 2) every WS row—150 stitches plus 4 hem stitches, continue to increase at collar edge until you have 24 (26, 28) stitches for the collar, following chart for size to marked spot on chart for armhole shaping.

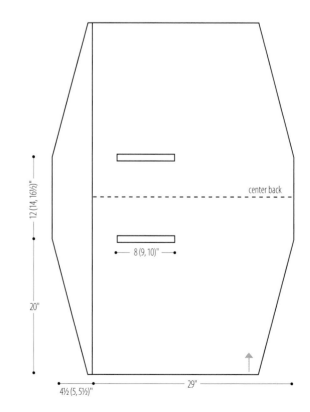

center back

12 (14, 16½)"

20"

4½ (5, 5½)"

8 (9, 10)"

29"

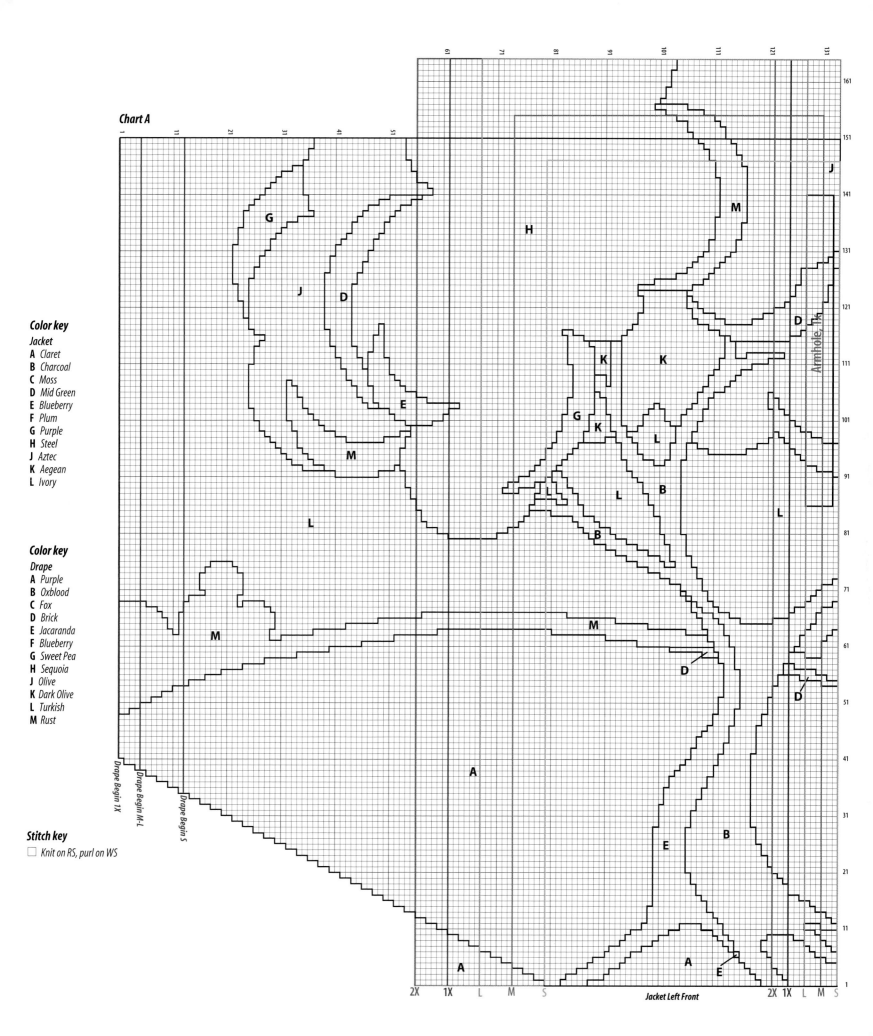

Chart A

Color key
Jacket
A Claret
B Charcoal
C Moss
D Mid Green
E Blueberry
F Plum
G Purple
H Steel
J Aztec
K Aegean
L Ivory

Color key
Drape
A Purple
B Oxblood
C Fox
D Brick
E Jacaranda
F Blueberry
G Sweet Pea
H Sequoia
J Olive
K Dark Olive
L Turkish
M Rust

Stitch key
☐ Knit on RS, purl on WS

Jacket Left Front

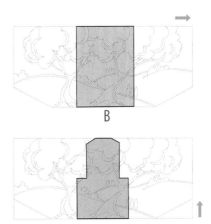

B

Jacket

Back
With B and smaller needles, cast on 109 (115, 121, 127, 133) stitches. Knit 10 rows. Change to larger needles.

Establish pattern Beginning with Row 1 (RS), work Chart B over 109 (115, 121, 127, 133) stitches. Work to same length as Left Front to armhole marked on Chart A.

Shape armhole

Note Chart B does not show armhole, neck or shoulder shaping. Maintain Chart B pattern over remaining stitches.

Bind off 15 (17, 19, 21, 23) stitches at beginning of next 2 rows—79 (81, 83, 85, 87) stitches. Work even to same length as Left Front to shoulder shaping marked on Chart A.

Shape shoulder

Bind off 9 (10, 10, 10, 10) stitches at beginning of next 4 rows. Bind off 10 (9, 9, 9, 10) stitches at beginning of next 2 rows. Bind off remaining 23 (23, 25, 27, 27) stitches.

Drape

Armhole Opening
Next row (RS) Work to the last 55 (60, 65) stitches on chart, bind off 45 (50, 55) stitches, k10, work collar stitches. Work only on these 10 stitches and collar stitches for 4 rows, on next row cable cast on 45 (50, 55) stitches in colors shown on chart over armhole bound off stitches. Place stitches on holder. With wrong side facing, join yarn at bottom of armhole and work to end following chart. ***Next 4 rows*** Work stitches below armhole. ***Next row*** Place held stitches back on needle and continue working across stitches completing a full row. Continue on all stitches for back placing a marker at last collar increase.

Back
Continue pattern and increases on all stitches. Work even to approximately 6 (6½, 8)" from armhole cast-on, mark row for center back. Count rows from left armhole cast-on to center back, also count rows from last increase to center back.

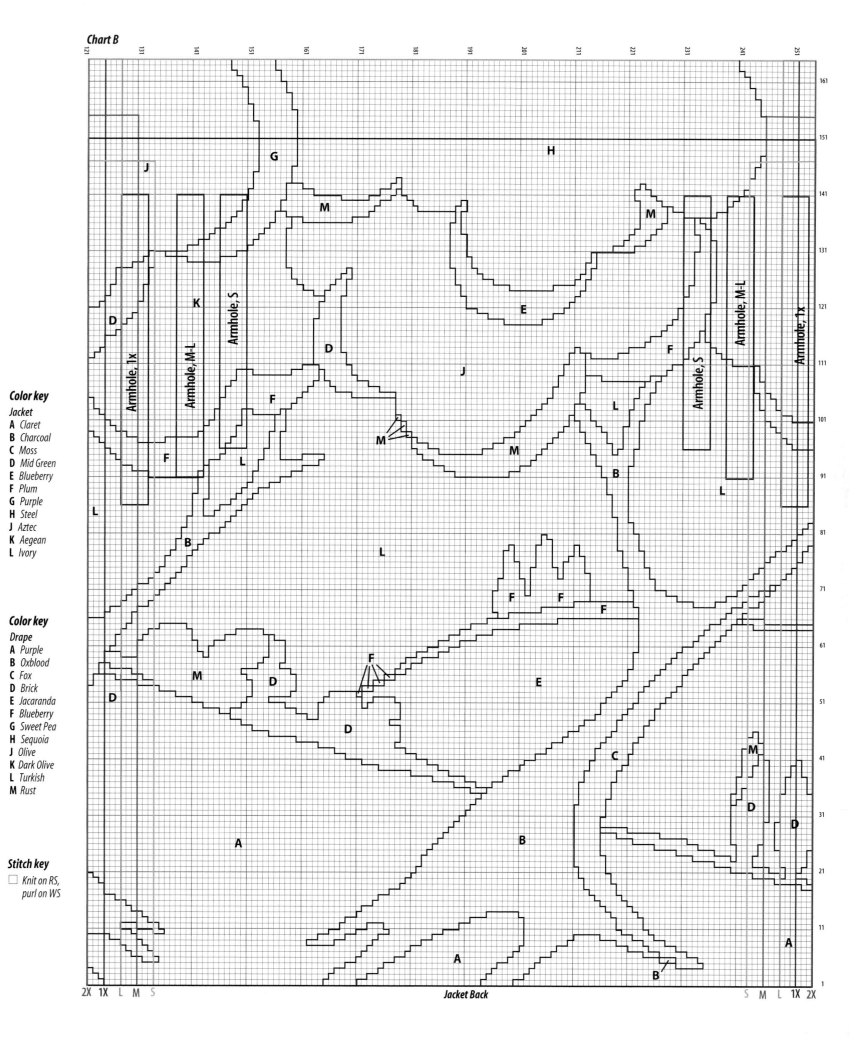

Chart B

Jacket Back

Jacket

Right Front

With B and smaller needles, cast on 63 (66, 69, 72, 75) stitches. Knit 10 rows making buttonhole on row 7 (RS): p2, k2, bind off 2 stitches, finish row. *Next row* Cast on 2 stitches over 2 stitches that were bound off. Change to larger needles.

Establish patterns Beginning with *Row 1* (RS), p2, k6, p1 (front band); pm; work Chart C over 54 (57, 60, 63, 66) stitches. *WS rows* Work Chart C to marker, purl to end. *Row 3* P2, k6, p1; work Chart C. *Row 5* P2, slip next 3 stitches to cable needle, hold to back, k3; k3 from cable needle (3/3 RC), p1; work Chart C. Continue patterns as established, crossing cable every 8 rows. AT SAME TIME place buttonholes after 3 cable crosses as follows (Row 7 of cable): P2, k2, BO 2, k2, p1, work Chart C.

Next row Work to bound-off stitches, cable cast on 2, complete row. Repeat every 3 cable crosses. Continue as Left Front reversing shaping using marked areas from Chart A.

Shape armhole

Note Chart C does not show armhole, neck or shoulder shaping. Maintain Chart C pattern over remaining stitches.

Bind off 15 (17, 19, 21, 23) stitches at beginning of next WS row—48 (49, 50, 51, 52) stitches. Work even to same length as Left Front to neck shaping marked on Chart A.

Shape neck

Next row (WS) Work to last 11 (11, 12, 13, 13) stitches and place on hold without working. Bind off 2 stitches at beginning of next 2 RS rows, decrease 1 stitch at neck edge at beginning of next 3 RS rows, then decrease 1 stitch at beginning of every other RS row, 2 times—28 (29, 29, 29, 30) stitches. Work to same length as Left Front.

Shape shoulder

Bind off 9 (10, 10, 10, 10) stitches at beginning of next 2 WS rows. Bind off remaining 10 (9, 9, 9, 10) stitches on next WS row. Mark shoulder shaping on front chart to match shoulders at back neck.

Finishing

Join shoulder seams. Sew sleeves into armhole opening, sew side and sleeve seams.

Neckband

With B, smaller needle, right side facing, and beginning at right front neck, knit across 11 (11, 12, 13, 13) stitches on holder, pick up and knit 27 (29, 30, 32, 32) stitches to shoulder, knit across 23 (23, 25, 27, 27) stitches on holder at back of neck, pick up and knit 27 (29, 30, 32, 32) stitches to holder, then knit across 11 (11, 12, 13, 13) stitches on holder—99 (103, 109, 117, 117) stitches. Knit 10 rows, working a buttonhole on row 5. Bind off. Block and attach buttons.

Drape

Center Back to Right Front

Work same number of rows to right armhole as from left armhole cast-on to center back; repeat armhole shaping. AT SAME TIME at same number of rows as from last increase to center back, begin decreases as follows:

Decrease row (RS) Work to first marker, sm, k2tog or p2tog, work to second marker, sm, k2tog or p2tog to maintain Corrugated Garter. Continue in pattern, working decreases every 8 rows at collar and every RS row at hemline — 124 stitches.

Work 4 rows of Basket Stitch. Bind off in pattern loosely.

Finishing

Sew sleeve seam reversing seam halfway through cuff. Sew sleeves into armhole opening.

C

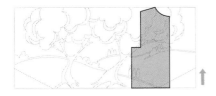

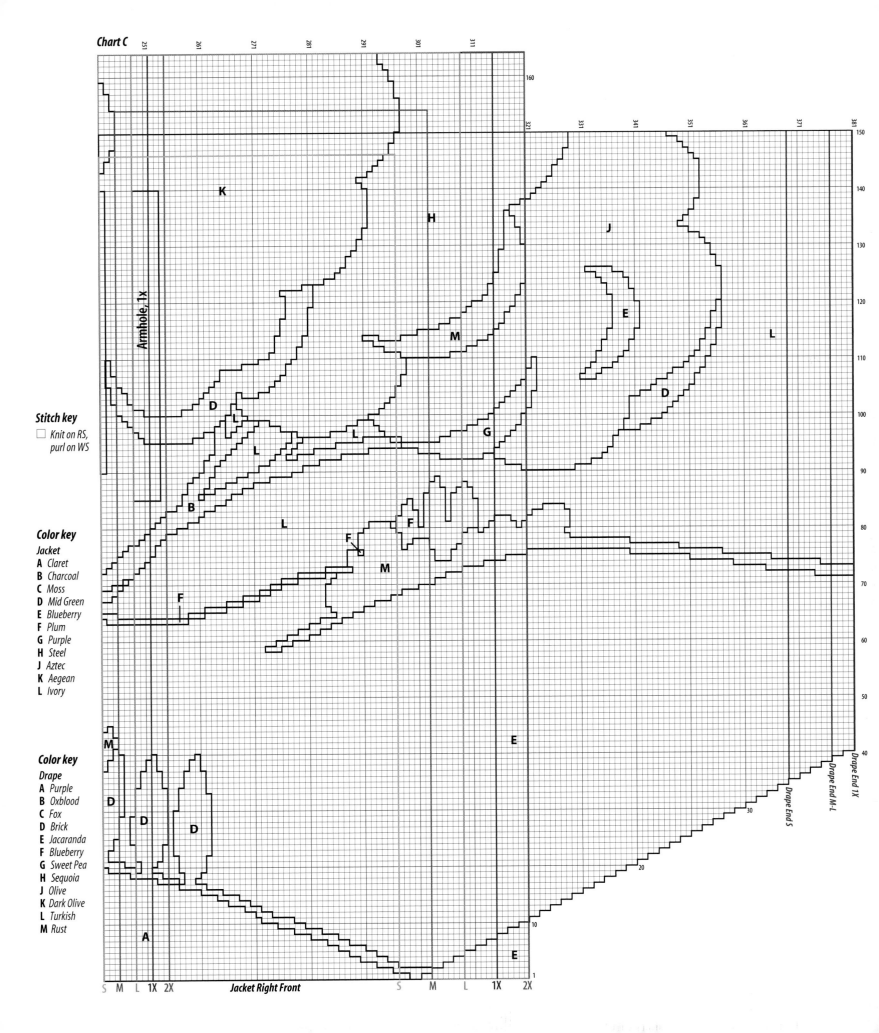

Chart C

Stitch key

☐ Knit on RS, purl on WS

Color key

Jacket
A Claret
B Charcoal
C Moss
D Mid Green
E Blueberry
F Plum
G Purple
H Steel
J Aztec
K Aegean
L Ivory

Color key

Drape
A Purple
B Oxblood
C Fox
D Brick
E Jacaranda
F Blueberry
G Sweet Pea
H Sequoia
J Olive
K Dark Olive
L Turkish
M Rust

Armhole, 1x

Drape End S

Drape End M-L

Drape End 1X

Jacket Right Front

S M L 1X 2X   S M L 1X 2X

ORBIT

Spots and circles inside and out of a frame create a shadow effect that can stand on its own. Add color-blocked sleeves and a striped back. Or go for broke with a Greta Vest front and an Orbit back, page 82. A little intarsia can go a long way.

131

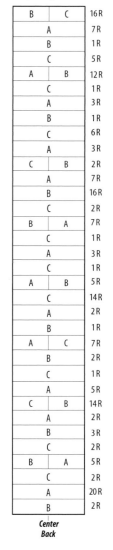

14½ (15, 16½, 18, 18½)"

2½ (3, 3½, 3½, 4)"

17 (16, 16½, 15½, 16)"

Sleeve

3"

8½ (9½, 10½, 11, 12)"

Orbit Sweater

Notes

1 See *Techniques*, page 160, for intarsia, SSK, p2tog, and bind-off in pattern. **2** Use separate lengths of yarn for each block of color. Bring new color under old at color change to twist yarn and prevent holes. **3** See *Intarsia Tips*, page 141.

Left (Right) Sleeve

With B (A) and size 3.25mm/US 3 needles, cast on 46 (50, 54, 58, 62) stitches, placing marker after 23 (25, 27, 29, 31) stitches. **Row 1** (RS) * K2, p2; repeat from *, end k2. **Row 2** P2, *k2, p2; repeat from *. Repeat Rows 1–2 until work measures 3", end with a WS row. Change to size 4mm/US 6 needles. **Begin Stripes & Blocks in stockinette stitch** Following diagram work 6-row stripes across all stitches; work color blocks by changing colors at marker. AT SAME TIME increase 1 stitch each end of row 3, then every 6 rows 15 (15, 16, 18, 18) times — 78 (82, 88, 96, 100) stitches. Work even until sleeve measures 20 (19, 19½, 18½, 19)" from cast-on.

Shape cap

Bind off 3 stitches at the beginning of every row until 18 (16, 16, 18, 16) stitches remain. Bind off.

Back

With B and 3.5mm/US 4 needles, cast on 102 (114, 122, 134, 142) stitches, placing marker after 51 (57, 61, 67, 71) stitches.
Row 1 * K2, p2; repeat from *, k2. *Row 2* P2, *k2, p2; repeat from *. Repeat last 2 rows once. Change to A and continue in rib until piece measures 2½" from cast-on. Change to 4mm/US 6 needles.
Begin Stripe Sequence in stockinette stitch Follow diagram, working 2-color sections by changing colors at marker. Continue until piece measures 25 (25, 26 27½, 27½)" from cast-on, end with a WS row.

Shape shoulders

Bind off 11 (11, 12, 13, 15) stitches at the beginning of the next 2 rows, 9 (12, 13, 14, 15) stitches at the beginning of the next 4 rows. Bind off remaining 44 (44, 46, 52, 52) stitches.

EASY +

S (M, L, 1X, 2X)

A 38 (42, 46, 50, 54)"
B 26 (26, 27, 28½, 29)"
C 32 (32, 34, 34½, 36½)"

10cm/4"

29

21

over stockinette stitch (knit on RS, purl on WS), using size 4mm/US 6 needles

1 2 **3** 4 5 6

Light weight

A 550 (600, 675, 750, 825) yds
B 500 (540, 600, 670, 725) yds
C 425 (460, 525, 575, 625) yds

3.25mm/US3, 3.5mm/US4 and 4mm/US6, or size to obtain gauge

3.5mm/US4 or size to obtain gauge, 40cm (16")

Stitch markers
Stitch holders

Large: 5 balls each TRENDSETTER YARNS Merino VI in Olive 9963 (A), Charcoal 305 (B), and 4 balls Ecru 7800 (C)

Stripes & Blocks

Color Key

A Olive
B Charcoal
C Ecru

6R 6 rows

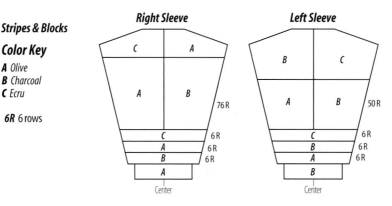

Right Sleeve

C	A
A	B

76R

C	6R
A	6R
B	6R
A	

Center

Left Sleeve

B	C
A	B

50R

C	6R
B	6R
A	6R
B	

Center

Stripe Sequence

B	C	16R
A		7R
B		1R
C		5R
A	B	12R
C		1R
A		3R
B		1R
C		6R
A		3R
C	B	2R
A		7R
B		16R
C		2R
B	A	7R
C		1R
A		3R
C		1R
A	B	5R
C		14R
A		2R
B		1R
A	C	7R
B		2R
C		1R
A		5R
C	B	14R
A		2R
B		3R
C		2R
B	A	5R
C		2R
A		20R
B		2R

Center Back

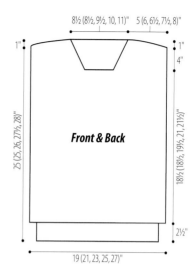

8½ (8½, 9½, 10, 11)" 5 (6, 6½, 7½, 8)"

1" 1"

4"

Front & Back

25 (25, 26, 27½, 28)"

18½ (18½, 19½, 21, 21½)"

2½"

19 (21, 23, 25, 27)"

Front

Begin as for Back, EXCEPT cast on and work 2 rows with A, then complete rib with B. Change to 4mm/US 6 needles and work Orbit Chart. When chart is complete, continue in A until piece measures 21 (21, 22, 23½, 23½)" from cast-on, end with a WS row.

Shape left neck and shoulder

Next row (RS) Work 40 (46, 50, 57, 61) stitches, place remaining stitches on hold. Turn and work 2 rows, slipping first stitch at neck edge. Bind off at beginning of every WS row 3 stitches once, then 2 stitches 2 (2, 2, 3, 3) times. P2tog at beginning of next 2 WS rows, then every other WS row 2 (2, 3, 5, 5) times — 29 (35, 38, 41, 45) stitches. Work even until piece measures same length as Back to shoulder, end with WS row.

Shape shoulder Bind off 11 (11, 12, 13, 15) stitches at beginning of next RS row, then 9 (12, 13, 14, 15) stitches at beginning next 2 RS rows.

Shape right neck and shoulder

Leave center 22 (22, 22, 20, 20) stitches on hold. With RS facing, join yarn to remaining 40 (46, 50, 57, 61) stitches. Shape as for Left neck and shoulder EXCEPT work neck shaping at beginning of RS rows using SSK, AND work shoulder shaping at beginning of WS rows.

Finishing

Block. Join shoulder seams.

Neckband

Round 1 (RS Beginning at right shoulder, with A and using 3.5mm/US 4 circular needle, pick up and knit 44 (44, 46, 52, 52) back neck stitches, 25 (25, 26, 30, 30) stitches along left side, 22 (22, 22, 20, 20) front neck stitches, 25 (25, 26, 30, 30) stitches along right side — 116 (116, 120, 132, 132) stitches. **Round 2** Purl. **Rounds 3–5** *K2, p2; repeat from * around. Change to B and work in rib until band measures 3". With C, work 2 rounds. Bind off in pattern.

Measure down body side seam from shoulder and mark distance equal to half sleeve width + ¾". Center sleeve between markers, stretching sleeve slightly. Sew sleeve to armhole. Sew underarm and side seams.

Orbit Chart

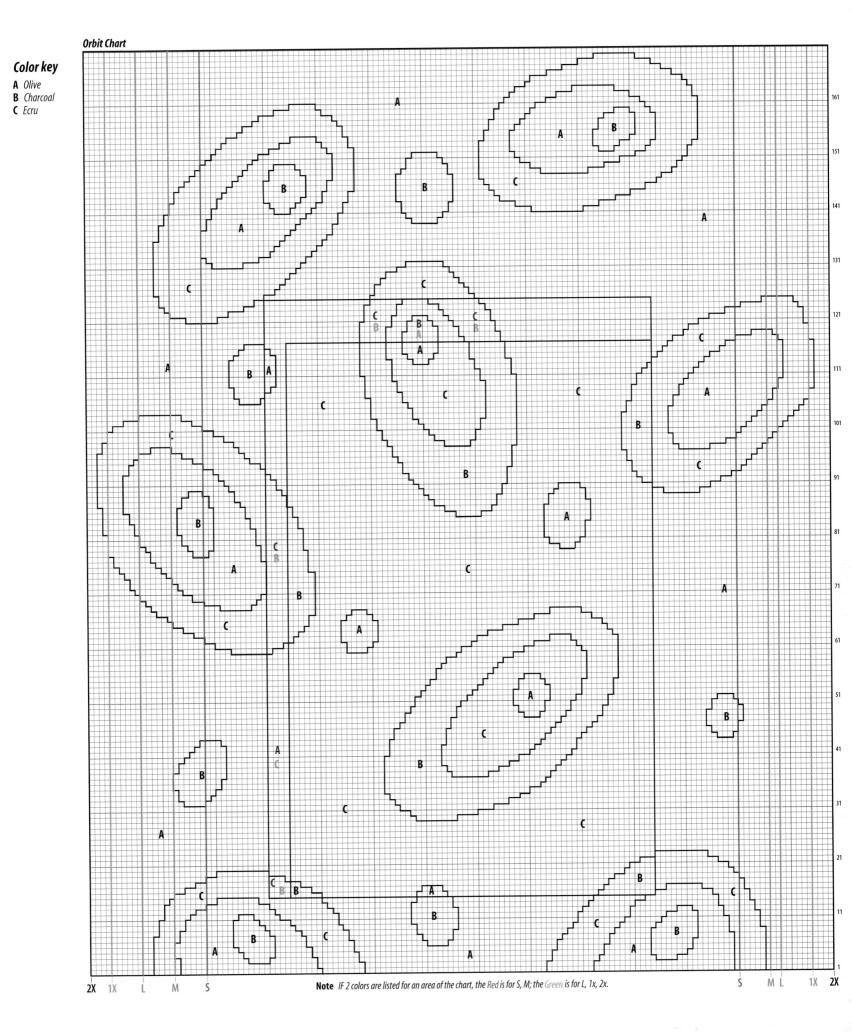

Color key
A Olive
B Charcoal
C Ecru

Note IF 2 colors are listed for an area of the chart, the Red is for S, M; the Green is for L, 1x, 2x.

Process + Practice

Process

Practice Pieces

Color

The Swing, Swagger, and Drape patterns are major projects. Select yarn carefully; use quality yarns that will reward your time and skills. With color choice, your first instinct is generally correct. Check your wardrobe for a color you love. Maybe you, like me, have a great pair of red cowboy boots you want to match! This color isn't necessarily the main color in your wardrobe, but simply a highlight to build a color palette around.

Local yarn stores are a blessing. Even there, it is sometimes hard to find a perfect color match — it may not exist or be out of stock — so try to straddle the color. If you are combining colors, you can pick a slightly darker and one slightly brighter shade and still wear it with the intended item. I did this with those red boots.

You've heard "Gray is the new black", and I agree. It's so versatile and harmonizes with many colors. But like many colors you do not need to wear it only with gray, black, or navy. The Lava Jacket uses two shades of gray and I combine them with two Olive greens — which proves pairing color is easy. I use gray again with the plum and pink in the stripe jacket. For a second stripe jacket, I pick a strong dark pink and fox, which I calm with chocolate brown.

I rarely use stark white with black. I prefer to use ecru or winter white. I have included a Metro coat in black and almond along with two beiges. It works well — the contrast is bold but the beiges create a true classic blend. However, if two reds were used instead of the beiges, the black and almond would be too stark and there would be no harmony. Winter white is so classic and elegant, but it too can be challenging to incorporate as a main color within such a strong color combination.

Metro

Design Stories

Reviewing the sequence of the book earlier this year I thought, "I can't use the Metro — it starts with pages of all the same design. But then I realised "that's the key!" Different color combinations, lengths, collars, cuffs and hats are what bring individuality to each piece.

I have created designs with color lessons in mind. With the Metro, I have shown nine color combinations, including the two below.

Pick four colors for the Metro Blocks, or use these blocks, page 7 as four contrast colors with a main color for the Fanfare, page 9. Add two highlights for the Stripe and Bobble, on pages 2, 5, 6, and 10.

Below shows yarn swatches laid on the top of the Metro's Stripe and Bobble. When choosing colors, use proportional amounts of yarns (as below) to judge how your constrast colors will work.

Proportion and balance

When I'm designing, I envision color use — both proportion and highlight. To balance the colors you choose, try to follow the dark, light, and highlight colors as I've used them.

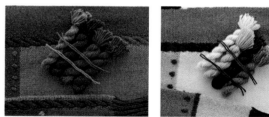

View colors in proportions — highlights simply as strands

Color relationships

Finding inspiration and proportion

So the choice is whether the orange should be a main color or a highlight. To balance the combination it would require two shades of orange/brown combined with perhaps, two shades of slate/moss, thus pairing colors.

Avoid using one bright color with three dark colors. Alternatively select four shades of slate/moss greens and keep the orange as the highlight.

Miters

Blue MC and 3 colors

The striping in Miters blends colors. This looks fantastic in black with three shades of gray. I rarely use brilliant white as the contrast is very high. I prefer to use ecru or winter white.

Neutrals

I originally picked chocolate and three beiges, which didn't quite work. The chocolate was too heavy. By adding the light olive highlight, this created balance in the combination.

Highlights

Alexis composed a shot, changing the camera angle to see a stripe of yellow through the carriage. This stripe brings energy to the entire shot. You can achieve this effect by adding a highlight to your color combination.

Just as Alexis used the yellow in the previous shot, the green scarf to the left, introduces an unexpected highlight to the A-line Metro.

Photographs are sources for color inspiration. This rusty garden gate makes me want to create a color combination of fox and brown with jade and gray. Shall I do Miters or the Metro?

Simple Intarsia

1 2 **3** 4 5 6

Light weight

5 colors of yarn
35 yds each

4 mm/US 6 circular needle

stockinette gauge over 10cm/4"

22 stitches
32 rows

Width 5"
Height 5½"
Strap 6"

Try the intarsia purse as a practice piece; it starts with Simple Intarsia. Learn how to join colors and work vertical color joins as you knit blocks of color. This is charted, but it could have been knitted from a diagram.

Small Intarsia Purse

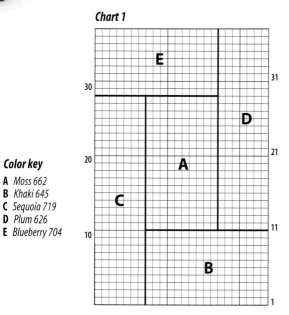

Note
See *Techniques*, page 160 for working from a chart, intarsia, cable cast-on, and wrap and turn for short rows.

Top back and buttonhole
With 4 mm/US 6 needles and A, cast-on 40 stitches. *Row 1* (RS) Knit. *Row 2* K10, bind off 20 stitches, k10. *Row 3* K10, cable cast on 4 stitches, k10 — 24 stitches. *Row 4, 5, and 6* Knit.

Next row (RS) Begin following Chart A. Knit 17 stitches with B, 7 stitches with C. Work 9 rows more in stockinette stitch (knit on RS, purl on WS). Cut B yarn. Continue working Chart rows 11–37 remembering to twist yarns at color change to eliminate holes between sections and cutting yarn not used in next section. At the completion of Chart A, keep stitches on left needle, cut D & E.

Chart 1

Color key

A *Moss 662*
B *Khaki 645*
C *Sequoia 719*
D *Plum 626*
E *Blueberry 704*

Make it easy

Bobbins and butterflies
Make a center pull ball or butterfly for working small areas of intarsia. Place an elastic band around the ball or butterfly to keep it firm and neat. Keep in mind that shorter lengths between the yarn and knitting makes for less tangles.

Needles
You might find it easier to work with straight needles rather than circular for Intarsia. You can measure the width of the fabric as you work, just spread the stitches along the 2 needles as you work halfway across the row. And a firm needle helps keep the multiple balls of yarn from swaying and tangling more then necessary.

The other side of intarsia:
Weaving ends at color joins

Above Tails have been trapped at color joins. Ends can then be sewn back into this woven tail — along or up a color join. *Immediately above* The vertical join that 'twisting' achieves.

Butterfly wrap

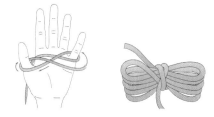

Make butterflies when using small amounts of yarn (5 to 20 grams) for colorwork.
Wrap yarn in figure-8 fashion around fingers. When finished, wrap yarn snugly around middle of butterfly, secure under center wraps, and slip off fingers. Knit from the tail.

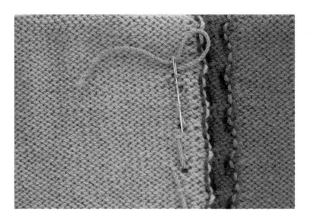

Contrast bobbles in a row of intarsia are worked from a length or butterfly of color, carried across the row or up the column, and caught every 4 stitches or rows.

Stunning Intarsia

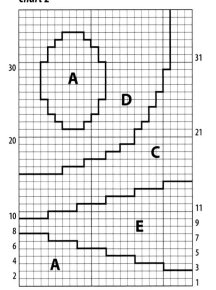

Strap

Cast on 80 stitches with B, knit across 24 stitches from live sts of back piece; with C, cable cast on 80 stitches — 184 stitches. **Row 1** With C, k80, k24 stitches of bag; with B, k30 stitches, turn (W & T). **Row 2** With C, slip 1, k84, turn. **Row 3** Slip 1, k73, turn. **Row 4** With C, slip 1, k43; with A, k20, turn. **Row 5** With A, slip 1, k124. **Row 6** With A, k184 — all stitches worked.

Begin Front

Row 7 With A, bind off 80 stitches, knit stitches 2–24 of Row 1 of chart 2, knit to end. Row 8 Bind off 80 stitches, work stitches 2-24 of Row 2 — 24 stitches on needle. Work Rows 3–37 of chart. Purl 5 rows. Bind off.

Join gusset strap to form sides of purse. Knot tops of strap. Sew on button.

Let's step through the first rows. Positioning yarn for the following row is the key to intarsia. Learn to think about adding stitches to an area of color. You don't need to count the 34 stitches between areas of pattern. Mark your progress on the outline of the shape you are working. Mark right-side rows, reading chart right to left and wrong side rows, reading left to right. Now, read don't knit!
Row 3 With E, k4, now looking at the next row above, we need another 4 stitches of E, so E needs positioning this row for the next row. K4 in A, weave E into wrong side of A as you knit, ending with 5th stitch of A. Complete row in A.
Row 4 With A, purl, you'll find E in position to work the last 4 stitches of A — 4 extra stitches in E. Complete row in E.

Row 5 Add 4 E stitches this row (don't count the total—think 4 more E), continue in A, check next row and place E accordingly. Complete row in A.

Thought process: Need 4 more E stitches next row E, prepare yarn placement this row, knit the stitches in A as graphed — position yarn by trapping E at the stitch *after* it is required for use — for 4 stitches, trap with 5th stitch. Continue working chart through Row 9.

Row 10 Count stitches as graphed. Join C, trap tail and weave E; prepare for next row: purl 4 E, trap C into 5th stitch of E.
Row 11 Yarn was placed row 10, last 4 stitches of E in C, complete row in C.
With E knit, you'll find C waiting in position to work the last 8 stitches.
You should be able to work your way through the complete chart, so continue knitting.

Chart 2

Color key

A Moss 662
B Khaki 645
C Sequoia 719
D Plum 626
E Blueberry 704

Trap the tail

1 One stitch before new color, trap the tail by placing it between the fabric and working yarn.

5 Knit another stitch then weave tail again to secure.

2 Knit the next stitch with the working yarn.

3 Drop old yarn and work next stitch with new yarn.

4 Then trap new cut tail by placing it between the new working yarn and fabric and knitting the next stitch.

Carry yarn to position for the following row, weaving it.

Why trap the tail:
Also referred to as weaving-in, trapping

1 It secures the end and makes for a neat and tidy edge stitch.

2 K1, trap, trap, makes a smoother fabric than trapping the stitches every stitch.

3 For garter, trap the tail every stitch.
For miters, trapping for 12 stitches secures the end.

4 When joining for a single stitch, catch the tail 1 stitch before color change, knit it then trap it with the next stitch.

5 When working a bobble in a new color, the tail can be trapped into the stitch as the bobble is worked.

Cast on in color for Metro

1 Catch second color.

2 Last stitch traps and secures.

3 Continue . . .

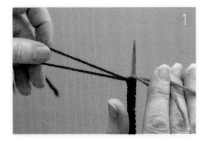

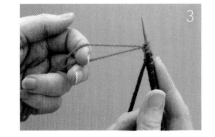

Cast on in color

1 Cast on and work to 1 stitch before first color change. Place new yarn under knitting needle.

2 Cast on last stitch of first color, new color is caught by that stitch.

3 With second color continue to cast on to next color change, leaving tails hanging. Do not weave tail into cast-on end.
Begin working stitches in pattern, making color changes on the wrong side. Weave in cast-on ends.

Miters

I love color, so when I discovered miters, I was in heaven. There was the challenge of them being squares; I don't design square garments, as there aren't so many square shaped people about! A little playing and planning, by turning the square into a diamond and either decreasing or increasing the stitches per miter gave me A-line shapes, flared skirts, and so much color so simply! For a simple start, try the Coco Vee or Miter Capelet.

Miters are modular knitting, worked one square at a time. It is far less complicated than it looks. Knit one color at a time in 2-row stripes. Work a 3-to-1 decrease over the center stitches of the miter every RS row. Each miter is picked up from previous miters; you do not sew the miters together.

Miter Hints & Tips

Use a double-pointed needle (dpn) to pick up loops from ridges of garter, then join yarn and knit from the double-pointed needle. This creates an even pick-up; and allows easy adjustment of stitch numbers to increase or decrease, for the A-line shaping.

Decrease When decreasing a number of stitches per miter, still pick up 1 stitch per garter stripe — then knit 2 loops together at the center of each pick-up side.

Increase Pick up 2 stitches instead of 1 stitch from a stockinette stripe.

Gauge Miter For garments made with miters of different sizes, work the size at the bust as a gauge miter.

Trap tails to avoid sewing in ends

The wrong side of the miter shows the ends from the color joins woven into the back of every stitch for 12 stitches (see page 163). This secures the ends without knots, leaving a nice even edge to pick up the next miter.

This swagger coat shows the dramatic result of increasing and decreasing the size of miters. Though the coat is wide at the hemline and narrow at the bodice, the number of miters does not change.

1 Using a dpn, pick up one loop per ridge, join yarn, and knit one stitch per garter stripe or ridge.

 Full and half-miters create garment hemline and front edge.

2 Work half-right miter.

3 Work full miter.

4 Connect the two miters with another miter.

Cast on different number of stitches to create different sizes of miters.

Bodice Decreases *page 39*

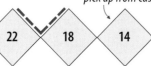

dec   *dec*

As you knit from dpn, k2tog in the middle of each side: no holes in pick-up, k2tog hidden in garter stitch.

pick up from cast-on

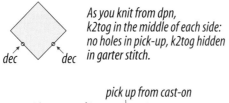

| 22 | 18 | 14 |

Skirt Increases *page 37*

	9
5	31 (33)
2	27 (29)
28 (30)	4
22 (24)	27 (29)
1	22 (24)
	3

Miter 9
No increase: pick up 1 st per stripe

Miter 5
Pick up *(1 st/garter ridge, 1st/St st stripe) 2 times, then 1 st/garter ridge, 2 sts/St st stripe; repeat from *.

Miters 2, 4, 7, 11, 15, 19, 23, 26
Pick up *1 st/St st stripe, 1 st/garter ridge, 2 sts/St st stripe, 1 st/garter ridge; repeat from *.

Texture

EASY+

1 2 **3** 4 5 6

Light weight

1 color of yarn
400 yds

4 mm/US 6 needles

stockinette gauge over 10cm/4"

22 stitches
32 rows

Width 12½"
Height 11"
Strap 10"

See page 64 for the
Dice Sweater

Dice Bag

Dice Plain stockinette always seems to takes so long to knit, so spice up the journey with a little texture. You'll soon be impatient to get to the next square of texture. The lessons in this design are about traveling stitches with the Celtic Cross and Fan and bobble, and creating 3-D stitches with the leaf motif and bobbles.

Notes
1 See *Techniques*, page 160 for working from chart. **2** For additional charts seen in purse, go to page 64.

Bottom
With size 4mm/US 6 needles, cast on 61 stitches. Knit 22 rows.

Back
Work 12 rows in stockinette stitch. *Row 1* (RS) *Establish pattern* Knit 11, *insert chart of choice from Dice sweater over next 15 stitches*, knit 9, repeat between * once, knit 11. *Row 2* Work across in established patterns. After completion of charts work 9 rows in stockinette stitch. Repeat from Row 1 once more. Knit 10 Rows. Bind off.

Front
With right side facing, cast on 15 stitches, pick up 61 stitches from opposite side of garter stitch bottom, cable cast on 15 stitches. Extra stitches will be worked in Corrugated Garter. *Row 1* Purl. *Row 2* Knit. *Row 3* Knit. *Row 4* Purl.
Establish pattern Repeat from Row 1 of Front EXCEPT make 3 buttonholes (yo, k2tog) centered with patterns and center panel on 3rd row of garter stitch border. Sew back of purse to front gussets. Sew buttons opposite buttonholes.

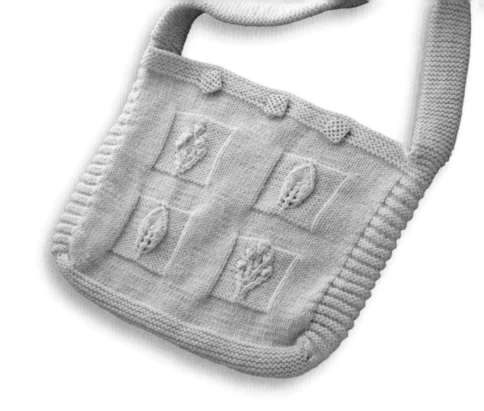

Strap

Cast on 6 stitches, pick up 10 stitches from top of gusset, cable cast on 6 stitches. Work garter stitch (knit every row) for 28". Sew bound off edge to top of gusset, fold cast-on and bound-off edges towards center of wrong side of strap and seam to close.

Chart A

15 sts

Chart B

15 to 16 to 15 sts

Stitch key

- ☐ *Knit on RS, purl on WS*
- ▦ *Purl on RS, knit on WS*
- ⊵ *pf&b*
- ⊿ *K2tog*
- ⊙ *Optional bobble (K1, p1, k1, p1, k1) into stitch, turn; p5, turn; k5, turn; p2tog, p1, p2tog, turn; SK2P*
- ■ *Stitches do not exist in these areas of chart*
- ⟋⟍ *2/1 RPC Slip 1 to cn, hold to back, k2; p1 from cn*
- ⟍⟋ *2/1 LPC Slip 2 to cn, hold to front, p1; k2 from cn*
- ⟋⟍ *2/2 RC Slip 2 to cn, hold to back, k2; k2 from cn*

Chart tips: Cable diamonds

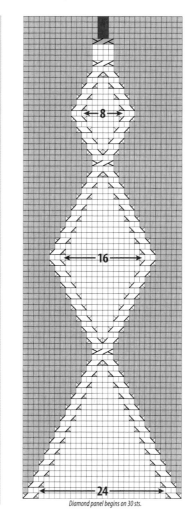

Diamond panel begins on 30 sts.

Greta is about classic texture — combining simple cables with cable stitch diamonds. Pairs of knit stitches move 1 stitch every right side row across the surface of the knitting. When moving the stitches, always hold the K2 to the front and the single stitch to the back. There is a logical approach to this — from the hem. The stitches move together, meet, cross, and open again. When they travel 16 stitches apart they change direction and close the diamond and repeat into a smaller diamond with 8 stitches in the center.

Before I start knitting I simply note 16 stitches in the centre of the first Diamond as a "turning point" rather than having to refer to the chart for each row. Charts do create a very clear picture of what you are knitting, but use them as a map, with landmarks for change rather than each step (or stitch). Note the shading for the Reverse stockinette on the outside of the Diamond and Stockinette inside, so when working the 2/1 cables, make sure to knit or purl the single stitch to match the field it is entering.

See pages 68 and 76 for Greta and Greta Vest.

Texture

To get this right you must work a swatch to check that your cast on technique will allow stitches to 'drop' fully and neatly. The 'thumb' or long-tail cast-on method works best.

For a flared drop-stitch hem, stitches have been added into the cast-on of the body and sleeves. Stitches to be dropped are purled on the RS for easy identification. When dropped they ladder back to the cast on edge. The pattern continues making new stitches which will be dropped. To do this, pick up and knit the yarn between two stitches of the previous row. Each new stitch will only ladder back to that row where it was created. Always work 2 rows beyond the drop before laddering down, this keeps the stitches on the needles even.

4 Wrong side row—3 dropped stitches (left to right), 3 columns of fully-, halfway-, and partially-dropped stitches.

5 Right side view—(left to right) 3 columns of partially-, halfway-, and fully-dropped stitches.

EASY+

1 2 **3** 4 5 6

Light weight
200 yds

4 mm/US 6 needles

stockinette gauge over 10cm/4"

23 stitches
32 rows

5 x 48"

Dropping Stitches

1 Drop stitches are worked as purls in a stockinette body.

2 Wrong-side view of stitches you will drop.

3 Drop every other rib.

Drop Stitch Scarf

Drop Stitch (D1) Drop stitch off left needle. Work 2 rows, then unravel stitch down to M1 or cast-on.

Scarf
Cast on 30 sts.
Row 1 K4, p4, k2, p1, k2, p4, k4, p2, k1, p2, k4.
Row 2 K2, p2, k2, p1, k2, p4, k4, p2, k1, p2, k4, p2, k2.
Repeat last 2 rows 14 times
Row 31 K4, p2, M1, p2, k2, D1, k2, p4, k2, M1, k2, p2, D1, p2, k4.
Row 32 K2, p2, k4, p2, k1, p2, k4, p4, k2, p1, k2, p2, k2.
Row 33 K4, p4, k2, p1, k2, p4, k4, p2, k1, p2, k4.
Repeat last 2 rows 14 times. Repeat Row 32.
Row 63 K4, p2, D1, p2, k2, M1, k2, p4, k2, D1, k2, p2, M1, p2, k4.
[Work Row 2, then Rows 1-63] 2 times. Work Row 2, then Rows 1-62. *Next row* K4, p2, D1, M1, p2, k4, p4, k2, D1, M1, k2, p4, k4.
Following row Bind off row working D1 without M1. Sew in yarns.

6 All stitches dropped.

7 Dropping stitches takes a little effort.

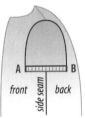

Adding a rib

Join side seam. With 3.75mm/US 5 ndls, work k1, p1 rib over underarm sts for 5 rows. Bind off in rib.
Sew edge of this rib to vertical edge of armhole (at A and B).

A   B
front | side seam | back

Pick up and knit 3 sts for every 4 rows around armhole. Work 5 rows rib. Bind off.

Seam the 5-row edge to the cast-off edge of the underarm.

Key
| *sew*
¦ *pick up*

Sleeveless knits require a non-rolling edge. The Greta and Orbit Vests both have double moss fabric around the armholes, but if you want a rib border, here is my process.

Square armhole: What to do?

Fitting sleeves
My patterns have a shaped cap sleeve set into a square armhole. The shaped cap edge is sewn into the edge of the armhole with the upper edge of the sleeve seam sewn to the underarm bind-off. For larger sizes the armhole is shaped slightly differently with an armscye (curved) underarm. Sew the cap stitches to that shaped area, leaving the initial armhole bind off to join with side sleeve seam.

Buttons

Looking for the perfect button?
Polyform clay could be the answer.

You'll need

- Polyform clay
  You can mix colors for
  the perfect match

- Toaster oven

- Sharp knife

- Knitting needle

- Texture tool
  I use a meat tenderizer

- Baking sheet or pie plate
  *Do not use for food
  after using with clay*

Layered pebbles

1 Prepare 3 colors of clay.

2 Roll them into logs of various
   diameters: ¼", ½", and ¾".

3 Cut and mold into pebbles.

4 Flatten, then stack your layers.

5 Pat them into shape, making sure
   to smooth out fingerprints. Jump
   to step 8 in Textured squares.

Textured squares

1 Soften the clay by kneading it.

2 Roll it into a log about ½–¾" in diameter.

3 Then score and cut it into equal sections about ¾" long. Cut a couple more than you think you'll need.

4 Shape them into cubes or balls depending on your desired finished shape.

5 Flatten them into button shapes.

6 Use the knife to further refine the shape into a square or triangle.

7 Imprint it with the meat tenderizer.

8 Make at least 2 holes in the button with a knitting needle for sewing button to fabric.

9 Place on baking sheet or pie plate.

10 Bake, following manufacturer's directions for temperature and time.

Fit & Style

neat over shoulder

sleeve length too long

small shoulder pad.

Details of fit cleans silhouette

Fit Jackets & Coats
Back width 2–2½" beyond bra strap
2"   2"

Fit Drape
Width between armholes in Drape styles.
1"   1"

Silhouette

Fit isn't just about getting a garment to wrap around your body comfortably and attractively; there is so much more. Of course, we start with the circumference of the body, usually at the bust. What knitter doesn't know about bust measurements and ease? Each of us already knows what size in inches (or centimeters) we like to wear, so we refer to the pattern for that size. But that doesn't always guarantee proper fit.

The key to great fit is across the shoulders. I believe that the shoulder seam for jackets and coats should end at the place where the shoulder becomes an arm, approximately 2–2½" (5–6cm) beyond your bra straps. I shape shoulders with several bind-off rows. The bind-off adds stability and keeps the final edge firm. When ready to seam shoulders, I choose a backstitch; it is firm and sturdy.

For the drapes — which are knit sideways without a shoulder seam — the required shoulder measurement is smaller because there is no stabilizing seam, approximately 1 inch (2–3cm) beyond the bra straps.

Confirm your gauge

Take time to check your tension (gauge) so, of course, a swatch is in order before you begin any garment. It is always a good idea to confirm your gauge: after knitting 4" on the project, spread the stitches out on 2 needles, measure the piece and compare to the pattern. If the numbers match, proceed. If not, then what?

The Swing, Swagger, A-line, and *Drape* rely on proper fit across the shoulders to enhance the line and create the style.

Greta

Dimensions of the Greta and Metro lower skirt sections are generous. As you start to knit the back, it may seem too wide. So after four inches, stop and check your progress. You don't have to rely on a 4"/10cm swatch, you can check the back of your coat to make sure it is the width you need and you are on gauge.

Estimate the bust measurement

The skirt tapers to the bust. It gradually decreases 10 stitches in each of the two 30-stitch Diamond panels and 2 (3, 4, 4, 4, 4) stitches at each side seam edge for a difference of 24, (26, 28, 28, 28, 28) stitches at the armhole. Subtract that number from your cast-on number to figure the number of stitches the pattern allows at the bust. Count in from each side seam half of the decrease number, mark, then measure between the markers. This is what the back will measure at the bust if you proceed with the pattern as written.

Double this measurement and compare it to your actual bust measurement. The pattern number should be between 2" to 3½" (9cm) larger. We call that extra amount ease. (Note that the two fronts of the Greta combined will be wider than the back to accommodate for the large button overlap in the shawl collar design).

So you have the numbers and find you need to adjust? Whatever adjustments you plan to make to the back will apply to the fronts.

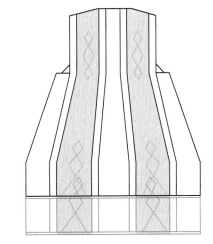

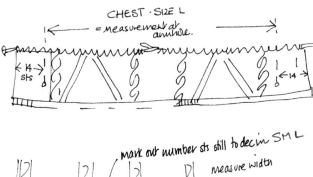

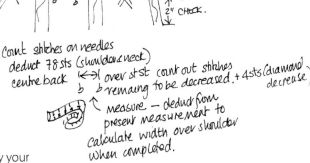

Sizing

Measure around the fullest part of your bust/chest to find your size.

Measuring

- **A** Bust/Chest
- **B** Body length
- **C** Center back to cuff (arm slightly bent)

ALTERATIONS from cast-on to bust

You need at least 1" ease in the back at the bust. Let's say your chest measures 36". Half of that is 18", so the back should measure between 19–22".

Too small? Simply start anew — put that knitting aside to compare to your change; it can be ripped out later. The choice is to knit a larger size of the pattern with the needles you have been using, or go up a needle size to achieve the correct tension.

A little small? Simply plan to omit one or two pairs of decreases in the panels — one pair for 4 stitches extra width, two pair for 8 and then adjust the pattern from there to the bind-off.

Radically small? You may need to eliminate quite a few decreases for less dramatic shaping. Or go up a size in the pattern and treat it as 'A little big'.

 A little big? Decreases may be added into the center back panel — work in conjunction with the last one or two pairs of decreases in other panels for 2 or 4 stitches less. Or if the tension is loose, change to one size smaller needle.

Radically big? Apply both of the above.

If you adjusted stitches in interior panels, add or subtract those numbers from the shoulder count. If decreasing in center back panel, deduct from back neck. Remember, changes to an interior panel need to be matched on the fronts.

Once you've figured out how to adjust for your bust do the same to figure the shoulder numbers; see if the underarm to shoulder decreases need to be adjusted.

Shape armhole

To get the proper shoulder measurement, the armholes need to be addressed next as they are between the bust and shoulders.

This pattern calls for a needle change. The smaller needle shapes the armhole a bit and also firms up the yoke fabric. If your fabric is already pretty firm, do not change needle size. Work 2 inches from the armhole bind-off then measure the width of knitting again. Be aware that there were 2 (2, 2, 0, 0, 0) decreases made in each of the two diamond sections, with 2 (2, 0, 0, 0, 0) more decreases in the next 2 inches. Refer to the pattern for the stitch count before shoulder shaping. Mark that number of stitches on your piece and measure. This is what your piece will measure at the shoulder if you proceed with the pattern as written. Remember, knitting will stretch slightly and blocking may add half an inch.

Calculate shoulders

Refer to Fit diagram for Jackets and Coats. Measure your back. This number will be between 12½" to 19" (32–48cm). You will have the opportunity to refine the gauge and numbers at the yoke when you shape the armholes.

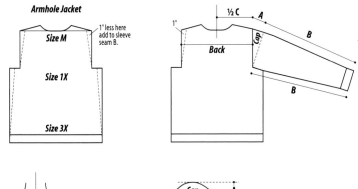

Armhole Jacket

1" less here add to sleeve seam B.

Size M

Size 1X

Size 3X

½ C   A

1"

Back   Cap   B

B

Cap   A

Back neck to wrist length. If you alter width over back neck you will shorten your sleeve. Deduct from one point, add to another.

Maintain back neck to wrist length. If you alter width over back neck you will shorten your sleeve. Deduct from one point, add to another.

Back neck to wrist = A + B + ½ C

Cap   A

B

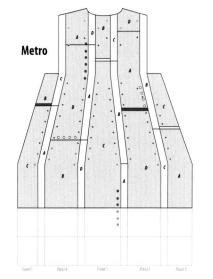

Metro

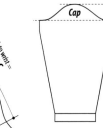

Adjusting length

Greta Swagger and A-line coat There is always the desire to add more length for drama or warmth! Both lengths are worked from a single set of instructions; we simply work the Swagger to Row 29 or the A-line to Row 69 — a 40-row difference — then begin shaping. To achieve a length between the two, simply add multiples of 8 rows to the Swagger length, then follow shaping directions from Row 29 of the Swagger. It really is that easy!

Metro

Apply principles as before: deduct the number of stitches remaining at bust from stitches on needles; divide the answer in half. Count in from side seams and place markers — measure between markers = chest size your tension will achieve. Add or subtract stitches into full panels or center panel. The Metro has less of a front overlap than the Greta Shawl collar; to allow extra ease over the bust line there are fewer decreases before the armhole shaping and extra stitches after the armhole. The number of stitches in the panels match front to back at shoulder.

Jackets—Lava, Stripe and Deco

These are boxy styles — with little shaping — but if you are a delightful pear shape, it is possible to add a little volume into the hip. Do the math first. Pick the size to suit your hip then deduct the number of stitches for your desired bust size from the hip numbers for the back of the jacket. You will decrease stitches from hip to armhole. Generally, you will need to work 4 to 6" before decreasing and complete the decrease 1½" before the armhole shaping — so deduct 7½" from the side seam length of 16" = 8½". We have 29 rows to 4", 7.25 rows per inch = 65 rows to work the decrease. Divide the number of decreases per edge into the 65. Round the result to even numbers for right side row decreases.

Examples Let's decrease from size 3X at hip (134 stitches) to 1X at the bust (118 stitches) — a difference of 16 stitches. That is 8 stitches per side seam. Divide row numbers (65) by stitch number (8) = 65 divided by 8 = 8. Decrease 1 stitch each side every 8 rows.

As you reach the armholes, cast off the armhole as in size 1X. Apply same decrease to front side seams.

Now let's shape from a 1X bust to a M shoulder. After the 1X armhole, you can reduce to the M shoulder by applying the same theory. Deduct the 68 stitches of M at the shoulder from the 80 stitches of 1X at shoulder, 12 stitches difference. Divide 12 in half and you get 6 stitches to be removed from each armhole. This decrease should be completed 2" before the shoulder so deduct 2" from the armhole depth. But what is the armhole depth?

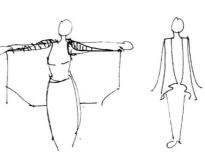

Select sleeve/armhole depth You split the difference between the 1X and M armhole depth so you work the L armhole depth — 9½" (unless you need the width of the 1X sleeve). 9½" – 2" = 7½". At 7¼ rows per inch we have 54 rows. 54 divided by 6 = 9. Decrease 1 stitch every 8 rows (again, even number for RS Rows).

Armhole depth What sleeve size to knit? I let the arm width decide the sleeve size — measure your upper arm and add 1" to 2" ease to this — see schematic to select sleeve width and therefore size, work armhole depth to match sleeve size.

Adjusting sleeve length The schematic gives sleeve seam length and depth of sleeve head (sleeve cap). Measure yourself from center back neck to cuff — let's say it is 29". If garment at shoulder measures 14", half of 14 is 7" — add sleeve cap length from schematic, 7" + 4" = 11". Deduct this from your measurement 29" – 11" = 18" sleeve (length to underarm).

Drape styles Because the drape is knit sideways, row gauge will effect the shoulder width. Since there are no shoulder seams — we knit the shoulders 2" narrower than the jacket or coat to allow for stretch. You can check how the sizes will work with your measurements. With intarsia designs you need to relate this to rows from center back in order to maintain the graph and shaping.

DRAPES
shape to create length in back. Fronts will still drape longer when open.

Lava Drape First the chart: Row 190 marks the center back. Check the shoulder back width from the pattern — 13", so half this is 6½"; 13" × row gauge = number of rows between arm ÷ 2 = number of rows from armhole to center back and center back to armhole. The first armhole begins 5 rows earlier, the width of the armhole. If your drape shoulder measurement does not match the pattern, or if you are not sure, compare your shoulders to the pattern, divide by 2, make that adjustment (+ or –) to chart placement.

Creating Swing In dressmaker's terms, we are knitting gored panels, frequently used in skirts, dresses, and coats. If a yarn has a firm twist, it will tolerate being knitted to a looser tension. I apply this with Miters where I stripe stockinette with garter on a larger needle to lighten the weight of the fabric and still maintain drape. With any knitting design, the thicker the yarn and longer the length, the heavier the garment. To combat and support this, I tighten the gauge as I move up the body toward the yoke. This supports the bulk of the skirt and accentuates the drape and flare of these styles.

Boxes Drape The beauty of this design is that you can knit it in any yarn weight. The finer the yarn the shorter the piece, as the stitch gauge creates the shoulder-to-hem length. Adjust length by adding or subtracting multiples of 10 stitches to the basket stitch repeat. 10 stitches make one block so you are adding 1 block to the length.

Jackets and Coats. When something doesn't fit at the shoulder, you feel the weight of the garment as you wear it. A jacket or coat can be pulled back into shape by firming and reinforcing the shoulders with stay stitching across the shoulders and back neck.

Start at armhole edge, work a running stitch through and into the seam of the shoulder for ¾", then gently ease the knitting in along that length, and work a back stitch to secure; repeat across the shoulder and back neck and tie off at second armhole. The width across the back of a garment can be reduced by 1 to 2"; this is perfect for repairing a knit that has stretched with wear. It also adjusts the sleeve length.

Shoulder pads come and go out of favor, but shoulder pads add structure to a garment, especially coats. They can also give a cardigan or jacket that final tailored edge. A shoulder pad will sharpen a silhouette, bringing focus to the body line.

HEMLINES
short Rows

Even if a garment length is onto the hip, with short row shaping, the angles distract ones eye from the hip line

MITRE Hemlines. again distract the eye.

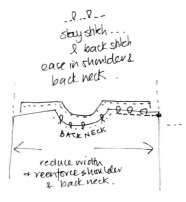

stay stitch --- & back stitch ease in shoulder & back neck.

BACK NECK

reduce width & reenforce shoulder & back neck.

BACK STITCH

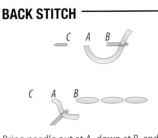

Bring needle out at A, down at B, and out again at C. Point C now becomes the point A of the next stitch.

RUNNING STITCH

Hats

Australian color at the drop of a hat

EASY+

1 2 **3** 4 5 6

Light weight

2–3 colors of yarn
total of 150–250 yds

4 mm/US 6, 16" circular needle
3.75 mm/US 5, 16" circular needle

4mm/US 6, double pointed needles
(dpn)

stockinette gauge over 10cm/4"

21–24 stitches
30–32 rows

Adult S (M, L)

Hats are an easy opportunity to play with style and experiment with color. A few examples are shown here with basic instructions to follow or bend to suit your fancy.

Choice 1
Pick the 2 or 3 colors you want for playing.

All the hats shown here use the same size needles and yarn at a similar gauge. Just cast on 99 (110, 121) stitches onto a 4mm/US 6 16" circular needle.
All these hats begin with 6 rounds of stockinette stitch for a border that rolls into a flattering, purl-curl edge.

Choice 2
You can drop to a size 3.75mm/US 5, 16" circular needle to work 5 rounds of k1, p1 ribbing. Or continue with the larger needles in Corrugated Garter (CG).

All these hats use easy Corrugated Garter as a strong design element. Rounds proceed straight up for 40 rounds (9 repeats). Or, use a contrasting color to work 4-6 reverse stockinette rounds at the top of the Corrugated Garter.

CORRUGATED GARTER
ROUNDS **1 & 2**
CC KNIT

ROUNDS **3 & 4**
MC PURL

Choice 3

Or stop the Corrugated Garter after 5 repeats then work 3–5 increase rounds for a softer, more beret-like shape. Change to 1 color, or continue to work rounds as before, but work Round 1 of each repeat as follows:

Increase for Beret or muffin top of Yurt:
Increase 1 * K10, knit in front and back of stitch (kf&b); repeat from * 9 (10, 11) times — 108 (120, 132) stitches.
Increase 2 * K6, [kf&b, k11] 8 (9, 10) times, kf&b, k5 — 117 (130, 143) stitches.
Increase 3 [K12, kf&b] 9 (10, 11) times — 126 (140, 154) stitches.

For a larger beret, continue with 2 more increase rounds:

Increase 4 K6, [kf&b, k13] 8 (9, 10) times, kf&b, k7 — 135 (150, 165) stitches.
Increase 5 [k14, kf&b] 9 (10, 11) times — 144 (160, 176) stitches.

Purl a turning ridge or knit 1 round before beginning decreases.

All these hats have similar top decreases. Match the number of stitches in your hat to the stitch counts after each decrease; begin your decreases with the instructions given in the NEXT line. If you have 110 stitches in circumference, begin with Decrease 6.

Have fun with color changes. Keep the top in flat stockinette stitch or insert a purl round after each decrease, as in these instructions. It's your knitting. Take joy in it!

Note Follow Garter Ridge Top directions below for decreases, EXCEPT:
For a stockinette stitch top Knit 2 rounds between each decrease.
For a Corrugated Garter top Purl 2 rounds, knit 1 round between all decrease rounds.

Garter Ridge Top

Decrease 1 K7, [k2tog, k14] 8 (9, 10) times, k2tog, k7 — 135 (150, 165) stitches. Purl 1 round, knit 3 rounds.
Decrease 2 [K13, k2tog] 9 (10, 11) times — 126 (140, 154) stitches. Purl 1 round, knit 3 rounds.
Decrease 3 K6, [k2tog, k12] 8 (9, 10) times, k2tog, k6 — 117 (130, 143) stitches. Purl 1 round, knit 3 rounds.
Decrease 4 [K11, k2tog] 9 (10, 11) times — 108 (120, 132) stitches. Purl 1 round, knit 3 rounds.
Decrease 5 K5, [k2tog, k10] 8 (9, 10) times, k2tog, k5 — 99 (110, 121) stitches. Purl 1 round, knit 3 rounds.
Decrease 6 [K9, k2tog] 9 (10, 11) times — 90 (100, 110) stitches. Purl 1 round, knit 1 round.
Decrease 7 K4, [k2tog, k8] 8 (9, 10) times, k2tog, k4 — 81 (90, 99) stitches. Knit 1 round.
Decrease 8 [K7, k2tog] 9 (10, 11) times — 72 (80, 88) stitches. Purl 1 round, knit 1 round.
Decrease 9 K3, [k2tog, k6] 8 (9, 10) times, k2tog, k3 — 63 (70, 77) stitches. Knit 1 round.
Decrease 10 [K5, k2tog] 9 (10, 11) times — 54 (60, 66) stitches. Purl 1 round, knit 1 round.
Decrease 11 K2, [k2tog, k4] 8 (9, 10) times, k2og, k2 — 45 (50, 55) stitches. Knit 1 round.
Decrease 12 [k3, k2tog] 9 (10, 11) times — 36 (40, 44) stitches. Purl 1 round, knit 1 round.
Decrease 13 K1, [k2tog, k2] 8 (9, 10) times, k2tog, k1 — 27 (30, 33) stitches. Knit 1 round.
Decrease 14 [K1, k2tog] 9 (10, 11) times — 18 (20, 22) stitches.
Decrease 15 [K2tog] around — 9 (10, 11) stitches.
Cut yarn and draw through remaining stitches. Fasten off. Or, continue for a 1" funnel before bind off.

Yurt hats use Corrugated Garter to create height with form. Left to right Blue with CG top, no muffin increase; Gray/Brick with muffin increase, top in CG; Navy/brick with St st top; single color muffin with CG top knitted in Kashmir to match Greta Vest. Page 157, Beret with extra increases.

Techniques

Cast-Ons

LONG-TAIL CAST-ON

Make a slip knot for the initial stitch, at a distance from the end of the yarn, allowing about 1½" for each stitch to be cast on.
1 Bring yarn between fingers of left hand and wrap around little finger as shown.

2 Bring left thumb and index finger between strands, arranging so tail is on thumb side, ball strand on finger side. Open thumb and finger so strands form a diamond.

3 Bring needle down, forming a loop around thumb.
4 Bring needle **under** front strand of **thumb loop**...

5 ...up **over index finger yarn**, catching it...

6 ...and bringing it **under** the front of **thumb loop**.

7 Slip thumb out of its loop, and use thumb to adjust tension on the new stitch. One knit stitch cast on.

Repeat Steps 3–7 for each additional stitch.

To cast on in colors, see *Jane's Intarsia Tips*, page 137.

CABLE CAST-ON

1–2 Work as for Steps 1 and 2 of Knit Cast-on (page 108).

3 Insert left needle in loop and slip loop off right needle. One additional stitch cast on.

4 Insert right needle **between** the last 2 stitches. From this position, knit a stitch and slip it to the left needle as in Step 3. Repeat Step 4 for each additional stitch.

Increases

KNIT INTO FRONT & BACK OF STITCH (kf&b)

1 Knit into front of next stitch on left needle, but do not pull stitch off needle. *2* Take right needle to back, then knit through back of same stitch (as shown above).

3 Now take both stitches off left needle.

PURL INTO FRONT & BACK OF STITCH (pf&b)

1 Purl into front of next stitch, but do not pull stitch off needle.
2 Take right needle to back, then through back of same stitch, from left to right...

3 ...and purl.

4 Now take both stitches off left needle.

YARN OVER (yo)

Between knit stitches
Bring yarn under the needle to the front, take it over the needle to the back and knit the next stitch.

Between purl stitches
With yarn in front of needle, bring it over the needle to the back and to the front again; purl next stitch.

After a knit, before a purl
Bring yarn under the needle to the front, over the needle to the back, then under the needle to the front; purl next stitch.

After a purl, before a knit
With yarn in front of the needle, bring it over the needle to the back; knit next stitch.

MAKE 1 LEFT (M1L), KNIT

Insert left needle from front to back under strand between last stitch knitted and first stitch on left needle. Knit, twisting strand by working into loop at back of needle.

Decreases

K2tog

1 Insert right needle into first 2 stitches on left needle, beginning with second stitch from end of left needle.

2 Knit these 2 stitches together as if they were 1.
The result is a right-slanting decrease.

P2tog

1 Insert right needle into first 2 stitches on left needle.

2 Purl these 2 stitches together as if they were 1.
The result is a right-slanting decrease.

SSK

1 Slip 2 stitches **separately** to right needle as if to knit.

2 Slip left needle into these 2 stitches from left to right and knit them together: 2 stitches become 1.

The result is a left-slanting decrease.

SK2P, sl 1-k2tog-psso

1 Slip 1 stitch knitwise.
2 Knit next 2 stitches together.
3 Pass the slipped stitch over the k2tog: 3 stitches become 1; the right stitch is on top.
The result is a left-slanting double decrease.

S2KP2, sl 2-k1-p2sso

1 Slip 2 stitches **together** to right needle as if to knit.

2 Knit next stitch.

3 Pass 2 slipped stitches over knit stitch and off right needle: 3 stitches become 1; the center stitch is on top.

The result is a centered double decrease.

SSP

Use instead of p2tog-tbl to avoid twisting the stitches.

1 Slip 2 stitches **separately** to right needle as if to knit.

2 Slip these 2 stitches back onto left needle. Insert right needle through their 'back loops,' into the second stitch and then the first.

3 Purl them together: 2 stitches become 1.

The result is a left-slanting decrease.

MAKE 1 RIGHT (M1R), KNIT

Completed M1L knit: a left-slanting increase.

Insert left needle from back to front under strand between last stitch knitted and first stitch on left needle. Knit, twisting the strand by working into loop at front of the needle.

Completed M1R knit: a right-slanting increase.

BO bind off
CC contrasting color
cm centimeter(s)
cn cable needle
CO cast on
dec decreas(e) (ed) (es) (ing)
dpn double-pointed needle(s)
g gram(s)
ER every row or round
EOR every other row or round
" inch(es)
inc increas(e) (ed) (es) (ing)
k knit(ting)(s)(ted)
k2tog knit 2 together
LH left-hand
m meter(s)
M1 Make one stitch (increase)
MC main color
mm millimeter(s)
oz ounce(s)
p purl(ed) (ing) (s)
pm place marker
psso pass slipped stitch(es) over
R row or round
RH right-hand
RS right side
rnd round(s)
sc single crochet
sl slip(ped) (ping)
SKP slip, knit, psso
SSK slip, slip, knit these 2 sts tog
SSP slip, slip, purl these 2 sts tog
st(s) stitch(es)
St st stockinette stitch
tbl through back of loop(s)
tog together
WS wrong side(s)
wyib with yarn in back
wyif with yarn in front
× times
yd(s) yard(s)
yo yarn over (UK yarn forward)

Bind off/Misc

BIND OFF IN PATTERN

As you work the bind-off row for fabrics other than stockinette and garter stitch, knit or purl the stitches as the pattern requires. The bind-off is more attractive and flexible than in all-knit.

FASTEN OFF

Work bind-off until only 1 stitch remains on right needle. If this is the last stitch of a row, cut yarn and fasten off stitch as shown above. Otherwise, this is the first stitch of the next section of knitting.

3-NEEDLE BIND-OFF

Bind-off ridge on wrong side
1 With stitches on 2 needles, place *right sides together*.
* Knit 2 stitches together (1 from front needle and 1 from back needle, as shown); repeat from * once more.

2 With left needle, pass first stitch on right needle over second stitch and off right needle.

3 Knit next 2 stitches together.
4 Repeat Steps 2 and 3, end by drawing yarn through last stitch.

Bind-off ridge on right side
Work as for ridge on wrong side, EXCEPT, with *wrong sides together*.

KNITTING IN ROUNDS

• After casting on, do not turn work. Knit into first cast-on stitch to join. Stop. Check to make sure that the cast-on does not spiral around the needle. If it does, undo the stitch, remove the spiral, then rejoin.
• Check your knitting at end of first and second rounds and make sure you have no twists.
• Mark the beginning of a round in one of three ways:
 1 Place a marker on needle.
 2 Use a safety pin in the fabric.
 3 Weave your leftover cast-on tail between first and last stitch of round.

WRAP & TURN (W&T)

Each short row adds 2 rows of knitting across a section of the work. Since the work is turned before completing a row, stitches must be wrapped at the turn to prevent holes. Wrap and turn as follows:

Knit side
1 With yarn in back, slip next stitch as if to purl. Bring yarn to front of work and slip stitch back to left needle (as shown). Turn work.
2 With yarn in front, slip next stitch as if to purl. Work to end.

3 When you come to the wrap on a following knit row, hide the wrap by knitting it together with the stitch it wraps.

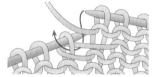

Purl side
1 With yarn in front, slip next stitch as if to purl. Bring yarn to back of work and slip stitch back to left needle (as shown). Turn work.
2 With yarn in back, slip next stitch as if to purl. Work to end.

3 When you come to the wrap on a following purl row, hide the wrap by purling it together with the stitch it wraps.

Purl a purl wrap
The first stitch of each short row is slipped (Step 2); this tapers the ends of short rows. When the wraps are hidden (Step 3), the mechanics of the shaping are almost invisible.

WORKING WITH 4 DOUBLE-POINTED NEEDLES (DPN)

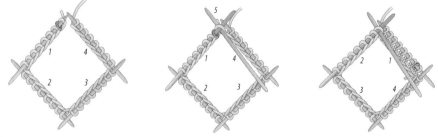

If instructions recommend working with a set of 5 dpn, arrange the stitches on 4 needles and knit with the fifth.
If instructions recommend working with a set of 4 dpn, arrange the stitches on 3 needles and knit with the fourth.

Working from charts

Charts are graphs or grids of squares that represent the right side of knitted fabric. They illustrate every stitch and the relationship between the rows of stitches.
Squares contain knitting symbols.
The key defines each symbol as an operation to make a stitch or stitches.

The pattern provides any special instructions for using the chart(s) or the key.
The numbers along the sides of charts indicate the rows. A number on the right side marks a right-side row that is worked leftward from the number. A number on the left marks a wrong-side row that is worked rightward. Since many stitches are worked differently on wrong-side rows, the key will indicate that. If the pattern is worked circularly, all rows are right-side rows and worked from right to left.
Bold lines within the graph represent repeats. These set off a group of stitches that are repeated across a row. You begin at the edge of a row or where the pattern indicates for the required size, work across to the second line, then repeat the stitches between the repeat lines as many times as directed, and finish the row.

Intarsia

For *Jane's Intarsia Tips*, see page 141.

SIMPLE INTARSIA

 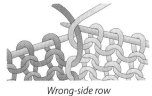

Right-side row   *Wrong-side row*

Making a twist:
Work across row to color change, pick up new color from under the old and work across to next color change.

WEAVING IN

1 One stitch before new color, trap the tail by placing it between the fabric and working yarn.

2 Knit the next stitch with the working yarn.

3 Drop old yarn and work next stitch with new yarn.

4 Then trap new cut tail by placing it between the new working yarn and fabric and knitting the next stitch.

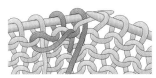 

Carry yarn to position for the following row, weaving it.

5 Knit another stitch then weave tail again to secure.

Specs: At a glance

Understanding pattern specifications

INTERMEDIATE   ◁ **Skill level**

STANDARD FIT

◁ **Fit**
   Includes ease (additional width) built into pattern.

S (M, L, 1X, 2X)   ◁ **Sizing**

A 32 (34½, 40, 45, 48)"   ◁ **Garment measurements**
B 26 (27¼, 29, 29, 29¾)"   *at the A, B, and C lines on the fit icon*
C 24 (26, 27, 28, 29)"

10cm/4"

     ◁ **Gauge**
22   *The number of stitches and rows you need in 10 cm or 4",*
18   *worked as specified.*

• **over Chart for Shell, using larger needles**

1 2 3 **4** 5 6   ◁ **Yarn weight**
   and amount in yards

• **Medium weight**
• **500 (600, 700, 800, 900) yds**

◁ **Type of needles**
   Straight, unless circular or double-pointed are recommended.

• **4.5mm/US 7, or size to obtain gauge**

&

◁ **Any extras**

• **Stitch marker**

Yarns

I have used pure new wool, in three weights. I call Merino 8 an Aran weight; it best shows the cables and texture stitches. Signatur Cable for the designs in color combinations is based on my own yarn and is the most common weight available, giving you a large color range to choose from in your local yarn store. Finally Merino 6, which knits to 23 stitches to 10cm. Not so different to 8 ply you say? Well, just enough to make a difference. Merino 6 is perfect for miters; it is a clean yarn without too much loft, so when we knit garter stitch the garment does not become too weighty or rigid.

When choosing a substitute yarn for designs such as the Metro or Harlequin where changes in needle size help shape the garment, work the 4" gauge swatch then work separate 2" swatches for the smaller and larger needles.

3 Light

TRENDSETTER YARNS/MONDIAL *Prima* (100% extra fine merino wool; 50g; 104yds)

TRENDSETTER YARNS/MONDIAL *Superwool* (100% merino wool; 50g; 135yds)

SIGNATUR *Pure New Wool DK* (100% merino wool; 50g; 110yds)

TRENDSETTER YARNS *Merino VI* (100% merino wool; 50g; 136yds)

TRENDSETTER YARNS *Kashmir* (65% cashmere, 35% silk; 50g; 110yds)

TRENDSETTER YARNS *Signatur Cable* (100% merino wool; 50g; 135yds)

4 Medium

TRENDSETTER YARNS/MONDIAL *Solare* (100% cotton; 50g; 100yds)

TRENDSETTER YARNS *Merino VIII* (100% merino wool; 50g; 100yds)

TRENDSETTER YARNS *Tonalita* (52% wool, 48% acrylic; 50g; 100yds)

TRENDSETTER YARNS *Merino Otto Shadow* (100% wool; 50g; 100 yds)

Other Yarn Choices

3 *Light*

BERROCO, INC *Pure Merino DK* (100% extra fine merino wool; 50g; 126 yds)

BERROCO, INC *Vintage* (50% acrylic; 40% wool; 10% nylon; 100g; 217 yds)

CASCADE YARNS *Cash Vero DK* (55% merino extra fine wool; 33% microfiber acrylic; 12% cashmere; 50g; 125 yds)

FIBER TRENDS/NATURALLY/NZ *Me* (80% merino wool, 20% cashmere; 50g; 111 yds)

FIBER TRENDS/NATURALLY/NZ *Pride* (100% pure NZ merino wool; 50g; 125 yds)

JOJOLAND *Baritone* (100% wool; 50g; 110 yds)

MUENCH YARNS/GGH *Maxima* (100% extra fine merino wool; 50g; 120 yds)

RUSSI SALES, INC/HEIRLOOM YARNS *Easy Care 8* (100% merino wool; 50g; 107 yds)

TAHKI •STACY CHARLES/FILATURA DI CROSA *Zara* (100% extra fine merino wool; 50g; 136 yds)

WESTMINSTER FIBERS/ROWAN YARNS *Pure Wool DK* (100% wool; 50g; 136 yds)

UNIVERSAL YARNS/FIBRA NATURA *Dolce Merino* (100% merino wool; 50g; 90 yds)

4 *Medium*

BERROCO, INC *Pure Merino* (100% extra fine merino wool; 50g; 92 yds)

CASCADE YARNS *Cash Vero* (55% merino extra fine wool; 33% microfiber acrylic; 12% cashmere; 50g; 98 yds)

KARABELLA YARNS *Aurora 8* (100% extra fine merino wool; 50g; 98 yds)

KNIT ONE, CROCHET TOO *Paint Box* (100% wool; 50g; 100 yds)

KOLLAGE YARNS *Fantastic* (100% merino wool; 50g; 93 yds)

PLYMOUTH YARNS *Boku* (95% wool; 5% silk; 50g; 99 yds)

PLYMOUTH YARNS *Worsted Merino Superwash* (100% merino wool; 100g; 218 yds)

SKACEL COLLECTION/SCHULANA *Merino Cotton 90* (53% wool, 47% cotton; 50g; 98 yds)

SKACEL COLLECTION/SCHULANA *Sumerino* (100% extra fine merino wool; 50g; 94 yds)

SKACEL COLLECTION/SCHULANA *Sumerino Print* (100% extra fine merino wool; 50g; 94 yds)

SKACEL COLLECTION/ZITRON *Ecco* (100% extra fine merino wool; 50g; 120 yds)

TAHKI •STACY CHARLES *Savoy* (52% silk; 48% merino wool; 50g; 108 yds)

UNIVERSAL YARNS/FIBRA NATURA *Sensational* (100% merino wool; 50g; 90 yds)

UNIVERSAL YARNS/WISDOM YARNS *Poems* (100% wool; 50g; 109 yds)

WESTMINSTER FIBERS/GEDIFRA *Extra Soft Merino* (100% extra fine merino wool; 50g; 115 yds)

WESTMINSTER FIBERS/NASHUA HANDKNITS *Creative Focus Superwash* (100% merino wool; 100g; 218 yds)

Specs: At a glance

Use the charts and guides below to make educated decisions about yarn thickness and needle size.

Yarn weight categories

Yarn Weight					
1	**2**	**3**	**4**	**5**	**6**
Super Fine	**Fine**	**Light**	**Medium**	**Bulky**	**Super Bulky**

Also called					
Sock Fingering Baby	Sport Baby	DK Light-Worsted	Worsted Afghan Aran	Chunky Craft Rug	Bulky Roving

Stockinette Stitch Gauge Range 10cm/4 inches					
27 sts to 32 sts	23 sts to 26 sts	21 sts to 24 sts	16 sts to 20 sts	12 sts to 15 sts	6 sts to 11 sts

Recommended needle (metric)					
2.25 mm to 3.25 mm	3.25 mm to 3.75 mm	3.75 mm to 4.5 mm	4.5 mm to 5.5 mm	5.5 mm to 8 mm	8 mm and larger

Recommended needle (US)					
1 to 3	3 to 5	5 to 7	7 to 9	9 to 11	11 and larger

Throughout this book, the photo caption describes the yarns and colors in the photograph. If a yarn is not available, its yardage and content information will help in making a substitution. Locate the Yarn Weight and Stockinette Stitch Gauge Range over 10cm to 4" on the chart. Compare the range with the information on the yarn label to fiind an appropriate yarn. These are **guidelines only** for commonly used gauges and needle sizes in specific yarn categories.

Equivalent weights

¾ oz		20 g
1 oz		28 g
1½ oz	=	40 g
1¾ oz	=	50 g
2 oz		60 g
3½ oz		100 g

Conversion chart

centimeters		0.394		inches
grams		0.035		ounces
inches	X	2.54	=	centimeters
ounces		28.6		grams
meters		1.1		yards
yards		.91		meters

Needles/Hooks

US	MM	HOOK
0	2	A
1	2.25	B
2	2.75	C
3	3.25	D
4	3.5	E
5	3.75	F
6	4	G
7	4.5	7
8	5	H
9	5.5	I
10	6	J
10½	6.5	K
11	8	L
13	9	M
15	10	N
17	12.75	

COLOPHON
SWING SWAGGER DRAPE
KNIT THE COLORS
OF AUSTRALIA

(Facing page, clockwise, from top) "Hi, I'm Jane Slicer-Smith, and I'd like to welcome you to Sydney, Australia, my home…" — The author videotaping in a green Metro Jacket with highlights of brick and fox; the Union Jack, the Southern Cross, and the Commonwealth Star — Australia's flag waves on top of another ubiquitous sight: a red corrugated roof; Opera legend Joan Sutherland; Opera House tiles.

(Clockwise from above) The Harbour Bridge spans Sydney Harbour — and frames the Opera House; a giant clown — with eyes and mouth wide open — welcomes visitors to Luna Park.

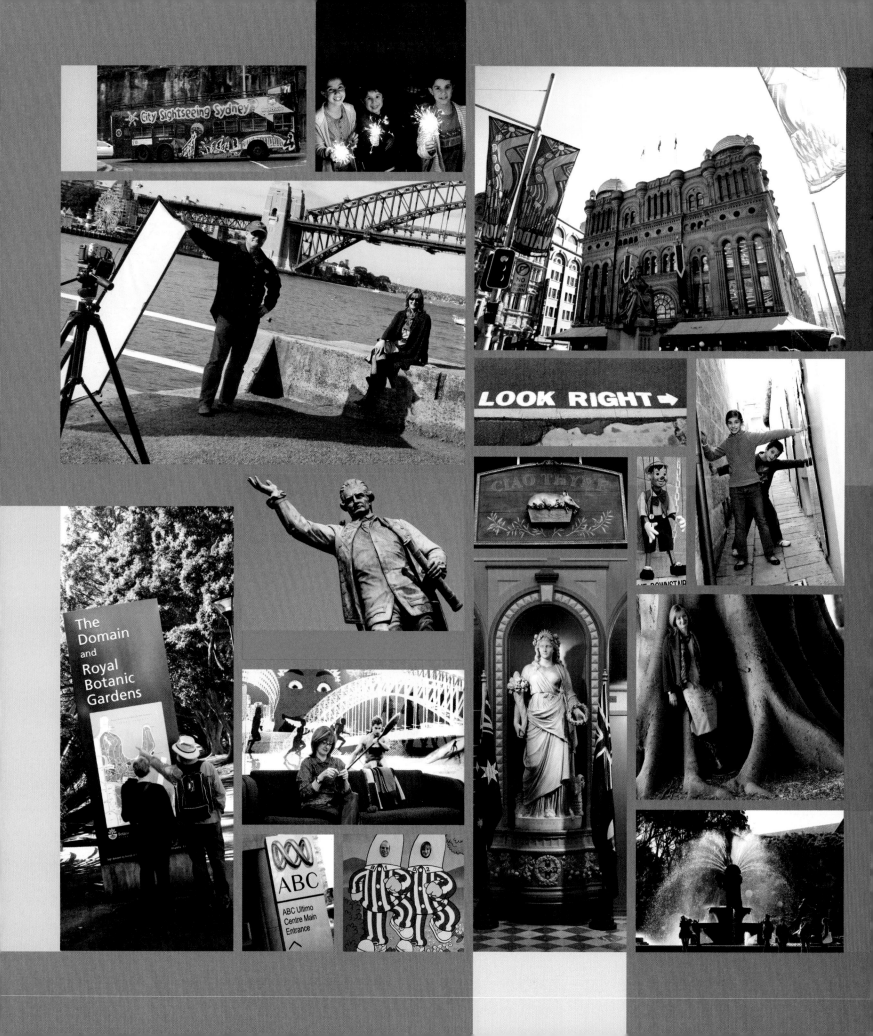

"Hi, I'm Jane Slicer-Smith, and I'd like to welcome you to my city, Sydney, Australia. Sydney life revolves around its beautiful harbor and that's why we're here. As you can see, it's another near-perfect day, like the last two weeks when Alexis, Elaine, my husband Brett, and I tripped around to bring you just a snippet of my Australia.

"It's fabulous that I can share part of my world. We traveled over the Blue Mountains with its Three Sisters, to Katoomba, then to the big country town of Bathurst, which was at one time the center of Australia's wool industry. We also drove up the beautiful Central Coast with its hidden bays and inlets. We've brought you architecture, countryside, flora, our unique wildlife, and all the beautiful colors that are Australia.

"Next week Alexis will have the pleasure of traveling to Australia's Red Centre and to Uluru, a monolith in the country's heart, sacred to the Pitjantjatjara and Yankunytjatjara, the Aboriginal people of the area.

"It'll be very interesting to see the colors of Uluru when Alexis is there; they change from year to year, between drought and wet. Three years ago, I saw Uluru after a wet season, so it was surrounded by desert plants. If there hasn't been a big wet, the landscape will be more monochromatic, with the exception, of course, of the color that floods onto the rock at sunrise and sunset…"

Cut! With the Harbour Bridge, the Opera House, and Luna Park as backdrop, Jane is taping a video for *Swing Swagger Drape, Knit the Colors of Australia*. So why am I waving 'cut'? The wind has come up and Jane's hair is everywhere. Brett, who's holding a giant scrim, tries to shield Jane from the wind. But it's hopeless. We'll have to wait.

"Hi, I'm Jane Slicer-Smith, and I'd like to welcome you to my city, Sydney, Australia, where I am so fortunate to live…"

What was *that* noise? I take my eyes off the video screen just in time to see a boat full of men in wet suits whizzing by at breakneck speed. Sorry, Jane, can we do it again?

"Hi, I'm Jane Slicer-Smith, and we're here on Sydney Harbour… Shall I wait until the train goes by? The helicopter, too? Or is that too far away?" A commuter train on the Harbour Bridge means just a click of the pause button. But a helicopter hovering overhead? It dawns on me: today is not just a perfect day — it's what the Australian media has dubbed 'Super Thursday.' The Pope is in town for World Youth Day.

Sydney is hosting 500,000 pilgrims, and as the papal flotilla passes by, they are lined up at Bennelong Point, on the Opera House steps, along Circular Quay, all the way to Darling Harbour where the Pope will address the young people's welcome celebration.

"I can't believe we totally forgot about Super Thursday," Jane says. "Will we be able to use any of the tape? No? All right. I always look at myself on videos and think I'm going to look like a puppet on a string anyway."

Jane is a natural in front of a camera — or in front of an audience or a class — but you don't argue with your author. Besides, the camera is still rolling, so why not just talk and not worry about the video?

"*Swing Swagger Drape* is all about shapes and, of course, color — for me, that's a big part of Australia's appeal; it's such a colorful country. I love it. Traveling with you these last two weeks — and constantly looking for shots — has me looking at my world in a different way and appreciating how lucky I am to live here.

"The book has been a long time coming, and a fantastic journey: of design, travel, and relationships — which is what knitting is really about: our relationships with the knitting world, with each other, and with color.

"It's a challenge designing for a book! It's about putting together a collection that will appeal to different levels of knitters. My garments are about style, shape, and drape; they vary between swing coats, A-lines, and the draped garment I'm wearing. Of course, color is the important element that brings everything together. I'm fortunate to have a fantastic team of knitters, so I can show multiple colorways. It's still now; let's do the Sydney part again."

Brett steps back to get his scrim out of view, and Jane repeats it all, without missing a beat. Was it the sailboat, swinging on the waves like a metronome, that helped?

We hear a ship's horn. At last, a sound that adds authenticity. "From Sydney Harbour, on a slightly cooler, windy day, this is Jane Slicer-Smith saying, I'll see you soon in America."

Colors of Sydney

(Facing page, left column, L to R, top to bottom) Art flourishes in Sydney, even on buses; Annie, Takis, and Taso demonstrate the New Year's fireworks at the Harbour Bridge; Brett and Jane video taping on Super Thursday; choosing a path around Farm Cove, Australia's first colonial settlement; Australia's colonial discoverer, Captain Cook; in the greenroom, waiting to go on 'Mornings with Deborah Cameron'; ABC Radio; a lighter moment.

(Right column, L to R, top to bottom) Now a shopping center known as the QVB, the Queen Victoria Building was a produce market; a necessary reminder — again and again and again; Annalies and Tass squeezed in the narrowest alley in Sydney; eatery; toy shop in The Rocks; personification of New South Wales; Jane and a giant fig tree in the Royal Botanic Gardens; Archibald Fountain.

Brett suggests we adjourn to a cafe at Luna Park. It's a perfect spot for an author shot. Jane is wearing her Metro Jacket, a complement to the row of palm trees that recedes toward the bridge. "I love green," Jane says between shots, "and the brick and fox highlights are like the red stems of the eucalyptus leaf we shot in Balmain.

"And these beiges, won't they go beautifully with the scribbly bark we found at the Reptile Park? Insects burrow under the bark, and when the tree sheds, the clean, blond trunk is exposed. It's like the insects left track-like whispers, tiny messages.

"There's also paper bark, like layers of torn blotting paper. We can montage those images next to the eroding rock pictures." Jane is doing layouts in her head, but there's no time to talk book production: the ferry is coming to Milsons Point, and I must get a shot as it crosses under the Harbour Bridge. I leave my tripod, my Hasselblad, my assistant, and my model; grab my Canon, dash toward the pier, and start clicking. The ferry moves fast, and I only get a few shots before it's out of range (see photo, page 167).

Time to get back to my model. But Jane is now surrounded by commuters. Some make their way up the hill toward the train station, but others take a leisurely stroll down the palm-lined promenade, ruining my shot. Brett to the rescue: he runs around asking people would they kindly walk on the other side. We have our author shot.

It's time to give Brett a well-deserved break. We join him for coffee — and an incredible view. "Luna Park is one of the icons of Sydney Harbour," says Jane, but the thing that makes it absolutely magical is the face of the clown which you enter the fun park through. "Look, the face will be so perfect with the aqua Dice sweater. Remember? The one where the model wore the lime green T-shirt? Let's combine those shots. Won't it make a great page?"

Jane, it seems, has just about laid out the whole book. Is it time to rethink our rule about no authors on photo shoots? That thought brings to mind my first shoot with Jane, just across the harbor. She tells Brett, "Alexis and I were photographing in front of the Opera House in 2006, when he was visiting his sister, Anna. Remember? After we greeted one another, we sat down on one of the benches to talk. And the next thing, he's running off, saying, 'You don't have to follow me!' He pulled his camera out like a school boy on an excursion. A ferry was coming, and the light was perfect. He got his pictures and was so excited.

"I saw this all happen and realized that when Alexis gets behind that camera, it doesn't really matter what is going on in the rest of the world. Later at a cafe, the food arrived and the next thing Alexis does is whip my food out from under my nose and start photographing it.

"When we shot at the Sydney Antique Center, I also got into the act. It's huge, with each room owned by an individual dealer and each section a different genre. I was looking for Australiana: the eighteen-inch-high cockatoos; the galahs; the say-nothing, see-nothing, hear-nothing koalas; the electric kettle with a kookaburra.

"I phoned the man who owns the Australiana, and got the OK to photograph his pieces. But it was too dark to do it in his booth. What to do? By that time, I was playing by Alexis' rules. It's amazing what you can do when you assume an air of authority. We found good daylight in the front display window. Alexis crawled around shooting. I'd hand him an Australian Noah's Ark of creatures to parade in front of his lens. It was extremely cramped in that window, but we didn't break a thing.

"Every now and again, a customer or staff member would walk by and look at us. It was a joy to share Alexis' single-mindedness regardless of how silly or inconsequential the subject. It was one of many unexpected pleasures in creating each element of this book.

"Watching somebody so engrossed in something they've done for so many years, yet with such passion, enthusiasm, and love; that's just how I feel about my knitting. I can't imagine the day I won't want to sit down in the evening and knit."

"Knitting is a family thing," says Jane's mom, Sheila Slicer, a world-renowned miniature portrait artist. "My mother, one of six girls who all knitted their own stockings and underwear, taught Jane to knit. Yorkshire, where we come from, had a lot of woolen mills and many generations of both women and men with nimble fingers."

Sheila is taking time off from Jane's booth at the Darling Harbour Quilt Fair. The show is a marathon five-day affair, but Sheila loves helping Jane. "My two daughters are my reward in life,"

A Distant Shore

Peace and Progress (above) — and trade — have marked Sydney's history. (Facing page first column, top to bottom) The Museum of Sydney and its Edge of Trees pillars symbolizing contact between Aboriginals and Europeans; the Museum's Trade exhibit includes cheroots from India; yes, that Captain William Bligh was Governor of New South Wales in 1806; so was Mrs. Macquarie's husband, whose name is commemorated on the Hyde Park Barracks Museum clock turret; "rats", reads a Barracks sign, "unofficially shared the building with its official 19th century occupants — convicts, immigrants, and asylum women"; a trio of buckets denotes hard labor; Baluderri (whose name means Leather Jacket Fish) was an interpreter for Governor Phillip of First Fleet fame.

(Second column, top to bottom) Bennelong gave his name to the homonymous Point, site of the Opera House; convict No. 1264; mending socks; The Australian Monument to the Great Irish Famine.

(Third column, top to bottom) Steel silhouettes give an eerie feel to the upper floor of The Hyde Park Barracks, built in 1819 by convicts; The Founding of Australia, January 26th, 1788; an empty plate, symbol of the Irish Famine.

(Fourth column, middle to bottom) The Hyde Park Barracks; The First Fleet; Barracks dormitories.

SIGNATUR HANDKNITS

she says. "I'm so very proud of Jane. She's given me immense pleasure. She's very determined—did you know? Even as a young girl, I'd sit her down, and she'd amuse herself for hours.

"When she discovered knitting, she decided to go to art college to study knitwear design. She won a prize from the Royal Society, worked in London, and visited many countries. She saw many cultures and was inspired by ethnic arts. Then she took a trip from Cairo to Nairobi—do you know about that? She decided to come to Australia because there was this appealing gentleman in the back of the lorry—did she tell you that?"

Well, no, but here's my chance to hear the answer to the question I had posed when I profiled Jane in *Knitter's 85*: Sydney is a long way from Bradford, where Jane Slicer-Smith was born. How did she make the long journey Down Under? But Sheila looks at her watch. "Has it really been that long?" she says. "I've got to get back; see you at tea time!" A quick kiss on my cheek, and she's off, her white pony-tail and blue-and-beige Mitered Vee Capelet billowing in the wind.

I've got a couple of hours before I meet Jane, Sheila, my sister Anna, her husband Tasos, and book editor Elaine Rowley—who's flying in today—at the Quayside Brasserie. As I walk there, the view that unfolds before me is like a video replay of my last visit to Sydney Harbour.

It's one of the most beautiful panoramas in the world: the famous Sydney Opera House spreads its wings in the midday sun; the Harbour Bridge soars high above the port; Circular Quay—Australia's watery Grand Central Station—bustles with ferries, water taxis, commuters, and tourists. Nearby, where ocean liners once brought immigrants like my sister Anna to the Distant Shore, a tall ship awaits today's tourists. And by a wrought iron railing, a designer in a fire-red coat awaits.

"I won an award for color from the Royal Society for the Encouragement of the Arts and the prize was a travel allowance to Paris or New York," Jane says. "I had to do a bit of fast talking to convince them that I should go to Africa instead. After all, weren't some of the oldest examples of knitting in Cairo? While there, I managed to talk myself into an overland trip to Nairobi, Kenya's capital.

"It was a fantastic thirteen weeks, one of those times when you step out of your life into another universe. Everyone in the group thought it was crazy to knit a sweater through red-hot Egypt and Sudan, but I got to wear it when we reached the Equator: Kenya and Kilimanjaro were quite high and cold.

"I had met a group of Australians on the trip, so my next stop became Sydney. Everyone in the U.K. thought I was even crazier to go to Australia than to Africa. What would I do there? I told them that Australia is the world's largest producer of wool, so I would continue to design knitwear. Their reply was, 'Fine, but how are you going to make a living selling knitting in one of the world's hottest continents?'

"In Sydney, it may be hot in the summer, but it does cool down in the winter. You actually wear more knits inside the house than when you step outside—where it might be a sunny, beautiful winter day, and then you peel off layers.

"The knitwear degree I earned in the U.K. was aimed at the machine-knitting industry. Within a month of arriving in Australia, I was designing for Japan's largest importer of British wool. I traveled to Japan three times a year and I loved it. Such beauty, such respect for crafts—for people: I'd never heard anyone being called a 'Living Legend' for their craft skills. What an acknowledgement, what a wonderful appreciation for the work of hands.

"I love the process of knitting. It puts your mind in a different space. You pick up your knitting and answers to unasked questions come to you. Knitting helps you sort things out—not just in your swatch, but in your mental sorting and filing too.

"Really, knitting is about learning basic skills and simple techniques, to manage needles and yarn; work with color is the next step. I want to encourage other knitters to indulge in what I really enjoy—the techniques of creating with color, be it intarsia, Fair Isle, or my current favorite: mitered knitting.

"Color goes down to my roots. I've always loved and been inspired by color, watched it influence my life. My mother is an artist, and I was painting with oils when I was six, decorating and painting my bedroom when I was ten. My Barbie doll had colorful, tailored ball gowns I sewed with the help of my grandmother, who was a seamstress.

"My grandmother got me started when I was five, but I didn't pick up needles again until I was seventeen. I saw something in a magazine, but the instructions worked like a foreign language. I

Australiana

"Australiana designs were huge in the 80s," says Jane. "It started when Lady Diana wore a sweater with a koala sitting on a branch.

"It exploded; everybody wanted their koala up a tree. A shop at The Rocks in Sydney, where I sold my designs, was running 2,000 knitters to keep up with demand.

"So I put a koala up a tree as well. I also had a kangaroo with a joey in the pouch, a kookaburra, rosellas, crocodiles, possums—if it walked, crawled, or swam, it went on a sweater.

"And my knitters loved it. They miss all that pictorial work now. You may know what the design is going to look like, but knitting brings that black-and-white graph to life.

"Finding matching buttons was frustrating. Then I discovered polymer clay and started making swirly geometric buttons for my Fair Isle sweaters.

"When I did the Australiana range, I had to learn to do leaves, blossoms, koalas, and kangaroos on buttons. And when I did my Living Reef sweaters, I created fish, dolphins, crabs, lobsters—if it swam, it went on a button."

(Facing page) Australiana, and Jane's mom, Sheila Slicer, and her miniature portraits of husband (Jane's dad) Robert, grand-daughter Rebecca, and Jane as a stunning teen.

CERTIFIED ORGANIC

AUSTRALIAN CERTIFIED ORGANIC RETAILER NO 1014R

EVERYTHING CERTIFIED ORGANIC/BIODYNAMIC

PADDINGTON UNITING CHURCH

PINK LADY/ROSY GLOW

looked at the picture and thought, I'll just make it up. So that's how I started designing. My four years at art school sharpened awareness of the elements of good design — color, shape, and proportion.

"I think of a garment as a three-dimensional canvas. Of course, my canvases swing, swagger and drape, and the wearers' shoulders simply support them. This is why tall, square-shouldered women can wear kimonos better than most body types. Presently fashion is focused on neck trims and enhanced shoulders, so we're seeing shoulder pads again. In dressmaking, most coats, no matter what the fashion, have a small shoulder pad. And like a well-fitting bra, they can make a real difference to your silhouette. All's fair in love and fashion — so why not 'power dress' by popping a shoulder pad into a casual cardigan?

"When I talk color, I can still mean a single-colored garment — the smaller and shorter the garment, the bolder the color. It's been great to see lime green being worn boldly the last few years. And once we've introduced color, we can start talking technique. Stripes and miters are a breeze. Even with intarsia I often have new knitters exclaim, 'Is that all there is to it?' This challenge of trying something new must be there in a book. My goal as a designer is to make you want to learn a new technique and as a teacher, to give you the skills.

"With the experience I have making garments to measure, I always approach design with the finished garment in mind. It's not just about how to write the pattern, but how to make the pattern flexible — which will save me time later when customizing. Now, as well as customizing my patterns for made to measure, I also customize patterns for clients to knit themselves.

"I first started designing for a store in Double Bay in Sydney, then began selling at a crafts market in nearby Paddington. Word spread, and I assembled a team of wonderful knitters to knit my garments, some of whom are still with me after 20 years.

"I love intarsia and Fair Isle, but mitered knitting is such a natural, simple technique for putting colors together. An exciting world of color opens to any knitter who can do stocking or garter stitch. People who see me knitting at an airport say, 'Look at all those colors!' With mitered knitting, you may have eight colors in a design, but only two colors are attached. You work two rows in one color, two rows in another, and diamonds of colored miters become amazing stained glass windows created with needles and yarn.

"When I first looked at mitered squares, I saw a lot of kimono shapes. As a designer, I know that to wear a kimono successfully you need the right body shape. If you are petite, have sloping shoulders, or a big bust, a kimono won't work. So my challenge was to turn mitered knitting into my signature shape — a structured look, with a slight A-line shaping, fitted over the shoulders, with fullness that enhances the body, and gives an elegant result.

"What do I love most about living in Australia? The journey to and from — those fourteen-hour flights! Your knitting, a couple of movies, and no phones! I do love living here. The people are wonderful and it's so green, so unspoiled. You can be waterside in a rocky inlet and think you're absolutely miles and miles from the world, but you're only fifteen minutes from the center of Sydney.

"Our house sits on a steep rock face with lovely views across eucalyptus treetops and the river below. And twice a week I go horseback riding in Centennial Park, our Central Park. Swans, geese, and strange Australian birds float in the pond while everyone — with their children, personal trainer, or dogs — walk, play rugby, cycle, jog, or ride horses.

"It's really a perfect way to start your day. Then you hop in your car, drive by the colorful movie set that is Sydney Harbour, over the Harbour Bridge, and fifteen minutes later you're back in your house, ready to start work by 9:00 a.m.

"But I also love to travel, and I know how lucky I am to be living in the knitting universe. I love visiting America, teaching, meeting new knitters, store owners and their pets. I love the kaleidoscope of Stitches Expos, the excitement of meeting others who share my passion. When my husband Brett and I walked into our first Stitches show, we entered another world: everywhere there were people knitting. With so many friendly knitters there, you could go to Stitches by yourself and never feel alone."

"Stitches East was in King of Prussia," Brett says. "We entered the hotel lobby, and there had to have been 100 women — on the couches, on the floor, on every available seat — knitting. I said to Jane, 'I think we've found knitter's heaven.'

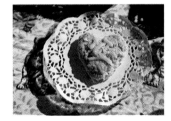

Paddington Markets

"Paddington Markets still carries through what I do today," Jane says. "I had a stall there for nine years, and it gave me the freedom to design without limits.

"I only sold finished garments then, so I could have six graphs, or ten pages of instructions. If I wanted eight colors, I used eight colors.

"Paddington Markets showed me what worked in terms of design, structure, the right fit, what works on a body in real life — not just on a model in a book."

(Outer band of photos, clockwise from upper right) Time for a sugar rush; with Sue; and her one-off dresses; rhapsody in beetroot red; waratahs; Pink Lady-Rosy Glow orchard apples; sweet bunnies; Mia, the hat lady; designer jewelry; with Nicole, a fine-porcelain-artist friend; one of the hat lady's happy customers; circles of proteas; waratah; custard apples; Nicole's wares; the national flower of Australia; is it a flower or a torte?; bird of paradise.

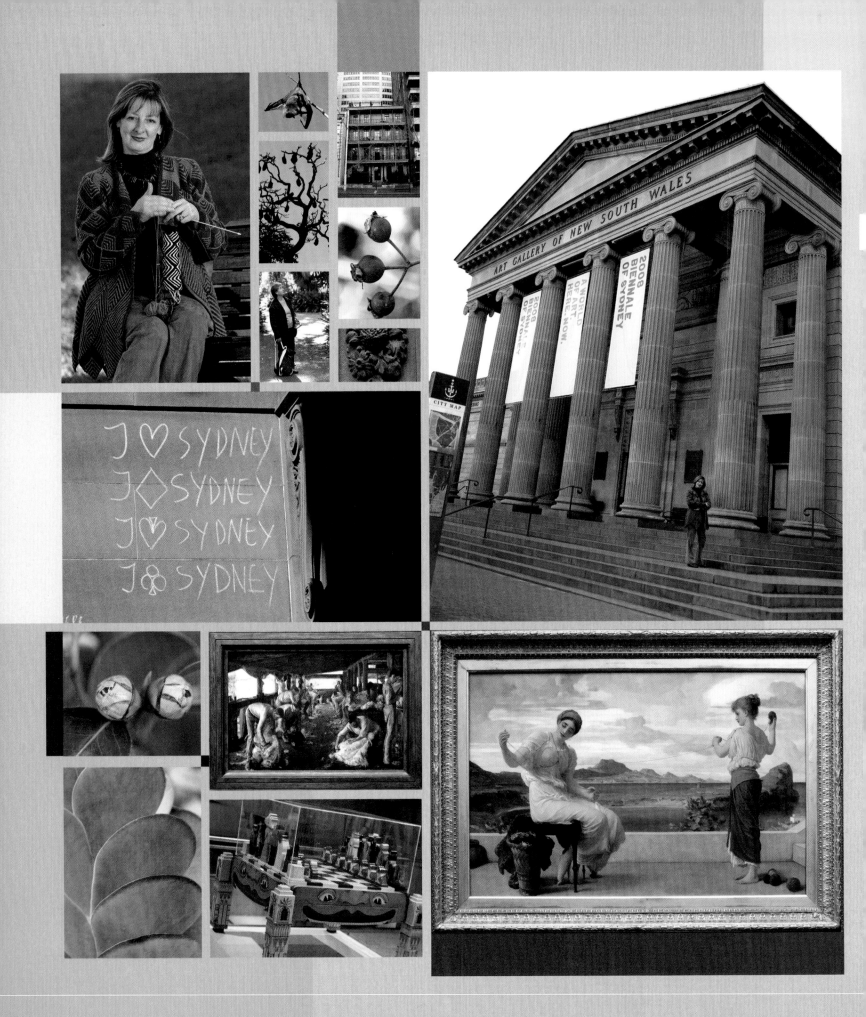

"When we saw this focused group of knitters, we thought, if that's what happens here, imagine what's happening across America. It'll be like painting the Harbour Bridge — you start at one end, and by the time you get to the other, you have to start again."

The only part of the Harbour Bridge I can see at the moment is a pair of red warning lights at its very top. That's because it's four o'clock in the morning, and the Sydney panorama is obscured by cover of darkness. Brett and I have set up my cameras under the lush canopy of the Royal Botanic Gardens — the perfect spot to take photos as the morning sun turns the crystal white of the Opera House iridescent.

But it's rather chilly. I remind myself that it's winter here and use a nearby trunk as a windbreak. It's a large Moreton Bay fig tree; Brett and I could play hide-and-seek in its folds. It isn't like we don't have time: four-thirty comes, soon it's a quarter to five and I tease Brett, saying that the sun must still be shining over Hawaii. He invokes scout's honor that the Internet site listed today's sunrise at 4:30 a.m.

I can now almost see the outline of the Opera House, but it'll be a while before I can start clicking, so I take out my small tape player, hit 'record', and hold it in front of Brett. What is it like to be shooting Jane's book?

"It's a dream," Brett says. "To be part of it, right down to actually helping the photographer, something I never imagined. And doing it in the city that Jane and I both absolutely love? Perfection."

A man materializes out of the darkness, in athletic shoes, shorts, and T-shirt working dumbbells, raising and lowering his arms as he runs. Meanwhile I'm shivering. Brett, what has it been like watching Jane develop into a world-class designer? "To see how she's respected and loved in the knitting universe," he says, "is wonderful. Jane always puts her whole heart into everything she does. She has a gift, but she works bloody hard at it. Like her father Robert, Jane is quick to see business opportunities and turn a half empty cup into half full.

"I would like Jane's Mom and Dad to come to Stitches and see the knitters' reactions to her designs — it's like the whole audience stops breathing. I never expected that. A lot of people may not even know Jane, but they'll watch a model step out wearing one of her designs, and suddenly there's a collective gasp."

I've been there, seen it with my own eyes.

And now — at last! — the first rays of the sun are painting a cloud violet. For my benefit, it has positioned itself right above the bridge, and soon, the sun glides down its graceful, lacy arc and touches the tallest Opera House sail. The sea fills with color, and steely gray becomes violet-blue. We've been standing here for almost four-and-a-half hours, and the sunrise is all over in a few minutes.

Later that day, we're back at the Royal Botanic Gardens for another author shot and find Jane already there, with lots of company. "Tourists love to stroll in the gardens," Jane says, "and take their photo at Mrs. Macquarie's Chair. Carved out of solid rock, it's where the wife of Governor Macquarie liked to sit in the 1800s, waiting for ships returning from the Motherland."

Now it's Jane's turn at the Chair. Brett holds the scrim, I set up my camera and tripod, and I realize I'm not alone. We've attracted a crowd, and Jane is being shot by Korean, Japanese, and Italian tourists.

Brett looks at Jane as if to say, 'How are you going to change to those beige trousers in the middle of the park, with the paparazzi still hanging around? The folds of the magnificent tree — that moments before had been a backdrop — become a dressing room, and Brett's scrim, the door. Jane emerges ready for her next shot.

The sun is setting fast as we roll our gear through the Royal Botanic Gardens for our last shot in front of the Art Gallery of New South Wales. I first ran into this classical building many years ago and I remember thinking what a wonderful setting it would make. Now, here I am, framing its Ionic portico through my wide-angle lens.

"It's getting dark," Jane says, "the lights go on, and Alexis plants me on the steps wearing the cover jacket. My arms aren't long enough for the sleeves, so I have to stand with my arms folded. Since there is not enough light, I have to keep really, really, *really* still. Gallery visitors are leaving, others are arriving for a function and Alexis — who's quite a distance from me so he can get the whole Gallery in his shot — shouts, 'Freeze! Please…'"

There are lots of stares. Jane does her best simulating a statue, and in the low light, in her beige jacket, her silhouette blends with that of the sandstone columns. You don't suppose some of the

The Royal Botanic Gardens

The Colony's first farm is an oasis in the heart of Sydney, a photographer's dream site, and Mrs. Macquarie's famous Chair.

My sister Anna and I walk through cool paths lined with flowers and herbs from around the world. Brett has the day off, and Anna doubles as my assistant. That's my sister — who can tell a fig tree a mile away — checking out some high-hanging fruit (facing page). It turned out to be bats who had found their Garden of Eden.

The Art Gallery of New South Wales borders the Gardens, and right under the bronze names of the great artists you can read, in chalk, that Aussies' love their city — in spades (facing page, middle left.)

During our Gallery tour we discover Frederick, Lord Leighton's, 1878 oil Winding the Skein — as our author had just done, right before her knitting shot. We also admire Tom Roberts' canvas of Aussie wool shearers, his 1894 The Golden Fleece (facing page).

At the Gallery's outdoor restaurant, we watch two colorful lorikeets fighting over a tube of sugar (above).

The Gallery's Ionic Portico becomes the set for our last author shot. It's getting dark, I am shooting at a very slow speed, and Jane valiantly tries being a column. I get the shot but don't want to leave. Lucky are those who get to stay (vintage house, facing page, to the left of the Gallery).

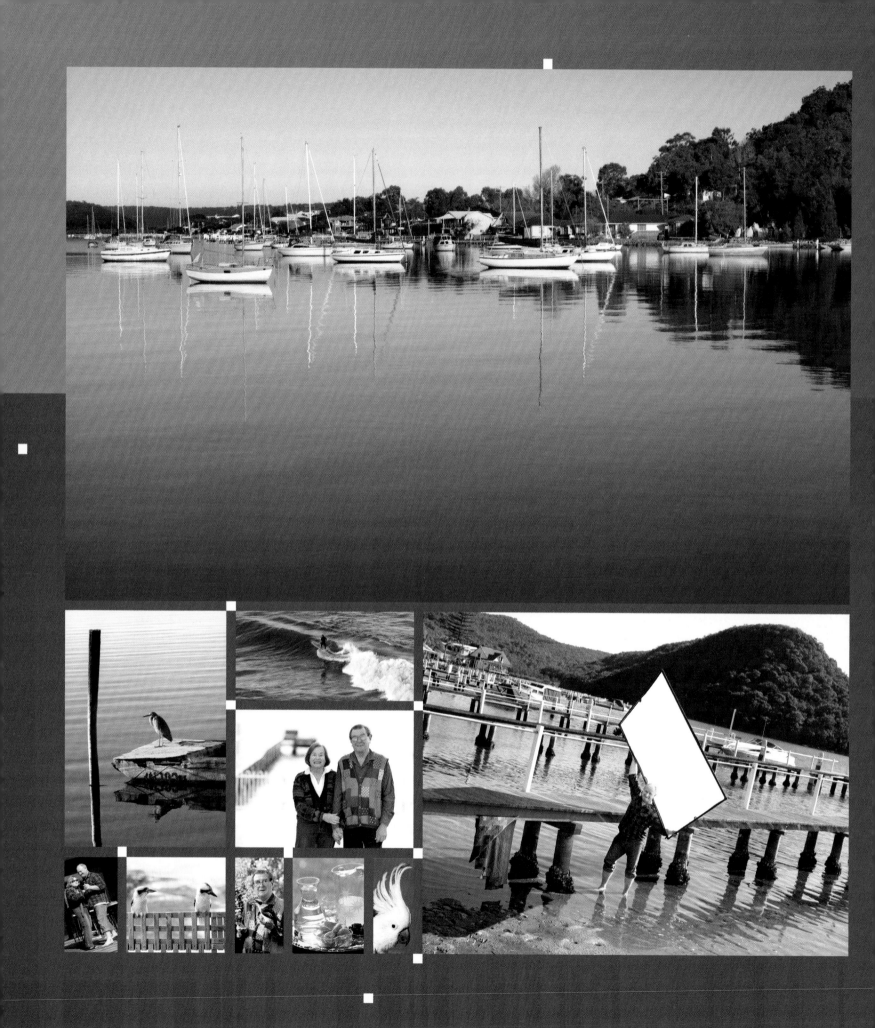

gallery-goers thought I was shouting at *them*? But Jane is unfazed, and says, "That's one of the things that makes this so much more than a book."

She picks up that thread later, over dinner, at Darling Harbour. "A year after my first visit to America, I realized I should think about doing a book and looked at those books I admire in a new way. It's *not* just about content or good designs: it's the whole package. To create the feel I want, my book benefits from a whole range of skills that I don't possess: the photography, styling, models, and location scouting, just to start. I want the book to reflect my aesthetic, and the layout to communicate my sense of color and style.

"Nothing will thrill me more than to see how knitters personalize my designs with their own colors, using the length options and silhouettes in the book.

"It's been fantastic to see my collection photographed. I've seen them all as individual garments during the design process. I've created capes and capelets, drapes, A-lines, and swaggers; I've put garments into different lengths and different sizings — always very aware that my garments are designed to fit the shapes of all women.

"*Swing Swagger Drape* brings together garment shapes, which I am known for — A-lines, drapes, swings — plus the actual garment fit, which I believe is most important. I hope the designs in the book will appeal to both basic and more experienced knitters.

"The shoot in Santa Fe was fantastic — a holiday with so many bonuses: the light was lovely and clear, the local art an inspiration. We shot the garments, I taught a brilliant class of 19 students, and we had some amazing coincidences of just being in the right place at the right time.

"Half way through the first day, red, blue, yellow, and black Harley-Davidson motorcycles pulled up in the Plaza. I shouted, 'Next shot, over here!' That fabulous yellow motorbike would look good with Lydia and my black-and-white. So, yes, I broke all the 'no author on a photoshoot' rules the very first day, didn't I?

"A lot of photo shoots I've done have been in cramped settings, very controlled studio shots, one model after another, one garment after another. In Santa Fe we criss-crossed the city taking photographs. It was interesting watching you select your location. Sometimes I wondered what you were thinking, then you'd say, 'Come have a look.' And I'd see this fantastic shot you'd seen in your mind's eye, framed in your camera lens. It takes an incredible talent to be able to transform colors, scenery, buildings, and landscape into perfect frames for my designs.

"When shooting at the train station, I noticed in some of the shots you'd pull back a touch to introduce a dab of the yellow from the carriage. You weren't just framing the model and the rails. I think a good photographer, like a good designer, has an instinct for color.

"When we were shooting in Santa Fe, it had to be 100°F — why were you making poor Nicola stand in the heat, on an open train car, with awful wire sides? When you had me look through the lens, I saw why. It was a beautiful shot. You framed and isolated the essence of what you needed, and the Mitered-Vee Capelet shone. I thought, 'I hope Brett doesn't look, because he's going to think he should have one of these cameras, too.'"

Our hotel's swimming pool and pergolas; the Plaza's adobe walls and timber colonnades; the sandstone Cathedral's wrought iron gates; narrow streets with massive, carved wooden doors and fountains became our backdrops. Santa Fe became our studio and Jane's garments looked stunning no matter where we shot them.

"What pleases me," says Jane," is seeing my designs look as good on any street, in any town, as they do in a fashion show.

"Santa Fe didn't just give us the crisp light of Australia, it also gave us its colors in both buildings and landscape. For example, the wrought iron gates were the perfect backdrop to the Metro Swagger in blacks and beiges. That's one of the most neutral garments in the book, in sandstone colors.

"Sandstone, which takes me back to my British origins, is what Sydney is built from. Remember the Art Gallery? We couldn't have photographed that particular garment in a better location than where it was — against a beautiful iron gate with sandstone walls. It falls into place beautifully — and will be a perfect complement to your shots of the Queen Victoria Building.

"Being on the shoot, I realized how much unseen work had been done before a single shot could be taken. It takes precise planning. Rick and Lisa had each garment already styled, accessorized with earrings, necklaces, and shoes in a plastic bag, ready to go. It all hung in the back of the van, each piece in the order to be shot.

Woy Woy Bay

When I told Brett we needed to take a few still-life shots of Jane's garments, he knew just the spot.

Woy Woy Bay could qualify as the paradise that Brett's father, Peter, believes Australia to be. Our greeting committee, a flock of pelicans makes a fuss on a wharf roof, and a cormorant (above) is too busy taking in the sun to notice I'm taking his picture.

(Facing page, clockwise from top) Protected by the hills that Peter calls his field of broccoli, Woy Woy Bay shelters sailboats — and mirrors them for a visiting photographer; Brett — ever the valiant photo assistant; sixty-seven years old and going strong, Cocko prances; cold lemonade, orange slices, and fresh strawberries for non-feathered friends; sausages for Junior and his dad; waiting until his father has his too; a spin on the porch for Florence and son; a cormorant enjoys the moment; taking advantage of a wave — even in the dead of 'Northern' Winter; Florence and Peter in their daughter-in-law's one-offs.

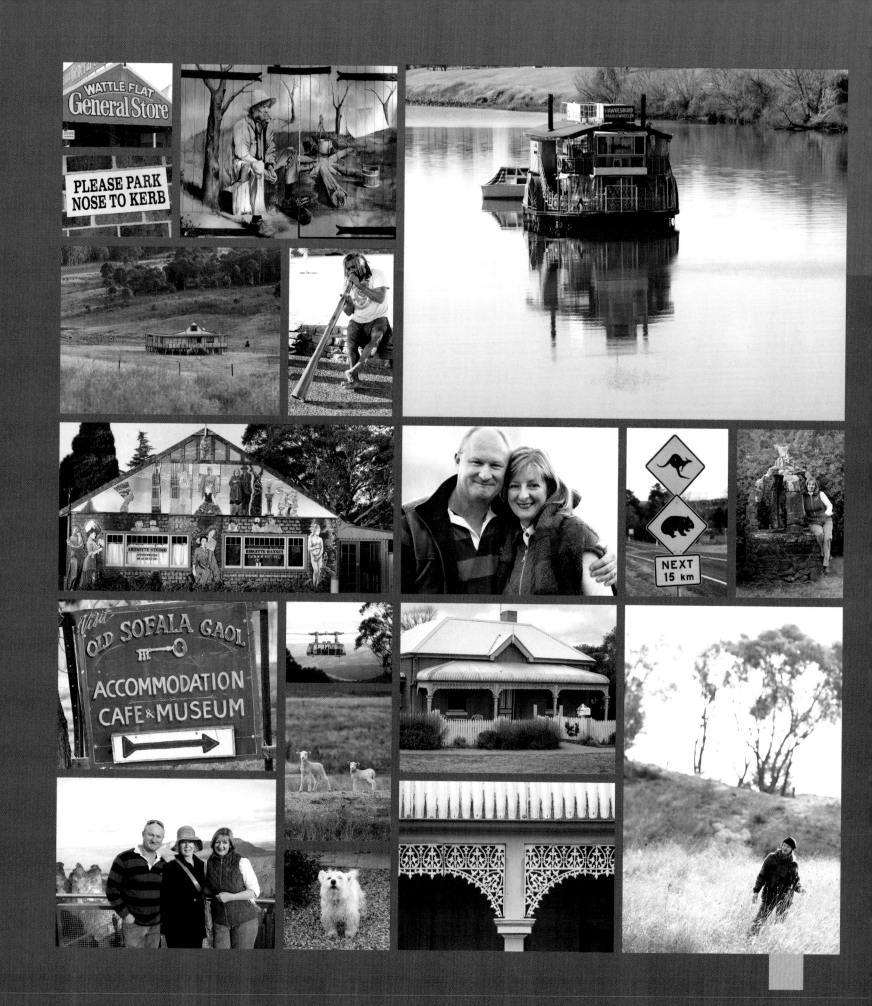

"It was great fun shopping for accessories with Elaine, Rick, and Lisa. Every outfit just worked. The styling brought it all together — and Lydia and Nicola's professionalism creates a wonderful picture. My greatest pleasure has been working with the whole XRX team and Sioux Falls became my home-away-from home — not bad considering I didn't know where South Dakota was three years ago! XRX has given me a fabulous opportunity to be an integral part of the book's evolution."

Next day, Jane leaves for Canberra, Australia's capital city, for a show and Brett and I have shots to do that do not require a model. Brett suggests Woy Woy Bay where his parents live.
As we drive north from Sydney, the city skyline is replaced by eucalyptus forest that stretches to the horizon.
"The road leading North from Sydney is on a natural escarpment, or spur, running northwest from the Harbour Bridge," Brett says. "This part of the city is built on a natural ridge that twists its way north. It seems as if we're flying, because we're so high up above the treetops. With each bend in the road, there's a new vista. There are almost no flat areas in Sydney and no straight roads — very confusing to tourists."
I bet they don't have trouble finding the Australian Reptile Park, coming up on our left. We follow a line of tourist buses and cars, and I hope I'll be able to take the perfect koala photo. *The Colors of Australia* without that cuddly creature? Unthinkable.
What we come upon is this bushland park teeming with Australian wildlife — and children. The star of the Park is crocodile Elvis, who seems to be taking a nap. "He's a twenty-footer," says a friendly park ranger, "and he's not sleeping — he's just sizing you up!"
With Elvis are his non-crocodile relatives: monitors, skinks, turtles, snakes, and blue-tongued lizards. I set up my camera, and instantly make friends. Kangaroos and wallabies begin to investigate just what kind of three-legged beast my tripod is.
Then, through an opening in the eucalyptus leaves, I spot a koala. You'll understand my enthusiasm when I tell you that I spent almost a whole day at the Taronga Zoo to no avail. The koalas at one of Sydney's premier attractions clung to their tree trunks, sleeping, not interested in posing. But this koala looks straight at me — a fuzzball on a forked branch. Its long black nails give it a secure grasp, and he sits there looking at me, surrounded by green. No unsightly wood enclosure anywhere to be seen.
My koala shoot comes to an abrupt end when my subject suddenly starts climbing down from its perch, faster than I thought possible. A park employee, arms full of leaves, doesn't attract just the koala, but hordes of screaming, delighted, children. Time to head on north.
As we approach the wharf at Woy Woy Bay, pelicans sun themselves on the roof. We are greeted by Brett's parents, Peter and Florence, who live on the water, in a white house bordered by red blooming hibiscus.
"Woy Woy is Guringgai Aboriginal for *deep water*," Peter says, "and the mountain you see opposite our bay is a national park. But I call it my 'broccoli field'. You can see why!"
Our conversation is interrupted by the arrival of Junior and his father, setting in motion a daily ritual. "Did you sleep well last night?" Florence asks Junior and holds a plate of chopped sausage. Peter takes one and throws it in the air. It does not go to waste.
"When the kookaburras first came," Peter says, "we fed them on the lawn. But then Junior started sitting on a chair, and now he eats from my hand." It was an amazing sight, and I've got the pictures to prove it. Junior and dad soon fly off, and Brett and I set up to do Jane's still shots on Peter and Florence's pier. Brett brings a long rod; we drape one of the garments over it and place it between two pier supports.
A perfect shot. The browns and ochres, ecrus, and blues of the miters are echoed by the water and the oysters clinging to the pier exposed at low tide. The soft breeze animates the garment and I worry about it dropping in the drink. So Brett gets a hammer and nails the rod down. But there's still a problem: half of it is in full sun. "No worries," says Brett. He rolls up his pants, grabs the scrim, and jumps into the bay. Way to go, Brett! When Florence comes out with a silver tray of fresh strawberries, orange slices, and iced tea, Peter — who has been watching the action from the pier — joins us.
"I thought to myself, gosh, these guys seem to be enjoying their work. But Brett was doing it all," he teases, "I could hear you, Alexis, saying 'Brett, you're the man!' while you were fiddling with your camera, and telling Brett what to do!

The Blue Mountains

Lacy columns, Aussie humor (see photos, above), and the Bush await you in the Blue Mountains.

(Facing page, left–hand column, L to R, top to bottom) The Wattle Flat General Store is for sale; Swagman driveway mural; parking instructions; an elevated house with a wrap-around veranda; didgeridoo player; mural in Blackheath; it isn't every day you can visit an old jail, a cafe, and a museum — all at the same time, at the same place — old Sofala gold town; the Skyway cable car, a great way to enjoy the view; Brett, Elaine, and Jane at the Three Sisters; lambs in Bathurst, wool center and jumping-off point for Australia's rich gold historic sites; Scottish Terrier letting the owners know a photographer is afoot.

(Right–hand column, L to R) No, it's not Oscar and Lucinda's cathedral, but a houseboat; time for a family portrait; watch out for kangaroos and wombats; I know what Jane is wishing for: the 9,143rd shot so this photo shoot can be over; a Bathurst home's tin-roof…; …and lacy trim say 'Australia' instantly; Jane almost gets lost in the eucalyptus–dotted Bush.

"Did you see the mud nests under our jetty? I call our place Capistrano. You can't stand around too long, because the swallows will dive bomb you every spring when they return."

Peter also wants me to meet one of his next-door neighbors, 67-year-old Cocko. "He fell out of his nest as a baby," Peter says, "and my neighbor rescued him." Over the fence, on a tree stump, Cocko puts on a show for us: prancing, flapping his wings, and displaying his curved, yellow, feathered crown.

That evening, with Brett fast asleep (he's just flown in from China), Peter, Florence and I stay up late talking and listening to Frank Sinatra on my iPod. I play Greek music; they sing backup to "Never on Sunday". Next morning when I wake up, the iPod is still on, and Brett and his mom are dancing on the porch. Junior watches from his usual perch as Florence serves sausages.

"When you come back, we'll have to make Woy Woy snags for you," says Florence. "You cook the sausage on a barbie, slice it down the middle, and fill it up with oysters."

As Brett loads the camera equipment in the car, Peter and Florence model two of Jane's garments from their own collection. I mention that no matter who I tell that I'm coming to Australia, they say, 'That's a place I've always wanted to go' Why? Is it Crocodile Dundee? The Great Barrier Reef? Hugh Jackman?

"Because Australia is an island paradise," Peter says, "that's your answer." Florence's response? She recites a poem she learned in school, along with hand gestures. "I love a sunburned country, a land of sweeping plains, / Of rugged mountain ranges, of droughts and flooding rains, / I love her far horizons, I love her jeweled sea, / Her beauty and her treasures, / The wide brown land for me."

It's time to see — and photograph — more of this wide brown land. Before our goodbyes, Peter says, "We've really had a lovely time, and you're welcome back here. You don't have to come professionally — come as a friend."

From Woy Woy Bay, my Australian journey takes me to the Blue Mountains and Sofala; from Alice Springs to Sydney's beginnings at Circular Quay where the First Fleet landed in 1788; from the Central Coast to Alice Springs and Uluru, Australia's ancestral spiritual heart. What was it like shooting the colors of Australia? Aussies make you feel at home — then you step outside, a cockatoo screeches, and you find yourself in a different world.

"When I was a child in school," says Jane, "if the art teacher said, 'Today, make me flowers that look like they grow on Mars,' I could have drawn the flowers of Australia. Look at wattle and banksia, or aptly named bottlebrush. You could take a hairbrush, melt the ends of the bristles, add a curl and a little nail polish, and presto! The words exotic, beautiful, and bizarre all come to mind. Banksias are certainly not related to the English rose — they *do* look like they're from a different planet. And now they're part of *The Colors of Australia*.

"It's been an incredible journey," Jane says. "I might cry when I actually see the book for the first time…"

Jane is right. At times I have felt transported to a different world: while watching Uluru glow into a red-hot ember, or when I first saw the waterhole of Serpentine Gorge at the base of two rock faces. The rock had been polished mirror smooth by time, wind, and rain, and a canyon full of color beckoned you to the other side (facing page, top).

After an endless night over the Pacific, I stepped onto a distant shore and discovered a dream time of my own. Yes, Jane; this *is* so much more than a book.

— *Alexis Xenakis*
Sioux Falls, South Dakota

The Big Red Center

If Australia seems to a visitor like a different planet, traveling to its Big Red Center has to be an out-of-body experience.

You can't have "Colors of Australia" in the title of your book and not include Uluru (also known as Ayers Rock).

I have to have an Uluru shot, but what if it rains? Last time Jane was there, cataracts cascaded down Uluru.

But here I am, and Uluru's waterholes are dry as a bone. It's a few hours before sunset, but I'm all set up: a video, my Hasselblad and Canon on tripods, and another handheld. That should just about do it.

That's a lot of heavy gear to be hauling around alone, but I'm in luck; Marcel Stolle, a new friend from Germany assists me as we join the crowd of Uluru watchers. Some, like the couple on the facing page, have brought supper and easy chairs.

After what seems like an eternity, it happens: the sun sinks below the horizon, and Uluru turns into an ember.

I'm transfixed, and I'm not alone. Our 'official photographer' campground is crawling with shutterbugs whose flashes keep going off.

Uluru-Kata Tjuṯa National Park, a World Heritage Living Cultural Landscape.

Uluru-Kata Tjuṯa National Park is a World Heritage Area renowned for its exceptional natural environment and the living culture of Aṉangu, its traditional owners. It contains outstanding examples of rare desert fauna and flora, whose fragile habitats are protected. Uluru-Kata Tjuṯa National Park's cultural significance comes from Aṉangu traditions dating back tens of thousands of years. The foundation of Aṉangu culture is Tjukurpa, which is the source of stories, ceremonies, landscapes, plants and animals, art and rules for living.

Lucky people find their talent, and with luck, work becomes passion. From crossing T's to dotting i's, the team at XRX deserve to be proud of their passionate skills: they have certainly 'done me proud' in this book.

Designing, editing and composing pages, framing a shot, montaging pages: it comes naturally to these individuals and leaps off the page when their talents combine. 'Simply' looking so very cool when you're really quite hot — our models Nicola and Lydia did it again and again, all so beautifully.

A heartfelt thanks to everyone who has proofed and mathed stitches and rows. You will glow with pride, as I will, when you open Swing Swagger Drape for the first time.